SPEAKING WILDLY

Other books by Jack Denton Scott:

THE WEIMARANER

ALL OUTDOORS

YOUR DOG'S HEALTH BOOK

FORESTS OF THE NIGHT

HOW TO WRITE AND SELL FOR OUT-OF-DOORS

THE DULUTH MONGOOSE

PASSPORT TO ADVENTURE

Jack Denton Scott

SPEAKING
WILDLY

illustrated by Lydia Rosier

William Morrow & Company, Inc.   New York 1966

*For Paul Palmer and Ted Kesting
who made it possible*

CONTENTS

	PREFACE	xi
1	PRINCE OF CATS | *The Leopard*	3
2	THE FABULOUS FAN DANCER | *The Peacock*	22
3	THE MIGHTY MONGOOSE	32
4	THE HUNTING ELEPHANT	42
5	THE BAFFLING BABOON	51
6	UNTOUCHABLE OF THE ANIMAL WORLD | *The Hyena*	65
7	HUSHWING THE HATED | *The Owl*	74
8	KING OF THE ICE | *The Polar Bear*	83
9	MONSTER IN YOUR BACKYARD | *The Shrew*	100
10	THE BLACK BRAIN | *The Crow*	109
11	MINISTER OF DEATH | *The Vulture*	121
12	THE BIRD NOBODY KNOWS | *The Hawk*	129
13	SAILOR OF THE SKIES | *The Sea Gull*	136
14	PROFILE OF A PARADOX | *The Porcupine*	144
15	THE POSSUM ISN'T PLAYING | *The Opossum*	153
16	THE FASCINATING FISHER	163
17	REMARKABLE RED | *The Red Fox*	174
18	THE STRIPED ENIGMA | *The Skunk*	185
19	TROUPER OF THE TREETOPS | *The Gray Squirrel*	195
20	HIS MAGNIFICENCE, THE MOOSE	205
21	SALT WATER DAFFY | *The Porpoise*	219
22	THE SAVAGE IN THE SEA | *The Shark*	234
23	LORD OF THE JUNGLE | *The Tiger*	251
24	IN DEFENSE OF THE WOLF	262
25	THE KING'S LAST STAND | *The Lion*	276

PREFACE

It has become a cliché to say that animals are more interesting than people. It also is not true. As a writer, I don't think there is anything more interesting than people.

But the vagaries of life are such that in searching for people, usually in the far places, I have found myself becoming interested in animals. While looking for the world's original gypsies in Ceylon, I was introduced to a mongoose fighting a hooded cobra; living with the aboriginal tribes in India's jungles, I was taken with the leopard and the peacock; searching for an arctic lake not far from the North Pole that had been lost from human sight for twelve years, and trying to get to know the ways of Norwegian sealers and sailors, I discovered the polar bear; while interviewing one of America's famed big-game fishermen, I was bitten by a hammerhead shark and became involved with what is probably the most savage creature in existence.

What follows is not the work of a zoologist, biologist, or practicing natural scientist, but the observations of a writer who wanders the earth getting acquainted with the wild ones off the beaten path. I have tried to bring them back to you alive.

J. D. S.

We ought not childishly neglect the study of the meaner animals because there is something wonderful in all of nature . . . We ought to investigate all sorts of animals because all of them will reveal something of nature and something of beauty.

ARISTOTLE

There cannot be found in the animal kingdom a bat, or any other creature, so blind in its own range of circumstance and connection, as the greater majority of human beings are in the bosoms of their families . . .

HELEN HUNT JACKSON

SPEAKING WILDLY

1

PRINCE OF CATS

The Leopard

He had twisted a dark cloth around his head into a turban; more of it was wrapped around his waist and then brought up and tied at the crotch. He bent in a quick, jerky movement before the pile of red-painted stones that rose from the roadside to form a little shrine. He had a small yellow chicken in his hands and was getting ready to sacrifice it to his gods. I had been hunting for two weeks, and he was hoping to help me find a tiger. Brown eyes glazed as he moaned and placed the peeping offering before his altar.

3

He was an Indian aboriginal, a jungle dweller known as a Gond, living in the Hoshangabad District of the Bori Range in India's central provinces, Madhya Pradesh. Although he looked terrifyingly barbaric, a man most people would be fearful to meet on a lonely road, he was one of the kindest, most honest men I have ever met.

Shobharam was his name. He lived in the two-hundred-hut village of Bori and had never ventured more than forty miles from his own part of the world. My dak bungalow sat on a hill within sight of his village. Shobharam was an assist-ant *shikari,* a skilled tracker and hunter.

He was an Animist, believing that natural things—rocks, trees, mountains, caves—have spirits, and that natural effects are due to these spirits. Now he was bowing before his holy rocks, preparing to kill the baby chicken to help find the destructive tiger. I left before he made the sacrifice and was one hundred yards from our bungalow when Rao Naidu, a Hindu, the chief *shikari,* came bursting out of the door and ran to meet me.

"We must go!" he said. "We'll cancel the plan we had for sitting in the tree waiting for our tiger. The people in Dhega have sent for us. Two tigers have made a natural kill. In day-light! Dragging a domestic buffalo from a herd before the eyes of the herdsmen!"

Two hours later my wife and I sat in a tree, Rao Naidu between us.

"The tigers will return to their unfinished meal in the early hours," he said. "We sit silently until then. We will hear them come. When I think the time is right I will flash the light. Then you and Mrs. Scott will shoot the cattle killers."

The moon was gone now after six stiff, motionless hours when a slight sound came from the dark, the barest scuff. Naidu flashed his light. Directly below stood a large, tawny leopard, eyes shining like topaz as he looked up. He had deliberately bypassed the dead buffalo to stalk a fresher meal

—us. Growling, he suddenly stood with his front paws on the trunk of the big *kowa* tree as I shot. He howled, ran thirty feet, then dropped dead. This was my introduction to the leopard, one of the most dangerous and fascinating animals I have met.

Everything about this regal, spotted cat is extraordinary. The worst of mankillers, he is said by some to be the best of pets. Although he is considered as ugly as death by all other jungle creatures, it was his dazzling beauty that nearly wiped him from the earth. While he sometimes seems to kill for the joy of it, the cat is a tender mate and a devoted parent. Arboreal, he is as much at home in a tree as on the ground, being so strong that he can carry an animal three times his size to the treetops. Courageous to the degree where he will attack an animal twenty times his size or instantly charge an armed man, the leopard is also noted for his patience and discretion.

This superb creature has a magic coat that makes him almost instantly invisible. He has sensitive whiskers on his chin and elbows, and special elastic tendons in addition to amazingly soft footpads give him a stealth that easily moves his 150 pounds almost soundlessly across dry leaves or puts him without detection within three feet of a man in a room.

The most ferocious leopard undoubtedly was the "Man-Eating Leopard of Rudraprayag." From 1918 to 1926, in the 500 square miles of Garhwal, India, this animal killed 125 persons before he was shot by Jim Corbett in Golabrai on May 2, 1926.

Before I left India in 1958 there was talk of a leopard that had killed one hundred women and children and currently seemed to be specializing in polishing off the experts who came to hunt him. He had recently climbed into *machans* (tree platforms) and killed four, completely discouraging successors.

Three days before my wife and I arrived at jungle camp in

the central provinces, Rao Naidu told us a leopard had entered a compound (huts protected by a high wall) and carried away a girl who was sleeping between two other girls, without awakening them. Naidu thought it was the same cat that stalked us in the tree. Seldom is there more than one man eater in a territory.

Leopards are not normally man eaters. The abnormal ones sometimes get that way by eating the unburied dead during an epidemic or by accidentally killing humans and, after finding how easy it is, concentrating on them. Sometimes physical incapacity or old age force the cats to prey on humans.

The normal animal, however, is such a master of the art of hunting that he has no need to resort to man for food.

Belonging to the family *Felidae,* the leopard is among the foremost of all carnivores or beasts of prey. The hunting of other animals as a way of life requires superior intelligence. Students of the great cats claim they have a brain development surpassed only by man, the higher apes, and the porpoise.

Ranging more widely than any other species of cat, the leopard owes his ascendency to his talent to take a variety of game, anything from a buffalo to a diminutive guinea hen, and to his ability to live undetected near man, his only enemy other than the lion and tiger. Inhabiting all of India, northeastern Asia, Manchuria, and Korea, the spotted cat is also found in China, the Malay peninsula, Java, Ceylon, the Persian Gulf, and Asia Minor. Leopards accompanied the lion to Africa and thrive everywhere there, even in the heavily forested Congo area that the lion doesn't enter. In the Pleistocene period (when most of the world was covered with glacial ice), he inhabited Europe, perhaps even North America.

Contrary to general belief, the leopard does change its spots. His coloration varies from the normal buff or straw color with black rosettes, which are composed by four or five solid spots forming a round figure enclosing a pale central area darker than the ground color, to a heavily coated gray in Persia and a rusty brown in Java. The southern part of the Malay peninsula, Burma, Java, Assam, Nepal, and Travancore and other sections of southern India have a black leopard. In Africa, the black cat occurs only in Abyssinia. This magnificent animal with emerald eyes is not a true type but a color phase resulting when normal yellowish hairs are invaded by a blackish brown pigment, melanin.

Like human fingerprints, no two leopard skins are exactly alike, the size and shape of rosettes varying in every animal. Natives in the Sudan believe that the markings of the leopard show the footprints of every game animal.

African leopards differ from Asian, having slightly smaller spots placed more closely. The jungle animals, called *gal baghs,* "spot tigers," by the Indian jungle tribes, are the largest, with tawny coats and fewer rosettes. The smallest, the most boldly spotted, are those living and preying upon domestic animals near villages.

An ordinary adult village leopard three years of age varies from 5 feet 4 inches to 7 feet in length (the tail often stretches an additional 38 inches) and weighs from 60 to 130 pounds. An average male measures 6 feet 8 inches and weighs 110 pounds. The large jungle dweller, however, often measures over 8 feet, and weighs as much as 180 pounds. The largest leopard on record, 9 feet 1 inch, was bagged by Lionel Inglish in Kashmir. Another weighing 186 pounds was also shot in Kashmir. But its size has little to do with its hunting ability.

Those who have studied the leopard say that it is the cleverest of predators. Armed with a pair of binoculars, I waited several hours a day for an entire month near a grassy clearing in the jungles, hoping to catch sight of something Rao Naidu had told me about. Often chital (spotted deer) came here to graze. Then one day I saw something rolling on the ground, playing with its tail like a house kitten. Chital are curious creatures and, as I watched, three came out to investigate the twisting thing near the edge of the jungle. The rolling object was a leopard. When one of the deer was within striking distance, the "kitten" was up off the ground on the chital's back so fast that I could scarcely follow the motion.

Major General William Rice saw a leopard take a camel in Western Kattywar using similar tactics. The cat suddenly appeared before the grazing camel, rolled on the ground, twisting and turning on its back until it got close. When the humpbacked animal curiously stretched its head down to examine the odd-acting object near it, the leopard instantly seized the exposed throat. The camel struggled, tossing the cat around, trying to beat it off. But the leopard hung on and finally pulled the camel to its knees and killed it.

The leopard has a variety of hunting tricks to prove that he is the smartest of the cat tribe. The hunter Syd Downey watched a large male prepare for his stalk of a buffalo calf by rolling in buffalo dung to disguise his body scent so he could get close without frightening the calf.

I saw a pair of leopards hunting langurs in the trees. Almost as agile as the monkeys, the cats, using perfect teamwork, finally herded all of the monkeys into a large *mahwal* tree, a giant creeper. This was a tree that looked like the perfect refuge, but the frightened langurs had to jump from the smaller trees to the ground in order to reach it. As the monkeys landed on the ground, one leopard, coming down a langur-abandoned small tree head first, leaped and quite easily got a straggler. The other cat calmly joined its mate in the meal while the terrified monkeys sat in the tree howling.

Natives claim that the leopard also simply sits under a

tree glaring at a monkey, so fascinating the animal that it is powerless to escape and finally drops to the ground at the cat's feet.

Leopards take the old cat-and-dog myth seriously. Dog meat is one of their favorite foods, and they use exceptional courage and cunning to obtain it.

J. A. Hunter, dean of African hunters, watched a leopard beguile a dog to its death. When the dog saw the cat it began barking furiously and ran for its master's hut. The spotted cat moved to the open ground and laid down, ignoring the dog. Then he began to purr, waving his tail gently from side to side, holding his head close to the ground as a dog would if he wanted to play. After a few minutes the dog became curious and moved closer to investigate, sniffing, still alert. The leopard looked harmless enough, but actually his hind legs were tucked under him in a position ready to spring. As the dog approached, the leopard continued to purr and to ignore him. Finally, the dog came within range. The cat's leap was so fast that it was a blur of motion.

An English hunter in India tells of a bold leopard who took his dog out of the bathroom while he was bathing. The door was open, facing the jungle, and the dog was sitting beside the zinc tub. Suddenly the man looked up and saw the cat with the dog in its jaws. He splashed water on the leopard and shouted, but the cat nonchalantly walked away with the dog. The man said the leopard seemed to know that it had caught him with his pants down.

In defense, some people have trained their dogs to track and fight leopards—without conspicuous success. An African farmer by the name of Cronje had six of his fierce, especially trained leopard dogs defeated by a single medium-sized leopard in just two minutes. Three of the dogs were killed, the others were terribly mauled. His Great Dane, an out-sized specimen weighing 120 pounds, was knocked spinning in the air with a single glancing blow delivered by a running leopard that didn't even slacken his speed as he slapped.

The spotted cat's strength is remarkable. African safari organizer Donald Ker told of locating a leopard kill, a three-hundred-pound young giraffe, high in the crotch of a tree. A friend told him that she found the trees next to her pigsty "blooming" with pig carcasses. A single leopard had killed ten full-grown pigs and propped them high in trees for seasoning and safekeeping. Jim Corbett's Rudraprayag man eater carried a full-grown man four miles, two miles up a steep slope, and another two miles through dense scrub jungle. Another hunter saw a leopard carry a full-grown donkey three hundred yards over rocky, hilly country.

Rao Naidu and I trailed a leopard that had killed a buffalo calf and carried it, without any part of the animal dragging on the ground, for three miles, up hills, across gulleys, and finally depositing the calf, at least twice the weight of the cat, high in the crotch of a tree.

Naturalist Dunbar Brander caught a leopard in a trap, but by the time he returned with his men, the cat had freed itself, inserting its free paw to bend the iron jaw back. Brander later regretted that he didn't have the jaw bent back to its normal position under conditions where he could have measured the force expended, because the amount of strength needed was incredible. The type of trap he used took the efforts of two men to set it.

The previously mentioned J. A. Hunter, who holds the world record for lion and rhino and has bagged 1,400 elephants, many of them the deadly "rogues," calls the leopard the "most dangerous game of all." He says that when a leopard knows it is being spoored it will climb a tree and lay on a limb overhanging the trail. If the hunter does not see him, the cat will usually let him pass, but if the man glances up, the leopard is on him immediately. Most animals when they find themselves discovered or cornered will grunt or snarl and run. Not the leopard; the instant he knows a man who is hunting him sees him, he charges.

An Englishman and his *shikari,* sitting in different *machans,* hunting leopards, saw one moving directly below. The hunter fired, wounding him. Instantly, the cat came up the tree and mauled him; then, before the *shikari* could even take aim, the leopard was up the other tree and killed the man.

When after leopards, the stalker has to watch the cover on both sides and behind and overhead. This gives the cat the decided advantage.

I trailed a wounded leopard with Rao Naidu, using shotguns (even a dead shot can't hit a leaping leopard at close range with a rifle) and four immense buffalo which we drove before us. Unlike other cats, the leopard doesn't growl or roar and betray his position when you hunt him in the grass or heavy cover. This day Naidu insisted on going first, I was second, three village *shikaris* followed, covering our sides and the rear. There were no trees, so we didn't have that disadvantage.

The buffalo were driven, one at a time, toward a suspicious rotting log that lay just to the left of our path a hundred yards ahead. The animals were frightened to begin with, so we couldn't tell by their actions whether they could scent a leopard nearby. One by one the clumsy beasts stepped over the log, then Rao Naidu started forward. He reached the log. The hidden leopard sprang. Rao jumped back and shot it with both barrels of his Purdey. That incredible cat had crouched silently beside the log permitting four buffalo to almost step on it, patiently waiting for the right moment.

One seasoned forest officer observes: "Some argue which is the most dangerous, tiger, lion, or leopard. Well, a leopard can hide his whole body where a tiger can't hide his head. He can leap on your back from a tree that a tiger or lion could never climb. He is a smaller mark to hit when charging and is full of courage."

Even the brave African Masai tribesmen, noted for killing lions with spears, fear the leopard. The elders of a village sent for a famed professional to try to get a cat that was killing their cattle. Two expert native hunters, *moran,* had been sent to get it. They spoored it, tracked it down, only to be badly mauled, nearly killed. This particular cat apparently killed for pleasure, destroying six calves in a night without eating their flesh.

Finally trapping the killer in a cave, four Masai poked him out into the open. He was shot, but not before he had terribly mauled all four natives. The entire action took place in three seconds. "He is the fastest and most deadly animal," concluded the professional hunter.

Nature has superbly equipped the leopard to be a perfect killing machine and faultless hunter. His chin whiskers and the bristle tufts on his forearms are sensory and tactile; connected to nerves, they instantly flash to his brain impressions gathered by touch. His upright ears are extremely sensitive, especially adapted to pick up the slightest sound, and his sense of direction in respect to any sound is remarkable.

After waiting eight long hours over a bait one night, I spooked a cautious leopard who heard me take a notebook from my pocket. It was a moonlit night, and I suddenly saw him appear one hundred yards away. His head went up, and he bounded off. Yet the person sitting beside me in the tree hadn't heard me make a sound.

The leopard's magnificent yellow-green eyes are the largest of the carnivores. A well-developed system of muscles within the eye contracts the pupil in bright light, protecting them from glare. In the dark, the pupils dilate to allow all available light to enter. Observers tell of leopards spotting a slight movement in a tree platform from more than a half mile.

Success as a hunter lies in the cat's stealth and ability to surprise. His feet are so heavily cushioned with noise-muffling pads that the leopard's sinuous movement may be described as the flowing past of a phantom. This gliding action is made by the simultaneous advance of his legs. As he walks, his hind feet are set precisely in the tracks of the forefeet, a perfect register resulting in his silent movement.

The leopard of Rudraprayag entered a dark room where two men sat smoking and took one. The unharmed man didn't even know the cat was in the room until he saw it silhouetted against the open door carrying away his friend. He had been sitting an arm's length from the victim, yet so noiseless was the approach and the kill, he claimed he didn't even hear so much as a quick intake of breath.

The leopard walks on his toes in a digitigrade movement that raises sole and heel above the ground, altering the balance of his body, throwing it forward, increasing impetus of movement, and giving extra speed and agility. One hunter had a leopard leap forty feet to try to get him.

The leopard's principle weapons of attack, claws, five on forefeet, four on hind, have a peculiar device preventing them from blunting by contact with the ground. The claw-bearing joint in its normal position lies folded back over the preceding joint, held in this reverted position by an elastic ligament. Folded back, the claw is off the ground, guarded by a sheath of skin completely covering it. When the leopard distends his paw to strike, a tendon connected to the limb muscles immediately pulls the reverted joint, drawing it downward and foreward and claws emerge instantly.

This ingenious armament is enforced with perfect canine teeth, longer and better separated than those of other carnivores. When the leopard closes his jaws, the canines interlock; when he opens them, the teeth stand clear and can drive full into the flesh of his victim. There are no contiguous teeth to prevent complete penetration. Supported on short, powerful jaws controlled by magnificent biting muscles in the wide cheek arches and long crest of the skull, the teeth are given increased strength by the short muzzle which concentrates a power lost to animals with pointed muzzles and snouts.

Corbett, Hunter, Ker, Carr, Downey, and other knowledgeable cat men credit these teeth with the leopard's ability to kill animals several times his size. "It kills by getting under the neck," Jim Corbett said, "into which its claws are deeply dug, then it chokes by sinking teeth into the throat. In most cases, unless those remarkable teeth have dislocated the neck, the animal it attacks is killed by strangulation. . . ."

Even his strikingly beautiful coat, glowing with "black roses," was designed to aid in the cat's profession of killing—and surviving. This spotted hide is such perfect camouflage that its pattern idea was copied by the U.S. Army in World War II for jungle warfare: repeating broken lights and shadows deceives the eye, breaks up the body mass, confuses and obscures contours.

I sat in a tree in daylight, waiting for a leopard to come back and finish its interrupted meal of a goat. Dried teak leaves, the tattletales of the jungle, were everywhere, ground cover was scant, and I was in a position where I could see an advance from any direction. Still I didn't know the leopard had returned until I heard him dragging the goat.

Yet with all these physical endowments the leopard's most important single asset cannot be seen: his brain. There are evidences that he has the ability to reason.

The Rudraprayag leopard opened a door that was closed with a chain through a hasp. He was so bright that he ate around odorless cyanide planted in the body of a man he had killed, avoided open ground where trap guns were set, and removed a thornbush obstruction placed to prevent his approaching the poisoned victim from the wrong position to set off another trap gun.

Another example of a seeming ability to reason was made by a leopard that removed the head of a young buffalo bait that had been tied to a tree. The rope was so stout that he couldn't break it by pulling, so he simply removed neck, head, and rope and carried off the body.

A naturalist who trapped leopards in India remarked upon their ability to "think." Traps were set close to camp; when a cat was caught the only sound that resulted was the closing clack. The naturalist noted that all other trapped animals would howl, but the leopard would silently and intelligently try to free itself, seeming to realize that noise would attract man and prevent escape.

If parental guidance means anything, then the leopard starts life with all of the advantages. Born into a family of from two to four cubs when the leopardess is three years old, the young come into the world blind after a gestation period of ninety-two days. Spots are merged, separating as the cub grows. Home is usually a cave, a cozy, hidden place under a rock ledge, a hollow tree, or an abandoned porcupine's hole. Mating in February or March, the parents remain together, often until after the cubs are weaned. Each takes only one mate and show strong affection. A professional hunter once put poisoned bait out for a female that had been killing a settler's stock. The next morning when he checked it he found the leopardess dead across the kill, her mate beside her, his head across her body in a caressing attitude. Refusing to leave his mate, he had to be shot.

A devoted parent, the leopardess starts training her offspring in the art of survival as soon as they can waddle. She encourages cubs to leap at her and each other and teaches them to stalk her moving tail. What seems like pointless play is really a lesson in timing and approach. As they attempt to attack the tip of the tail she quickly flips it out of their way, keeping them at it until they can actually catch her tail despite her efforts to avoid them.

An English tea planter observed an Indian leopardess correcting a cub when it broke and ran at an unexpected noise. Leopards freeze to the ground first, they never run and expose themselves at the sign of danger. So to teach the important lesson, with two other cubs watching, the mother picked the errant one up by the scruff of the neck, brought it back to the place where it had been frightened, then placed her paw on the cub, pushing it to the ground. When she removed the paw, the cub lay still for a long time, his lesson apparently learned.

Even before they are weaned, she teaches them to climb trees—by example. She climbs a tree trunk, barely keeping out of their reach, tempting them to follow. By observation and imitation they develop the skill and craft of hunting, learning how, when, and where to wait for prey and when to leap to strike effectively with tooth and claw.

When they are about half grown, the mother takes them stalking. An Indian friend and I have watched a female with three cubs carefully kill a *ghooral* (wild goat), exaggerating all of her movements, the crouching stalk, the leap, the kill, while the youngsters watched, much as students observe a teacher's lesson on a chalkboard.

Spending most of their daylight hours in dense forests or inaccessible rocky areas, "lying up" places between meals, the leopardess and her young rarely return to the same lying-up place the second time. Seldom do they follow any pattern of movement or the same jungle trail. The parent teaches the cub that one of the first lessons to be learned in the brutal life of the jungle is unpredictability. She also teaches them economy, showing them how to carry game up a tree, "banking" it high in a crotch.

From the time they are weaned at four months, during a life span of sixteen to twenty-three years, their lives are dedicated to hunting. Graduate steps in learning this precise art come when the mother locates the game, disables it, then sends the cubs in to finish it off. When the cubs are six months old she starts them on solo hunts by locating small

game, pheasants, guinea hens, and jungle fowl, finally working up to monkeys. If there is trouble, she springs in for
the finishing touches, showing them exactly how it should
be done.

This prolonged, patient tutelage results in the young leopard's complete mastery over his domain. The young often
remain with the mother, improving skills and polishing
techniques until they are a year old or until the mating
instinct forces them to leave.

Courage, however, is not an acquired characteristic or a
lesson learned. It is something the leopard is born with, one
of his finest qualities. Rarely will a normal tiger or a lion
enter human habitation, but a village leopard will often
try to force his way into any building or area where it scents
its prey, depending upon bold approach and knowledge of
man for success.

I have known a leopard to kill a calf in the midst of an
Indian village, snarl, spit, and defy the owner and six of
his neighbors who were frantically waving axes before he
nonchalantly turned and went off into the night.

A leopard's self-control is to be admired. A zoologist shot
a cat that emerged from a beat, using a .577 rifle, blowing
out a large portion of the animal's entrails. The leopard,
scarcely breaking step, finding the dragging entrails an im-
pediment, removed them and continued his escape, although
he died minutes later.

A friend told me of wounding a leopard, having the plucky
animal descend the opposite side of a hill on bare ground
and come at a gallop for him across a gully from a distance of 150 yards. Most animals, including the vaunted
lion and tiger, would have run in the opposite direction.

When provoked, leopards will even charge elephants without fear. A British army captain, mounted on a huge tusker
(whose hunting abilities and fearlessness were being touted
by the mahout) and after two leopards that had been haras-

sing an area, was about to give up when he found the cats crouching in thick bushes.

Despite heavy thumps on the head by the trainer, the elephant would not advance. One leopard growled and charged. The elephant swung around and retreated at full speed with his trunk in the air, the leopards in full pursuit, uttering fierce coughing, grunting growls. One attempted to spring on the great beast's hindquarters.

The leopard uses his voice to advantage, starting with the hoarse, grating "meow" as a cub, graduating to the growl used when angry or wounded. Before charging they give short, coughing grunts. The spotted cat also "saws," a sound exactly like wood being cut with a saw. In making this sound the leopard keeps his mouth partly open, expelling and inhaling air back and forth across his soft palate. Some observers say the cat does this to frighten game into exposing itself.

Zoo goers don't seem to be intimidated by the sight or sound of the leopard. Zoologists tell me these cats, especially the black ones, fascinate people and with few exceptions are the center of attraction.

Experts at the New York Zoological Park claim that the leopard is tractable in captivity, has an uncertain temper, is extremely alert, is always on the defensive, and is not to be trusted.

Even behind bars they can be dangerous. A black leopard in the Zoological Gardens, Regents Park, London, reached through his cage and caught a nine-year-old boy with his claws, severely tearing the boy's face and scalp. The boy's life was saved by his brother-in-law, who kept jabbing an umbrella down the cat's throat. In thirty seconds, even restricted in his cage, with an umbrella in his throat, the damage the leopard did to the two boys was enormous.

Yet some claim that leopards make fascinating pets. Old African hand John F. Burger considers the leopard the finest pet of all. He has raised five, all caught young, and claims that none showed signs of aggression or treachery.

He gave one of his leopards the ultimate test. Once he passed the cat's cage without stopping to pet it, briefly offering his cheek for a quick kiss. This wasn't enough. The leopard tried to pull him closer, hooking a claw in his eyebrow. With blood streaming down his face, Burger decided to test the old theory that the leopard will revert to type and turn savage upon tasting blood. He entered the cage, closed the door, and sat down. "The leopard was apparently sorry for what he had done," he said. "He sat for a half hour licking the blood from my wound, purring."

Burger, who is seldom without a leopard, says that they are "big, lovable, playful, and affectionate creatures who know only one master whom they look to for food, affection, and understanding."

Michaela Denis, wife of explorer Armand Denis, who wrote the book *Leopard in My Lap,* won't commit herself that far. She had a pet leopard, Tahui, whom she raised from a cub and took everywhere. He would walk on a leash and played a game with her, dropping on her shoulders from a tree.

But the "playful" Tahui once attacked a plumber in Mrs. Denis' garden, tearing off his raincoat. Michaela Denis spoke softly to her pet, took him by the tail and collar and pulled him off the man, then knelt to tickle his ears. The leopard yawned, his savage mood vanished, and he began to purr.

"I'd never take liberties with him though," Mrs. Denis said. "When feeding him, I'd keep away. He'd growl and forget friendship."

Mrs. Elizabeth Kimloch was presented with a leopard cub by her husband, a game warden for Uganda in Central Africa. She bottle fed the kitten, then graduated it to bits of raw meat, and finally white mice. The leopard cub ate the mice whole, leaving the tails in a neat row by his dish. Mrs. Kimloch said that at six weeks he was the affectionate companion of the family. But as he grew older he began to stalk and claw her neighbor's dogs, and they reluctantly sent him to a zoo.

Sinclair Cleland Scott, an African hunter, had two leopard pets that "playfully" tore off his clothes, gnawed his arms, ripped his furniture, and refused to be housebroken. Despite this, because of their beauty, he kept them for several years until one was shot by an annoyed neighbor and the other was destroyed for roughing up an Italian prisoner of war.

It is this famed beauty that nearly wiped out the African leopard. About twenty-five years ago leopard skins were so popular, bringing $40 right from the trap, that African suppliers could not keep up with demand. Traps were brought into Africa by the thousands, and Arab traders became rich, demanding from natives several leopard skins in payment for one $4 trap.

At this time, leopards were considered vermin and trapping was indiscriminate. In two years the cats were almost exterminated in the Wakamba country and the Kenya Lowlands. The British government, finally realizing what was happening, put the leopard on the game license and confiscated all traps.

But so many thousands had been trapped that there now was a nature imbalance and famine resulted. Wild pigs and baboons, the natural prey of the leopard, had multiplied to such an extent that there was insufficient food for them, and they began raiding crops. Moving in hordes, they laid waste to cultivated areas.

The leopard has made somewhat of a comeback in Africa, but as late as 1957, government agents were continuing to trap and poison wild pigs and baboons that were still overrunning the country.

Once more the leopard's beauty is betraying it. Its skin is being coveted again. At this writing, it is one of the most popular and expensive furs in the United States. We can only hope that Africa has learned its lesson. Unfortunately, the leopard is considered vermin in Asia. In most regions there is no limit on the number that can be taken. It would be unfortunate if India repeated Africa's mistake, upsetting that delicate balance of nature and making the jungle a poorer place by wiping out one of its most beautiful and interesting residents.

2

THE FABULOUS FAN DANCER

The Peacock

The next leopard I met was a strange one. He stood like a man when he saw me, and his spotted hide hung about him as loosely as a cloak. It happened one quiet afternoon in the Indian jungle. I had come through a copse of young bamboo, moving cautiously, trying to get a color shot of a peafowl, the wariest of creatures, when I saw a bird. A big male.

Tropical sun seemed to strike sparks from the peacock,

its breast a shimmer of blue as it stood tall as an eagle three hundred yards ahead. I made this a careful stalk, Nikon camera at the ready. As I got closer, I could see the bird was ignoring me, staring, hypnotized, at something before it.

Halting, I located the object: a leopard creeping through the grass. I quietly lowered the camera, unslung my rifle, and put it to my shoulder. Suddenly, the cat sprang to its feet, its hide fell off, and an alarmed voice shouted in Hindi: "Don't fire!" The bird fled, crouching, swift as a snake.

My leopard was a frightened Indian Gond. A professional fowler, he had cleverly draped himself in the cat's hide, perfect even to the mounted head. Clad now only in a loincloth, he held a short bamboo spear in one hand, a net over his shoulder.

This was my introduction to the most beautiful and dramatic of birds: the wild peacock. Clever, shy, a master of stealth, the peacock's only nemesis other than man seems to be the leopard. Fascinated by the spotted cat, it will often stand and stare until killed. Aware of this, natives in some areas don leopard skins to get close enough to net the peacock alive for sale or to spear it for supper.

Everything about this fabled bird is unusual. Currently worshipped by thousands, its colorful feathers are said to contain magical qualities that will cure the ill, protect the evil, and encourage the brave. Although naturalists list it among the most selective and alert of creatures, its plaything is a deadly snake. It rhumbas and fan dances, cries like a cat, utters an alarming English word, and has almost killed itself with conceit. A wild jungle dweller, it takes captivity calmly and has been known to frighten horses and threaten cars. Among the most ancient of feathered creatures, it is today a modern television symbol of color.

The Far East is native ground for the two true species of peacocks, both related to the pheasant family, the blue breasted of India and Ceylon and green of Java and Burma.

Both have crests: the Indian, fan-shaped: the Burmese, long and narrow, knife-shaped. The Indian bird, called the "common" peacock, is the one known by us all; domesticated in Judea during the time of Solomon, brought to Greece by Alexander the Great, it gradually spread westward, touching human life and fancy in many ways.

Fascination with the peacock is almost as old as India. A spray of peacock feathers is still the implement of conjuring and is carried by most Indian mendicants who claim skill in magic. It is believed that a favorite Indian god, Lord Krishna, wore peacock feathers on his head, giving the peacock the dignity no other bird can aspire to have. The priests of Benares use a wand of feathers with which to punish or absolve worshippers for their sins. In the Punjab, smoking a peacock feather in a pipe is an antidote against snake bite. I have seen feathers sold in many Indian bazaars, their burned ashes guaranteed as a remedy against vomiting. Among the nomad Basuis, a tuft of peacock feathers is carried by these robbers and counterfeiters of coins as a magical remedy to prevent detection.

In southern India, the fat of the peacock, the bird that struts so gracefully, is believed to cure stiff joints. Pliny recorded that peacock dung served as a remedy for several eye diseases and that the tongues were eaten to cure epilepsy.

All Hindus revere and protect this bird they call "Mor," believing that their god of war Kartikeya, son of Siva, rode a peacock. It is also the royal emblem of the kings of Burma, who claim to trace their descent from the sun. Even the early Christians engraved the bird on the tombs of the martyrs in the catacombs of Rome as a symbol of eternity and immortality.

Odd beliefs extend to mating, many in the Far East believing that the hen conceives by licking the tears shed by the peacock. Actually, breeding is prosaic, varying only in locale. In Ceylon, the season runs from January to April; along the foothills of the Himalayas, March to April; elsewhere, it doesn't begin until the rains break, usually from June to September. All breeding in the wild seems to be governed by rainfall, mainly because natural food (insects, frogs, lizards, worms, and vegetables) is more abundant.

The peacock normally has a three- to six-hen harem, but I have seen two old Indian peacocks trailing 92-inch jeweled trains, each with ten obedient mottled-brown, green-necked peahens in procession. Mating is preceded by the fabled dance and much strutting with the showy tail spread.

If unhunted or in a Hindu-protected area, peahens will lay eggs on the jungle edge or even in a clump of bushes near a village. They are partial to the thick and thorny *Ber* bushes which grow in a protective mass where three to eight pale cream eggs are laid in a natural hollow which the peahen sometimes fills with leaves, small sticks, and grass. I have found their eggs in a hollow limb of a banyan tree and even in nests on the thatched roofs of huts.

Sitting close, the hen hatches the eggs in thirty days. The peacock takes no interest in the eggs or his young (peabiddies) which start life off with drab brown down. The crest comes in ten days, the first flecks of green touching the neck in six weeks. In two more weeks cocks can be distinguished by speckles on the back. Young peacocks begin to show off when they are the size of a partridge, but even within a few hours out of the egg they raise their tiny tails in a strut.

It takes two years for train plumage to develop. The first year the peacock has a buff breast, speckled back, a green neck, and a short gray tail. During the second year his breast turns black, he gets his father's blue neck, and his back turns green and gold. The third year brings a Prussian blue breast: the neck and shoulders are shaded in green and purple-blue, running to a deep metallic green on the abdomen. His back, from shoulders to rump, becomes brilliant bronze-green, each feather black edged. He also gets his brown tail, which often grows to 46 inches. Another year brings his weight from 9 to 12 pounds, often with a 19-inch wingspread.

The train or "nautch" projects beyond the tail, from 40 to 54 inches in full breeding plumage, giving him a magnificent tail train from 80 to 92 inches. Train feathers, which he carries during a 35-year life span, shedding in late summer, growing back by December, are also bronze-green with a copper sheen near the tips, each feather having a distinct eye formed by a deep-blue heart-shaped spot with four rings of smalt, blue-green, golden-bronze, and gold and rich brown.

The unfurling of this fantastic fan in its sunburst of color has awed and impressed since the beginning of recorded time. The raised nautch takes the shape of a shield from which a thousand eyes seem to peer. In Sanskrit, the bird is called the "thousand-eyed" creature.

I saw those eyes the first time when a peacock did a fan dance at the New York Zoological Park where I went with a couple of school chums the day after we had learned that in Roman legend, Juno, wife of Jupiter, transposed the hundred eyes of Argus to the peacock's tail after he was slain by Mercury. Our bird opened his great train by shaking himself until he rose in a multicolored halo. Before we had a chance to see it properly, he swung around presenting his backside, stiff grayish-brown tail, and a puff of black feathers, giving the impression that he was wearing winter underwear. When we moved in front, he turned again and again, until finally he decided to let us see him. The great fan with its green, gold, bronze eyes rose and trembled, impressing us so that no one said a word for five minutes—a rare feat for boys that age.

The caution that old Indian peacock displayed in delaying our seeing his fan was a natural carry over from the wild. From the time jungle peacocks are large enough to unfurl their tails, they automatically let the hens precede them into the open. If it is safe, they then show their gorgeous selves.

At night, they roost on the lower branches of tall trees, again the hen going first. Regular in habit, they frequent the same feeding ground morning and evening, returning to a favorite tree at dusk.

I have heard them calling at intervals all night. One cry is exactly like a child's plea for "help!" But the sound most often heard resembles an old tomcat on a backyard fence, a cross between a "meow" and the clear sound of a trumpet, coming out a surprisingly loud "phi-ao-phi-ao." They also utter a shrill "ka-oan-ka-oan" alarm call.

Naturalists call them the most alert of jungle creatures. Stuart Baker, for example, says that they are "as sinuous as a snake, as stealthy as a cat, and as wary as an old bull bison in watching for foes."

I spent nearly two weeks in 1960 in India in a camera "hide," camouflaged, trying to get the impressive love dance and then the mating in a close-up on film. Moving a few yards every day, I managed to get within two hundred yards. Then the suspicious guardian hens took off, rocketing like pheasants, rapidly overtaken by their frightened lord, his train streaming like a tail of flame. I never got the picture.

But I did have a box seat at a show even more unusual than the mating dance while sitting in a tree *machan* waiting for a tiger. The tiger didn't come that day, but I never noticed. I sat enthralled with a dozen young peacocks performing under my tree. There wasn't a female in sight, thus exploding the theory that they only strut when hens are around. They actually were dancing with each other, strutting and bowing, paired off, first a forward dance, then an equally graceful backward movement, almost a rhumba, the jeweled fans quivering, the sun striking lights, and not a noise coming from them. It was sheer Oriental splendor. Then, suddenly, as if by silent signal, the dance stopped, the ocellated nautches were folded, and they quietly made their way single file through the jungle.

I've savored that sight often since then, realizing how lucky I had been to get that close to the rare group of dancing peacocks—the wariest of birds.

Even skilled hunters trying to shoot them for the pot (young peacock is more delicious than turkey or pheasant) usually turn to easier game after spending several days on a useless stalk. The peacock, even with his cumbersome train, crouches and gracefully slinks through grass and undercover so fast that nothing can overtake him. Wisely, he never takes to the air until he is many yards from danger. My companion in the jungle said they moved "like feathered snakes."

Jungle legend has it that peacocks and snakes are mortal enemies. In areas where they are protected or revered, landowners often entice them into their gardens to discourage snakes, even though the peacocks usually end up eating the better grains and fruits.

Naturalist William Beebe in a seventeen-month quest in the Far East for exotic pheasants had his most difficult moments trying to approach peacocks. In the jungles of Ceylon he finally got close enough to see one playing with a deadly Russell's viper. The bird circled and pursued, keeping at a distance, but tempting the viper to strike again and again. Seeming to know of the danger, the peacock cleverly kept out of the snake's striking range. "The bird didn't attempt to kill the snake, he just teased it," said Beebe. "Then tiring of the game he ran down a slope and flew away, the full light of his train a wonderful colored tapestry. . . ."

It took the patient naturalist several weeks of waiting and a hands-and-knees approach before he saw a wild peacock in what he called a "mating display."

Like the turkey, the wild peacock does strut and quiver his fan more often before his harem, usually when he is feeling fit after feeding in the morning. But the peahens don't pay much attention. Of the fifty times I have seen wild peacocks displaying their glory before females, only twice did the hens stop pecking or lift their heads to see their master burst his color for their appreciation.

The Mogul Emperor Shah Jahan who created the Taj Mahal appreciated that display so much that he spent ten million rupees and seven years building the "peacock throne." Supported on twelve pillars of emerald, it was surmounted by two peacocks, fans unfurled, and blazing with diamonds, sapphires, rubies, and emeralds.

Domesticated and enshrined by such history shakers, to-day the blue-breasted Indian jungle peacock is distributed worldwide on private estates, zoos, and aviaries, accepting captivity gracefully—even arrogantly. There are interesting characters among them.

Caroline Sherman had one named Sir Roger de Coverley on her Virginia farm who waited at the gate until the guests' horse and buggy arrived, delighting in fan dancing before the terrified horses that had never seen such a creature.

Flannery O'Connor, who raised them in Georgia, told of an old Negro woman saying "Amen! Amen!" reverently when one of her show-off birds did his fan dance. She said that none of her peacocks would budge an inch for a car or a truck. They stood and tried to fan the vehicles away.

One in California almost killed itself with conceit. He was observed watching himself in a plate-glass window, preening and turning, when a few minutes later the owner heard sounds of battle. The peacock had decided that the reflection wasn't his after all and was a bloody mess by the time they dragged him from the window.

Lucifer, once the peacock pride of the Bronx Zoo, fell for a black turtle, Geraldine. Zoo keepers said that as soon as he saw the turtle he fanned his tail and walked out of the peacock section. For three years he lived with her in the turtle yard behind the service house. He had to fight it out on several occasions with another peacock, Oswald, who came over to discover what he saw in Geraldine.

An ill-tempered but obviously beauty-conscious elephant, "Lizzie," adopted one of the birds at the Philadelphia Zoo, guarding the colorful charge carefully, chasing away all intruders. The peacock seemed to appreciate the whole business.

There is a community of contented peacocks in Arcadia, a heavily populated section of southern California. Brought there by Elias Baldwin in 1870, six pairs soon became two thousand. The great Baldwin estate was finally broken up, but the birds stayed, taking over the countryside. Finally, 127 acres of the Baldwin grounds were established as Los Angeles State and County Arboretum, a botanical garden and sanctuary for the peacocks. They didn't seem to appreciate it, deciding that it was just as pleasant to spend their time on the resident's lawns and fences.

Along Old Ranch Road they had pedestrian right of way, roosted in trees, gobbled petunias, and teased the dogs, but few residents objected. After all, how many people are lucky enough to have peacocks in their gardens?

One resident put it this way: "Every night this peacock calls his harem, and they roost in our tree. In the morning as we have breakfast he is still there, his tail hanging like a bouquet of flowers. It's a thrill I wouldn't trade."

Most tame peacocks seem to like people, or at least put up with them. An English woman had one named Aquila that she taught to erect his fan on command. He would also eat from her hand and tap on the dining-room window when she was late with his food.

A game farm operator in Connecticut had an Indian peacock that followed him like a dog, and a woman in Georgia had forty that roved her property freely, calm, collected creatures that refused to budge or get excited, even for a roaring tractor.

Generally, though, peacocks are more ornament than pet, keeping their distance and remaining tame so long as they are fed at regular times and are not molested. Occasionally, like swans, they take a violent dislike to people and will attack on sight. On a New Jersey farm, one came rushing at me, rattling his quills as if he was going to commit murder.

People who keep peacocks claim that once you've owned them you are hooked forever. Their beauty and flaming color is such that you feel something vital has gone from your life if the rainbow bird isn't around.

Even as I write I can see the birds in their wild jungle, strutting as proudly as dancers of the Ballet Russe, and hear Rao Naidu saying, "See how the sun burns on their feathers? That is why they stay so beautiful. They have a special knowledge. They are the only living creatures that know how to capture the sun. . . ."

3

THE MIGHTY MONGOOSE

S. V. Rao Naidu is an unusual man. Although his profession is *shikari,* professional hunter, he uses it as an excuse to live in the jungles where he does more watching than shooting. He is a Hindu, of the warrior caste, the *Kashatriyas,* believed to have been born from the god Brahma's arms, and he graduated from Hislop College and from a technical college, Dayal Bagh, in Agra. He became a hunter because he loves the jungle more than the bee swarm of cities. Unlike most of us, he has the courage of his convictions, is a nonconformist of the highest order, and yet respects another's thoughts and profession. A lithe five feet ten inches, his hair is the shade of a crow's wing in sunlight, his complexion is toast-brown, and his voice is soft.

He always speaks softly; the primitive people of the jungle respect him, for he not only has taken the time to learn their language, but he knows their problems and is helpful in many ways. When they need meat, he gets it; when they want to know more about the frightening world outside their jungles, he tells them; when they are sick with dysentery or aching with rheumatism, he has the medicine and the salves that bring relief.

He also is my wildlife mentor, teaching me what goes on behind the green screen of jungle. There is no habit of an animal that he doesn't know, no bird sound or track in the dusty road that he can't identify. I look forward to and treasure the hours in the wilderness with him. They are better than money in the bank; I can spend and respend those moments.

So I was delighted, full of the same old excitement, when in the fall of 1960 Rao and I again arrived to set up housekeeping in a dak bungalow in the jungles. Piles of cleared bamboo burning by the roadside brought a pungent but pleasing perfume. It was dusk, the peaceful, purple time, and shadows were just beginning to stand still. The cat cries of my friends the peacocks, retiring in their trees, came as true a tone as that of a cat on a backyard fence. Our home for the next two months, the whitewashed house with its thick, red tile roof, sat starkly on a rise overlooking the village of Mulni in the cup of valley three miles away, flags of cooking fire smoke unfurling from its two hundred huts.

The dak hadn't been occupied for months, not even overnight by traveling forestry officials who had first call, and when we walked into its stale air a faint spiral of animal musk rose. Smiling, Rao said, "We're in luck. A mongoose is living here. There will be no rats—or snakes."

For the first time, he was wrong. Exploring, I opened the bathroom door and jumped back at what lay coiled on the stone floor: a cobra. As I froze, Rao slammed the door, peering through a crack he made by slowly opening it a half inch. Finally, he said, "It is dead." As we stood over the fearsome thing, Rao took a knife from his pocket. Tapping the snake's head with the blade, he pointed out distinct tooth marks. "Mongoose," he said.

Suddenly there was a slight rustling at the door. We jerked around to see a gray animal, perhaps three feet long with a narrow head and bushy tail, regarding us. Our host, the mongoose, had come to greet his visitors.

This was not nearly as dramatic a scene as Rudyard Kipling described when he made his mongoose, Rikki-tikki-tavi, world famous. But it was exciting enough for me. Evidently, our mongoose had recently taken up residence in the dak, had finished off the cobra, and was returning to dine on it when we arrived. Kipling's fictional Rikki had defended his master in a fight to the death with a cobra that slithered through the water drain of the bathroom. It is largely through this *Jungle Book* story that the mongoose attained his international reputation as an invincible snake killer and friend of man. Mongooses (not mongeese) are also hailed as the Pied Pipers that rid Hawaii of rats and saved its sugar industry. It is said that they are so cunning that they combine forces to defeat an enemy, so courageous that they attack animals ten times their size. Abundant personality and affection has made them valued house pets since the days of the Pharaohs.

Believed to have originated in Africa of the civet cat family, mongooses are now also native to Spain and Asia where they adapt themselves to every condition of terrain and climate. There are even mongooses that live on crabs, cleverly cracking the shells by dashing them against a hard object held between hind feet.

The most popular of the thirty species is the one Kipling heaped with glory, the common Indian mongoose. His fur is a salt-and-pepper shade, his walk as cocky as a dachshund's, and his fifteen-inch tail tapers like a turnip. His small, rounded ears are perhaps the most amazing in the animal world. Constructed of folds that can be overlapped at will, completely closing off the opening, this, plus well-developed, nonretractable digging claws, enables the mongoose to enter the underground dens of snakes, rats, and other animals as effectively as a shovel. His tongue is also unusual, containing a thorny section which the natives believe holds the antidote to snake poison but which is a patch of rough papillae used for removing meat from bones. Armed with forty sharp teeth and remarkable aggression, mongooses are carnivorous, living on reptiles, frogs, ants, scorpions, rats, lizards, and any bird or insect they can catch. They are valuable residents of areas where they help keep this prolific horde in check—an important counterweight in nature's law of balance.

This balance was so seriously upset in Hawaii in the 1880's with the accidental introduction of five species of rats, including the large, destructive Norway, that the entire sugar cane industry, mainstay of the islands, was seriously threatened. The bounty system, with planters offering cash for rat tails, proved less than ineffectual when it was discovered that the Chinese who were delivering the majority of tails were freeing the tailless rats so they could continue breeding more bounty. Finally, in 1883, the *Planters' Monthly* suggested that the Indian mongoose be introduced, adding that the animal was "a great ratter, better than the cat." The Hilo Planters' Association quickly put up $1,100 to bring in seventy-two mongooses. After the animals had been there a year one planter, in a speech before his organization, said all Hilo cane fields had been infested with rats twelve months ago, that now there not only wasn't any rat-chewed cane, but no rats. The planter, Mr. Austin, estimated that mongooses had already saved them $50,000.

Actually, all rats weren't eliminated. Being clever animals, some learned to live in trees where mongooses couldn't reach them, and they soon discovered that their swift and deadly enemy hunted only during daylight—so the smart ones slept aloft by day and foraged by night. But the largest and most harmful, the Norway, fled into ground holes and was fair game for the Indian annihilator. Although they were doing a remarkable job, the mongooses soon had detractors who claimed that they were taking chickens and ground-nesting birds. Planters countered with scientific research proving that an examination of stools showed that 80 percent of mongooses lived on insects. They also pointed out their economic worth, stating that on four islands inhabited by them the destructive rat population was small, while on the two islands without mongooses, the cane-and-fruit-eating rats were still in command. As a result of this experiment and another in Jamaica, the mongoose's fame has spread, bringing him with telling effect to Puerto Rico, Grenada, Santa Cruz, Cuba, and Barbados. Meanwhile, in Hawaii, the mongoose has become the most common animal—and the most controversial.

Part of the controversy is the question: Is he really the great snake killer that Kipling and others claimed? I may have part of the answer: I saw a contest between cobra and mongoose in Ceylon, conducted by the island's most colorful people, the gypsies, in an arena surrounded by chin-high bamboo matting to prevent the contestants from escaping. We stood outside, looking over the enclosure. The cobra was large and black,with the painted spectacle on the back of his hooded head, and he came out of his basket hissing,

full of life. The mongoose was in a cautious cat crouch, his
beady eyes watching every slither of the cobra. We were
told that both were wild and had been caught a few days
ago. The fight promised to be a good one. The cobra twisted
to the center and raised one third of its length off the
ground, its hood spread, waiting. The mongoose, tiptoeing
as gracefully as a ballet dancer, made a wide circle around
the snake. Neither rushed to the attack. Then, two gypsies
with long paddlelike sticks, began gently pushing them
toward each other. The mongoose turned and glared at
the gypsy, bristled, seemed to swell, his fur standing out,
and the pushing stopped. (I am told that this fluffing of fur
throws the snake off and confuses him as to the actual size
of the mongoose, often causing him to strike short.) Suddenly, the mongoose darted near the cobra, tempting it
to strike. It did, missing by a foot. This strike-and-dodge action went on for twenty minutes, with the cobra's lunges
becoming less vicious, the mongoose closing his circle until
the snake was missing him by mere inches. Finally, after the
cobra made an especially strong strike, the mongoose, in a
marvelously agile motion, sprang behind, grabbing it by the
neck. There was furious action now; the mongoose seemed
to be riding the neck of the writhing, thrashing snake. In
five minutes it was over. The mongoose rose from the still
snake and shook itself, an exhausted little animal. A grin-
ning gypsy came running, picked him up, placed him in a
small cage and gave him a piece of root, *suthaclavara mulle*
(only Ceylon gypsies are supposed to know exactly what it
is), said to destroy cobra poison.

This is another mongoose mystery: Can they absorb cobra
venom without harm? The Ceylon gypsy root and the herb
manguswail, the Indian antidote to snake poison supposedly
used by the animal, are acknowledged by experts to be
sheer superstition. But mongooses are known to have been
bitten and yet walk away from the fight apparently un-

harmed. Clifford Pope of the Chicago Natural History Museum tells of a fight between a mongoose and a cobra where the mongoose was bitten in the region of the mouth more than once without any seeming ill effects. Mentioning this in *Animal Facts and Fallacies,* Osmond Breland says that the poison was probably absorbed so slowly from the mouth region that no harm resulted.

S. H. Prater, O. B. E., C. M. Z. S., in *The Book of Indian Animals,* says that the mongoose, less sensitive to snake venom, is able to withstand doses of poison potent enough to kill other animals of equal size But he also points out that immunity is not absolute, that a mongoose injected with sufficient venom dies like any other creature.

There is also no doubt that the courageous animal is sometimes bested in a snake fight. But some observers claim that when a large and dangerous snake is sighted, mongooses will gather forces for attack. Hunter Hans Coudenhove was assured by natives of Taveta, Africa, that it was a common tactic for several mongooses to join to do battle with a python. I saw the cooperative effort when a male and female polished off a large jungle rat in India. Working as a team, one flushed the rat from a bamboo thicket into the waiting jaws of its mate.

Mongooses are affectionate mates, often traveling in pairs, but the male leaves the female in complete charge of the nursery department. This can occupy much of her decade of life with breedings as often as five times a year, with two to four offspring in a litter. Usually, she gives birth to her young in an underground den dug for the purpose, but some have been known to use empty huts or unoccupied rooms of dak bungalows. Protective to the extreme, she will savagely attack animals of any size that approach her young. The eyes of the young open in sixteen days, and within a few weeks they are toddling beside their mother as she takes them afield to teach them the facts of life. When she goes for

an insect, they follow her motions precisely, quickly learning
the art of hunting until they are strong enough to take
creatures of their own size. With a powerful neck and jaws,
keen vision, and extreme speed and accuracy of attack, the
mongoose has little trouble furnishing her numerous litters with food or in passing on her proficiency. Their enemies are man, the big cats, and hawks. But they protect
themselves effectively with a sentry warning system—posted
mongooses utter shrill yelps in time of danger. I saw a mongoose in South Africa sitting up like a begging dog watching the sky. Using binoculars, I spotted a hawk far up in
a lazy hunting glide. When the mongoose's yelp came, five
others that had been stretched out in the sunshine they love
scuttled for their dens long before the hawk could set his
wings in a dive.

Many who have spent time in the wild places of India
and Africa eventually end up adopting the unique animal
as a pet—or being adopted by one. An English soldier, R. A.
Sterndale, had one, "Pip," a constant companion. Under
complete control, Pip obeyed finger commands, would sit
up and look for the game bird every time Sterndale put a
shotgun to his shoulder, and without any prior training,
would run and get the downed bird, as skillfully as an experienced bird dog—with one difference: he kept the bird.
Sterndale said he was absolutely fearless, once putting to
rout an enormous greyhound, perhaps twenty times his
size.

Easily tamed and housebroken, mongooses are clean and
intelligent companions. A friend had one that would sit in
a chair after his meal, picking his teeth with a claw, as sedate
as an English clubman using a toothpick after a roast beef
dinner.

One fan had a mongoose, Rikki-Tikki, for eight years,
an esthetic who loved to rise on his hind legs and smell
flowers in bloom and was fond of music. When his owner,

Hans Coudenhove, took him for a walk and Rikki refused to return with him, he would play the guitar he brought along and the mongoose followed entranced. He also climbed on his master's lap when he wanted his back scratched; he reached up and stroked the man's face, keeping at it until he got what he wanted.

More curious than a cat, mongooses explore everything in the house or camp they inhabit. When they arrive in a new place they minutely examine the premises, squeezing through or scooting under any space they can, slowly at first, then repeating it at full speed—insurance if they ever need instant escape. A trick many owners have discovered when they want to locate their pets is to place a key ring on the floor. In seconds, the mongoose is there examining each key. Great lap climbers, they usually sleep with their owners, using their winning personalities as a persuasive power for food, favors, and to evade punishment for wrongdoing.

This personality saved one mongoose's life, upset an entire city, inspired a song, and involved a Secretary of the Interior. It started in 1962 when a sailor gave a male mongoose, Mr. Magoo, to the Duluth, Minnesota, zoo.* In the mongoose manner, Magoo quickly captivated zoo visitors and all went well until the United States Fish and Wildlife Service pointed out that in 1900, mongooses, because of their reproductive powers and carnivorous tastes, had been banned in the United States (except Hawaii). The suggestion was that "Mr. Magoo should be dispatched humanely."

Immediately, the Duluth radio network began a "No Noose for the Mongoose" movement, and indignant letters and phone calls flooded Mayor George Johnson's office. He responded with a "Save Magoo" campaign that gained momentum daily. At the Purdue-Minnesota football game, a "Save the Mongoose" banner was paraded around the field.

* Jack Denton Scott, *The Duluth Mongoose* (New York: William Morrow, 1965).

A disc jockey wrote a satiric ballad of the sad plight of the mongoose to the beat of "Davy Crockett." Trans-World Airlines suggested that it be permitted to fly Magoo back to his native India. The hubbub finally reached Washington, where Secretary of the Interior Stewart L. Udall decreed, with the wisdom and solemnity of Solomon, according to a report by *Newsweek,* that Mr. Magoo didn't undermine the intent of the law, "That there was no threat as long as Mr. Magoo is not two."

Whether in the zoo or the jungle, the mongoose is a conspicuous charmer, a versatile animal with bewildering facets to his character. His courage can take your breath away. Once while moving through some grassy flatlands on the back of a beautifully trained hunting elephant, I was astounded to see a pair of mongooses come tearing out of a clump of grass and stand glaring at our huge mount. The elephant lifted his trunk and then his right foot as if to squash these belligerent little nothings. Suddenly, one mongoose shrieked and darted to the right; the other started to climb the elephant's left leg. I felt the big animal trembling; his right foot came back to the ground and he stood silently as if held, a thrall of fear. With this, the mongooses ran back a few paces, looked directly up at the elephant, turned, and moved away in a dignified, slow walk.

The elephant quieted and started forward, increasing his pace, muttering like an irascible old gentleman disgusted with the antics of a couple of youthful cutups. This is the only time I have ever seen a hunting elephant lose his magnificent aplomb.

4

THE HUNTING ELEPHANT

The roads to the camp where I met my first hunting elephants were bog soft some of the way in. Winter rains had been falling for a week and it became questionable whether we should continue with our tiger hunt plans. We had driven from New Delhi to Kotdwara, a medieval village on the edge of the lower Shvalik Range, the foothills of the Himalayas, eighty miles from Tibet, and sat in our jeep watching the mountain people streaming into the trading town with milk, monkeys, fruit, and skins that they would use for barter.

Our destination was forty miles deeper into the jungle wilderness, and the forest guard with the gold and red peaked turban who stood at the entrance to the road shook his head as Giriraj Singh, one of the owners of Indian Shikar and Tours, signed the book, attesting that we would travel at our own risk.

"We don't know what the rains have done," the guard said. "We are recommending no one enter the forests. Of course you have the jeep. . . ." Giriraj smiled and told the guard that he thought we would make it.

As we drove he said, "It would take a much worse storm than we've had to stop this vehicle."

I shared his optimism. World War II had proved to me that it would take the bottom of a swamp or 5 feet of snow to baffle a jeep. But as we got deeper into the jungle, the mud rutted beneath our wheels and we had to go into low-low and four-wheel drive and even then we had rough going.

"About four miles more," Giriraj said.

The road ahead looked flat and hard, and he took the jeep out of low-low drive and spurted ahead. We never made it, sinking to the top of the wheels. We had difficulty getting out of the vehicle onto the safety of the shoulder of matted jungle grass.

Giriraj told us to wait, that he would go to camp for help in yanking the station wagon out of the mire. It was an hour before we heard him shout and saw him plodding toward us on the back of an elephant. There were three other men with him, and they quickly took over, hooking a chain to the bumper of the jeep, giving the big animal instructions. The elephant had the jeep out and on hard ground in less than ten minutes. We were safely in camp in another fifteen minutes.

I mention this episode for two reasons: It historically

annotates the beginning of my love affair with the elephant
and explodes the modern myth of the infallibility of the jeep.
I had used the jeep hunting in central India and the Land
Rover (its British cousin) in Africa, and I had always credited it with making big-game hunting possible. Here, even
without roads softened by hard rain, the jeep could do little
good in hunting the tiger. Again, the elephant came to the
rescue.

The tall, fall grass of this mountain section grows to a
height of 20 feet. It is impossible to walk in it to hunt
cats, and you can't drive the jeep. The answer: four elephants
with *mahouts* (which, loosely translated, means "rider of
the great") move through an area where a tiger has been
located, driving the animal back where you sit in the tree
machan. The big, gray, beating elephants come through,
breaking trees, trumpeting, enough to scare anything, even
the hard-to-intimidate tiger out of the grass. You can't hunt
without them.

They also transport you to the *machan* so that all you
have to do is stand up, reach a foot over, and you're treed,
ready for the tiger wait. In short, the elephant is master in
this terrain.

The first day in the Shvalik Range area we started out
single file, four elephants and twelve men, three on each
animal. Suddenly, a breeze came up, whipping off my light
canvas hat. It fluttered to the ground four feet in front of
the elephant behind me. Without orders from the *mahout*,
the animal carefully picked it up with his trunk, moved up
beside me, reached over, and deposited the hat on my lap.
The same animal picked up his rider's *ankus* (pointed
steel goad, a training tool) that the *mahout* had dropped—
without being instructed.

I have hunted Indian bison (gaur) with a brave elephant,
sitting on her back facing down the charge of the angered
bison; I have hunted tiger, or watched from the safety of

a tree while the elephant hunted the tiger and drove it toward me; I have shot partridge and jungle fowl from the back of an elephant who was as steady to shot-and-wing as the finest bird dog; I have joy ridden along a moonlit jungle road on the back of an elephant with my wife, probably the most romantic and memorable ride I've ever had—and the safest. I have stood and talked with elephants while they ate their dinners, watched them while their *mahouts* bathed them in the river, rubbing their bellies with a rock until the giants groaned in delight.

Out of this experience has come a growing contempt for the men who shoot them: "I got this tusker in my sights. He couldn't see me, didn't even know I was there. I let him get within twenty-five yards, then got him twice in the brain pan." This school of writing and sport sickens me.

Shooting elephants is a "sport" that exists only in Africa. The Far East is more intelligent in this regard, some of the Indian princes realizing two thousand years ago that the beasts were friends of man and as such must be protected. Unfortunately, in areas like Sumatra and Ceylon, and to some extent Burma, some elephants are being shot to "protect" farmlands, and the push of civilization is taking its toll in elephant tusks. But the sportsman can't shoot elephants in most of Asia. The animals are protected by rigid law.

In fairness to the African big-game hunter and in the interest of objectivity, however, it should be pointed out that the big slaughter of elephants in Africa cannot be blamed on the man with the high-powered rifle. The pachyderm population of 6,000 for Kenya, 11,000 for Uganda and 100,000 in the Congo is cruelly preyed on by the natives. *The London Times,* October 31, 1957, reported that the director of the Royal National Parks of Kenya claimed that more than 3,000 elephants had been killed in just one game area during the previous two years. An antipoaching party scouting an area 25 miles long by 20 miles wide between the Galena and Tana rivers had counted more than 1,280 elephant carcasses in a period of nine weeks. The natives kill them for food and ivory, but the British are imposing strict laws with jail penalties and huge fines, and the slaughter is slowing. What will happen to the big animals when all of Africa becomes independent is cause for alarm because, paradoxically, most Africans care little or nothing for the wild animals of their continent.

Some authorities place the world elephant population at slightly more than a quarter million. Naturalist-writer Richard Carrington, who made extensive field studies in Africa, believes that there are at least that many in Africa and about half that number in India. One thing is certain: There aren't enough around to justify shooting them. And let's be factual: Unless the elephant is a rogue, an overworked word where these big animals are concerned, what skill is involved in bagging a target the size of a garage? Sure, some of the elephant-eliminators have told me that you must hit one very small, one very particular spot to down an elephant. If you miss, if you don't kill on the first shot, your life is in grave danger. It should be.

The elephant is the last of the great prehistoric mammals, a living monument to what has gone before in the dark times, a significant symbol of man's attainments, his emergence from the abyss. Consider that the elephant, whose ancestors go back more than fifty million years, was once one of the large populations of earth with more than three hundred species and relatives. Now it is down to two species, the Indian and the African.

Elephants have been friends of man for centuries. They have been and are being used as beasts of burden, as a means of transportation, as protectors in time of war, for show and entertainment, and in India in sports afield.

The principal method of capturing wild elephants, especially in India, where their training originated dating from the second millennium B.C., is an annual roundup called the *keddah*. The one I saw had as its trap a large triangular stockade with a funnel-shaped opening at one end into which the wild animals are herded. The funnel was formed by running out two sides of the triangle beyond the base about five hundred yards. The entire stockade was made of large tree trunks with an opening called the *Kan gula* (ear hole), also made of logs, a solid shield of a door that could be raised or lowered. The stockade encloses a large jungle area that has a pond or a stream, the theory being that the elephants to be driven toward the fenced area will be attracted by the water which they love.

The next step, at least as I saw it, was to gather as many men from the local villages as could be assembled. There must have been close to a thousand in the group this day. The dry season was selected and any streams between the herd of elephants and the *keddah* had their courses changed so the animals would not stop in the drive toward the stockade. The object is to keep the beasts thirsty so they will enter the *keddah* without objection.

Once the herd is located, it is completely surrounded by the beaters, and the drive begins. It may start close to the stockade or fifty miles away, and can take from a couple of weeks to four months. Often, if the beat is too far away from the *keddah*, a new one is quickly constructed, saving time, money, and tempers—and driven elephants can have terrible tempers.

The beaters splay out in a rectangle and move the animals forward slowly so they won't panic and break back through the line. When the drive gets close to the stockade, the beaters quickly form new lines parallel with the funnel, which means that the driven elephants are enclosed by the two protruding arms of the *keddah* and the three sides of the advancing men. The forward push continues until they enter the gate. It clamps down like a portcullis. The day I watched the mass entry which was spurred by the firing of blank cartridges and shouts, the elephants seemed to enter gladly, immediately making for the water, a large pond in the center of the enclosure.

The next day, the *mahout* enters the *keddah* on a trained elephant and attempts to get a noose around the leg of the animal they have selected for domestication. This is an involved process which hinges upon separating the animal from the rest of the herd. The Indians nearly always select females, working on the basis that the tusker is unpredictable, especially during mating season, and cannot always be depended upon as a hunting or working animal. Cows with calves cause trouble, and I watched patient *mahouts* working on two cows all day. The roars, the trumpeting, the screaming! But finally they made it, and the nooses were fastened. This is done by a trained man who slips from the tame elephant's back, strikes the wild beast's hind foot, and cleverly nooses it as it is raised. If, for a variety of reasons, this doesn't work, an enormous trained elephant will then butt the captive from the rear until it is submissive enough to noose.

The Indians do not believe in training elephants through fear. The first step is to assign a *mahout* who will live with the elephant, perhaps for the rest of his life. The animals I rode with Indian Shikar and Tours were all at least twenty-five years old before they began their training as hunting elephants. According to Shem Sher Jung, the rajah who was senior owner of the *shikar* organization, the temperamental streak is gone at that age; the animal is quiet, sometimes almost placid, and will take to specialized training more easily.

Jung tells me that the captive female elephant is placed in a stall between two others who are already well trained or at least well advanced where she is left alone with sufficient food and water. In this manner the wild one can see that she is safe, that nothing alarming is going to happen. Once the captive starts eating normally and quiets down training begins.

The trainer stands in front of the animal with two assistants on tame elephants on either side, controlling the captive. Four other men then run their hands gently over the wild one's hide, uttering soothing words. Often, the elephant doesn't take to this and starts whipping her trunk. The trainer then uses his *hawkus* or *ankus,* the pointed metal rod with the curved hook on the side. The elephant will take a limited amount of punishment with the sharp point of the goad, then she will fold up her trunk in protection and quiet down, enduring the hands of the men attempting to soothe her.

After she has submitted to this, she is led to a stream and her *mahout,* again using the sharp goad, will induce her to lie down in the water where she is bathed and has her belly rubbed and water splashed on her. This delights her, and after a while she looks forward to the bath as a reward. Then comes the ordeal of getting her accustomed to the *khatola* or *char-jarma,* a huge pad with an oblong frame lashed on it, the riding saddle. Long rides with several people aboard finish this phase. Then come the hunting lessons.

Shem Sher Jung tells me that this usually takes four years, beginning with the elephant being ridden into a field where barking dogs are driven out of the brush toward her. When she becomes staunch to this racket (and this can take a long time), the trainers then ride her into the jungle, throwing lighted firecrackers ahead of her and cracking a bullwhip over her head.

When the elephant becomes calm about all of this, she is taken out with a pair of experienced animals, with a *houdah,* a boxlike saddle, and the gunner stands and shoots at whatever game is flushed. Imperfections are corrected until she is as steady to shot as a polished field trial pointer.

A mixture of wheat, salt, and water, actually a huge loaf of bread, is fed to the hunting elephants daily. One animal needs ten pounds a day, plus all the ficus (a variety of fig) leaves he wants. Young bamboo, kans, and tiger grass are also part of the diet.

The "riders of the great" have their own language for the elephants.

Shem Sher Jung translated a few words as we were swaying along a jungle road one day on his favorite hunter, Champa Kali, a small, powerful animal with superior intelligence. "Dhut" means stop; "Mall," go; "Bhit," sit; "Tul," special canter lifting the left leg; "Jhuk," drop one shoulder and bend sideways; "Mall agah," go forward; "Dub," knock down a tree; "Tali," step on the tree once it is down.

The rajah claims that a hunting elephant can understand thirty words and several phrases. This makes him more intelligent than the dog, who normally masters a dozen words or commands.

Nights when the campfires had flickered out and the stars were misted with a chill light, we would go into our tents, climb under blankets, listen to the soothing sounds of the elephants as they softly trumpeted to one another, and be lulled to sleep in as wild a place as I have ever visited. Somehow, with those big, intelligent animals out there, the camp was surrounded with a sense of security.

5

THE BAFFLING BABOON

Animals still exist in Africa because of farsighted men who set up preserves, places of patrolled protection. South Africa probably has the best maintained and most efficiently patrolled preserve in its Kruger National Park.

As is usual in my quests, I had gone to South Africa to see people, but I spent the most interesting time of my life in that vast national park, looking at the animals in their natural element: crocodiles coming like death out of rivers;

zebras looking like the wallpaper in a child's room; giraffes suddenly standing in the road, props for a Walt Disney production, a strange animal with fewer vertebrae in its neck than a mouse, a creature that can see backward without turning its head; elephants plodded the dirt roads in majesty; Cape buffaloes, seen from the rear as they disappeared into the brush, reminded me of women in skin-tight slacks at bowling alleys.

One afternoon, when the sun was bright and heavy, we stopped our car under the umbrella spread of an acacia tree and sat watching a herd of feeding wildebeests, a curious horse-buffalo sort of animal that looks like it has come off a cartoonist's drawing board. Suddenly, there was a thump on the roof and a hairy hand shot through the window and grabbed my necktie. Another hand stretched out, palm flat.

What peered through the open window looked like someone in a Halloween fright mask: the face was grayish black; a long, bony ridge overhung cold eyes; coarse, black hair stood straight up from the head; fangs hung under a dog-like snout. He made no sound.

In addition to the visual shock, I was beginning to have slight trouble breathing and couldn't decide how to loosen that grip. Then the South African sitting beside me carefully placed a cracker in the outstretched palm. "Meet our jungle beatnik," he said, laughing. "Just in time for breakfast."

Immediately, I was released, and the animal leaped into the road munching the cracker. I quickly did two things: rolled up the window and removed my necktie. This was my first intimate meeting with the baboon, one of the most frightening and fascinating of animals.

Manlike in his social organization, concern for his young, and in his frustrations, the baboon sits on the evolutionary ladder just below the anthropoid apes. Baboons hold council meetings, post sentries, and have a language of their own. They can count, reason, and use mechanical gadgets. They are so fierce and strong that two are a match for a leopard, yet at times they are so gentle that people have entrusted them with children.

The most intelligent of all monkeys, baboons have inhabited Africa for millions of years. Their color—yellow, green, ginger, gray, black, and brown—changes with locale. The most unusual, the Mandrill, has a scarlet nose, brilliant blue cheeks, and a violet and rose rear. Next to the gorilla, this vicious pastel nightmare is the most feared animal in the deep Congo forests. The largest baboon is the brownish-black South African Chacma: he is best known and said to be the most intelligent. A big male stands almost five feet and can weigh 100 pounds. The stone-gray Abyssinian Hamadryas, worshipped as a god by the ancient Egyptians, carries a cloak of long hair on his shoulders and a tuft on his tail like a deformed French poodle.

For an overall description of the baboon, my small nephew's reaction after seeing his first at a zoo is quite accurate: "A big monkey with a dog's face, a crooked tail, and the seat of its pants worn out." The 18-inch tail is held at an angle to the body, the end portion drooping, and the skin around it obscenely bare and heavily calloused, permitting the baboon to sleep sitting up, even on small branches.

At a game park in Kenya, where I had gone to observe the sunset and the vast sweep of violet African dusk, I saw two adult male baboons climb out on a branch smaller than my wrist. Sitting easily on that perch, backsides balancing them perfectly, one fell asleep immediately, the other sat and stared. One hundred yards away I saw a troop of thirty dozing in five thorn trees. In each tree a baboon sentry sat staring until I got into my car and left.

A troop finds safety from its greatest enemies, lions and leopards, in trees which provide refuge, bedroom, and playground. As leopards are adept climbers, the baboons post a sentry in the lower branches of each tree to remain on duty several hours; he is then relieved and moves up to join his family for the night. One observer, who sat up four nights watching, reported this changing of the guard occurred promptly at 11:30 each night. Once hidden in a tree *machan,* I saw a big leopard sitting on its haunches like a dog, watching baboons retiring in a half-dozen trees. There was much wailing and barking, evidence that they also saw the cat, but finally it became dark and silent. But every time the leopard made the slightest advance, the baboon sentry in each tree barked. No match for baboons *en masse,* the cat finally gave up in disgust.

Baboons also find safety in high rocky areas. A photographer related an unusual incident that occurred when he was trying to get some 16mm action of the Gelada baboons of southern Abyssinia to include in a documentary he was filming of that area.

"We started up a steep rocky hillside where my guide said the baboons were likely to be found," he told me, "when I saw two looking at us. They began jumping up and down and barking, and soon several more baboons appeared. Within seconds it seemed like the mountain was falling. The baboons were actually rolling rocks down at us. We got out of there fast."

Most of those clifflike areas are accessible only because of the baboon's agility. Naturalist Eugene N. Marais, who lived for years near a troop in South Africa, tells of their using a retiring place in a cave on the face of a sheer cliff. "It looked like no animal without wings could ever reach it," he said. But under the nightly terror of many prowling leopards below, the baboons found a way. A narrow ledge, inches wide, ran across the cliff. Each night the baboons had to travel a full mile hanging by their fingers to this ledge, hind feet against smooth cliff-face. Below was a five-hundred-foot drop onto rocks. Baboons are seldom quiet but there was dead silence on this perilous journey led by large males, followed by females, mothers with pickaback babies, then youngsters. One false move meant death. "We watched this nightly performance with horror," said Marais, "always expecting a mother carrying an especially large youngster to fall." Yet, such is the baboon's strength, grace, and balance that there was never a mistake.

There isn't evidence of this grace on level ground. The animals lope along in an awkward quadrupedal canter, eternally in search of food. They are especially partial to corn on the cob—a small troop, advancing abreast, army fashion, can quickly strip a large field. Then they move off clumsily on three limbs, carrying the corn under one arm.

African farmers report that previous to such a raid a baboon scout will be sent ahead to look the field over. If it is safe, he summons the troop. Then two sentries are posted in trees, often back to back so they can scan the entire area. If there is danger, the lookouts bark, sometimes even pointing at the enemy. Bill Olds, owner of the Springbok Tour Agency in Johannesburg, South Africa, told me he has seen cases of punishment when sentries didn't do their duty properly—rough cuffing and mauling were meted out.

As a result of this use of sentries, and their extraordinary appetites, baboons are destructive pests, the bane of African farmers who use ingenious schemes to try to outwit them. I watched one farmer try. It is a fact that baboons are unafraid of women, often approaching and mocking them, invading gardens in full sight of the lady of the house. After having an entire cornfield destroyed, one South African farmer decided to dress as a woman and shoot as many baboons as he could.

"I hope to kill the leader and disorganize the entire raiding troop," the farmer told me. That evening, as the baboons approached his fields, he walked out in his wife's dress with a gun under his arm. The baboons came on unafraid. When he got within range, he began firing, killing several and frightening off the entire troop.

Apparently, he didn't get the leader, because the troop was back again in a few days. When the farmer tried a repeat performance, the baboons fled long before he was within gunshot.

"Yet," the farmer said, "a week later, when I was away, these same baboons came close to the house completely unafraid of my wife who stood in the yard."

On occasion, farmers will leave loaded shotguns near the cornfield, and often the curious baboons will pick them up and pull the trigger, injuring themselves and others. But baboons cannot be caught twice by the same trick.

Like crows, they seem to know when a man is carrying a gun; they often are unafraid and will surround and sometimes attack an unarmed person if he is interfering with their social activities, such as disturbing a meal. A Bantu in Kruger Park told me that he had once thrown a spear at a belligerent baboon in a corn field, only to have the animal dodge it, pick it up and hurl it back.

But they aren't completely destructive. Besides farmers' crops, they eat more than fifty forms of plant life in East Africa alone and are great destroyers of the harmful locust. They also relish the deadly scorpion, that stinging insect that can make man or beast sick. Their technique is fascinating. I have watched a baboon scout a scorpion under a rock, lift the rock, and swiftly pinion the stinging tail. Then he quickly plucked the tail and popped the body into his mouth, all in a swift, beautifully coordinated motion.

Their diet is currently causing scientific consternation and study. Long considered herbivores, they have suddenly taken to eating flesh, even killing for it. Although they are rare cases, baboons have been observed killing lambs and eating the entire carcass. I saw a big male kill a vervet monkey in an East African park refuge. Current studies in this startling change in baboon diet may indicate when and how man became omnivorous.

Unlike most wild species, baboons are not always loners in their quest for food. A team of American scientists photographed baboons grazing with impalas, gnus, and zebras in what appeared to be a mutual-assistance pact—the grazing animals have a keen sense of smell, the baboons have superior eyesight. As a result of this teamwork, if a predator approaches, the baboon shrieks and heads for the trees; if an impala winds an enemy, it gives a sharp barking sound. "A mixed herd of impalas and baboons is almost impossible to surprise," the scientists concluded.

This, in my experience, is an understatement, for the baboon alone is almost impossible to take unawares. I spent most of one day trying to approach a troop of wild baboons, near a deep forest, not the game-park types accustomed to humans. Using a 16mm motion picture camera, I wanted to get close for some long, continuous runs. Finally, creeping on my hands and knees in high grass, I managed to get within 500 yards, but never closer.

African white hunter Donald Ker claims that baboons have the keenest vision of any animal, equal to ten-power binoculars. Using glasses, Ker spotted baboons not visible to the naked eye on the open plains and watched them scamper off as he moved a few steps forward.

Other recent observations of wild baboons in East Africa by anthropologists S. L. Washburn and Irven DeVore have brought remarkable conclusions. Their scientific studies of the baboon's social habits—mating, group organization, feeding, and other daily routines—reveal patterns of interdependence that may shed light on the early evolution of the human species. They report that a baboon troop ranges an area of 3 to 6 miles from sleeping tree to feeding territory, with the troop carefully organized: in the vanguard are the less dominant males with a few larger young baboons with females and youngsters following. In the center are females with infants, the youngest baboons, and then a rear guard of the most dominant males. Females and young are so protected that no matter how a predator approaches it has to face adult males.

Troops, from 12 to 200, are staggered in a hierarchy of dominance, usually with several males ruling, forming a council, putting down troublemakers, enforcing a peaceful community pattern of living. The scientists' observations disprove theories that sex is the bond keeping baboons together, the council actually preventing fighting or rivalry over females.

Like humans, baboons are afraid of the dark, have a fear of falling, of snakes and, like our world, theirs is divided into enemies, allies, and neutrals. I have seen baboons step calmly aside to make way for elephants, giraffes, and hippos; watched them hie to the trees and scream madly at cheetahs; observed them dozing in the sun with alert zebras surrounding them.

The anthropologist team also discovered that sociableness holds the wild baboon troop together, with ties between mother and infant, between youngsters in a play group, between mating adults, and between dominant males. They found that life in a troop is the only possible one for the wild baboon. If one strays or drops out hurt, it is quickly killed by predators. These recent findings differ greatly from studies made by zoologists of caged baboons in which sex and fighting over females seemed to be the order of the day.

Another naturalist discovered that baboons have a language consisting of shrill alarm cries, contented chucklings and grunts, dissatisfied barks, silly, happy chatterings, mourning wails for their dead, cries denoting pain, groans of dread, and calls for assembly and for action. He observed that at night there was a continuous soft mumbling among them which sounded so much like human talk that he was almost convinced that baboons were capable of articulated speech. One native told him, "Baboons can talk, but they won't do it in front of white men for fear you will put them to work."

In the troop this scientist was studying he observed that the older baboons never took much notice of the play of the little ones, until on one occasion the youngsters came closer to his huts than they had before.

"Suddenly," he observed, "there was a *basso-profundo* shout by an old baboon and immediately, without a moment's delay, without looking at us again, the little ones rushed up to the circle of the older ones. Each one went immediately to its mother. There was a short silence; then from the same old baboon came a deep bass grumble and immediately the whole troop began to move. They did not run, they walked slowly away from us, every mother with her baby on her back, toward the sleeping place."

He concluded that there was no doubt about the meaning the two sounds the old baboon made. The first was a command to the little ones to return immediately; the second a command to the entire troop to move to the sleeping area, or at least get moving and follow the leaders. Actually, baboon activities seem to revolve around their young.

A single offspring is born once a year after a seven-month gestation period. Remarkably responsible parents, they defend their young with vigor and bravery.

A game park ranger in East Africa told me of seeing a leopard attack three female baboons near a cliff. The one nearest the leopard had a youngster on her back. Immediately, she handed it to the baboon behind her who was in a higher, safer position and stood and faced the leopard. The cat killed her before the ranger could reach them.

In South Africa, Alexander Lake heard a female baboon wail and saw several male baboons head for the sound. She was wailing over her baby that apparently had eaten poisoned corn and was having convulsions. Lake walked over to the baby, now surrounded by adult baboons, and poured hot coffee down his throat. Eventually, the baby seemed to recover, and its mother took it away. Lake points this out as an example of the baboon's maternal instinct and ability to reason. Usually they tear anyone apart who touches one of their young, but these just stood by, seeming to want his help.

This maternal instinct is so strong that kittens, lambs, goats—even human babies have been adopted by baboons. A farmer told me of a captive baboon on a farm in the Transvaal becoming so attached to a baby that she curled up in the crib, tenderly holding the baby in her arms. The child's mother noticed that the presence of the animal was soothing, with the result that she soon began calling her to aid as a baby sitter.

Baboons respect mating, and the wooing pair is left alone much like young lovers in human society. After watching a troop in South Africa for some time, I observed that the female runs faster and longer than the male and that often several young males make a love chase. The baboon belle outruns them, then, when the panting swains catch up, she calmly makes her choice. There is no fighting, no contest involved, the female often choosing the last tired male to arrive.

The pair's newborn clings to his mother's long underhair for two weeks, riding in this precarious position wherever she goes. After that jolting and hazardous period he makes clumsy attempts to walk, then giving up, he moves to his mother's back in a comfortable jockey position for another month. Often, association between mother and baby is amusing. Mrs. Osa Johnson watched one hold her offspring by his tail, suspending him over a pool for a drink with the youngster doing more looking at his reflection than drinking. Then another playful youngster nipped the mother and she let the baby slip to give chase. Sinking, her baby came bobbing up, spluttering and coughing. His mother rushed back, pulled him out, and tried to soothe him, but he would have none of it. Screaming and sobbing he struck at her, scolding her furiously.

After six weeks the pampered offspring starts taking solid food and moves away from its mother for a few hours a day to join other youngsters. This play group is where they practice fighting, hiding, tree climbing, outhunting one another in a search for insects and plants; it is the basis for the baboon's education. They play much like children, "king of the mountain," "tug of war," racing, yanking tails, and somersaulting. When the roughhousing gets out of hand, an old male will bark at them and interfere if he thinks it necessary. In four months, the young baboon's movements are so well coordinated that he joins juvenile society for good.

Maturing at six years, baboons live in the wild state for twenty-five years, sometimes doubling that time in captivity. As adults, they have little trouble protecting themselves and are as fierce and almost as strong as anything in the wild. Their 2-inch fangs are longer than a lion's; their method of fighting is terribly effective. The enemy is gripped by powerful jaws, usually on the underside of the throat. Then the baboon grasps the body with fore and hind feet, pushing away violently. Dogs have no chance against them; even the leopard, for its size the strongest and most dangerous animal in the jungle, has been bested by baboons.

A French biologist tells of a remarkable feat of courage he observed when a large leopard crept to attack a young baboon on a cliff ledge, passing below two waiting male baboons who had seen the cat coming and positioned themselves for attack. As the leopard passed immediately below, the baboons leaped. There was a moment of confused struggling, then he saw the leopard lying on its back with one baboon between its forepaws while the other gripped it from behind and prevented it from using its deadly hind claws. The first baboon had the leopard by the throat, so from the beginning the leopard could not use its great canine teeth. The fangs of the baboon did their work, and the huge leopard was soon motionless. The baboon that had grabbed the leopard by the throat struggled only a few yards away before he also died on the ledge.

The biologist called this teamwork, one holding the leopard's hind legs so the other could reach the cat's throat—an example of the baboon's power of reason. He gave other examples: the captive baboon that took its feed bag to its sleeping box every night using it as a cover when it was cold; of two baboons in the Pretoria South Africa Zoo who learned to use cups to dip in a running stream when they were thirsty—they also carefully saved full cups to douse annoying spectators.

Scientists have proved that baboons not only have the power to reason, but to count. "Cowboy" has been taught by Dr. Jack Findley to push a button that turns on a light when the animal is hungry. The color of the light (orange, red, green, blue, or white) determines how many beep tones —coming from a sound box hooked to light switches—he must let pass before he pushes a second button that stops the sound and releases a food pellet. If he pushes the second button before enough beeps or after too many have sounded for the particular light color, he gets no food. Although each beep lasts two seconds, the time between varies. This prevents the baboon from merely marking total time before pushing the second button.

Cowboy is doing well. He eats as he wishes and gets plenty of food by pushing the right buttons two hundred times a day. Fifty button pushes give him enough for a meal. Dr.

Findley is hoping, now that Cowboy can count, to teach him to add. This can be done by turning on two different colored lights simultaneously, teaching Cowboy that he must stop the sounds only after the total of beeps produced by each light has passed.

I knew an English soldier who owned a baboon, Oscar, who sat at the table with guests pretending to chat, mumbling away like a dowager at a tea party. He also drank with the guests, holding up his glass for a refill, even filling it from his own bottle, rinsing and putting it away. He was allowed only two light gins and lime a night, but one night when the drinking became involved, Oscar revolted when he was stopped on his usual two, took his gin bottle to a treetop, and got roaring drunk.

Usually, baboons do not make the best of pets, often becoming surly and dangerous as they grow older. In South Africa I once saw a "pet" pick up an African and throw him and the chair he was sitting on through a window. Another, belonging to a friend of mine in Kenya, grabbed a horse's leg, flipping both horse and rider to the ground. But occasionally one will make not only an excellent pet but a helpful companion. A farmer in the Transvaal had a baboon that led his ox wagon, obeying all commands, keeping the oxen under control. This animal even went out and found water when there was a drought.

The classic story of a pet and an example of the animal's power of reasoning is of Jackie, owned by James Wide of Uitenhage, South Africa, recorded by respected South African naturalist, F. W. Fitzsimmons, author of *Monkey Folk of South Africa,* and *The Natural History of South Africa.* Among other helpful tricks, like pushing him on a handcar, Wide, a legless railroad switchman, had trained Jackie to throw the active railroad switches. The baboon knew each switch by name and would insert the lever and throw the switch when told. The switches were locked, but Jackie knew how to unlock them and, without command, he would throw the switch back when the train had passed.

One day, Wide became so ill that he couldn't get out of bed. Jackie kept trying to rouse him but failed. At nightfall, he heard the express train whistle four times, the signal to open the switches. He took the keys from a wall peg and, carrying a lantern as he had seen his master do, hurried out to the correct switch for this track and train. First he pulled the lever, giving the distant "all clear," then he unlocked the switch and opened it. As the train roared safely by, the engineer saw the baboon by the rails waving the lantern. It was weeks before the line discovered that the fate of many people had been in Jackie's hands.

Less dramatic but most significant are the current accomplishments of a female baboon, Ahla, owned by Mrs. Aston, a goat breeder in Okahandja, South West Africa, reported by Professor W. Hoesch in a German zoological journal. Mrs. Aston had been having trouble with wandering goats, losing two or three a day, when Ahla arrived, a gift from a friend. A few days later, given the run of the farm, the baboon was interested only in goat activity. Soon, she left with the herd every day, riding the back of the biggest billy, supervising the order of march, and controlling the grazing plan.

Now there were no lost goats. Ahla maintained strict order even when the goats were given salt. Baboons detest salt, yet for the sake of discipline, she took her share. She recognized each animal in the large herd. When a goat gives birth to three kids, Mrs. Aston often takes one away, giving it to a doe with one. Ahla won't permit this. She immediately returns the kid to its mother. She grooms her charges daily, picking lice from their hair. Although former studies have compared baboons favorably with humans, it was never previously known that the animal could rise, unaided and untrained, to such a position of leadership.

6

UNTOUCHABLE
OF THE ANIMAL WORLD

The Hyena

I'm not certain what emotion held me one day while I was sitting in a Land Rover in a game preserve in Kenya. But held I was. We were watching a herd of grazing wildebeest as we sat in a welcome pool of shade thrown down before us like a Persian carpet by an enormous thorn tree. One of the animals was giving birth to a calf.

Suddenly, as if by some terrible kind of black magic, eight spotted, doglike creatures appeared and tore away the half-born calf, ripped off the mother's udders, then attacking on all sides, literally tore the wildebeest to pieces. I couldn't do anything to help for two reasons: I had no gun, and it is forbidden on a game reserve to interfere with the laws of nature.

The attackers were spotted hyenas, at once the most repulsive and incredible of animals, and this was my introduction to them. Since that time I have seen them in many places, but that first sight stays with me and is my lasting impression of these strange, brutal, nightmarish, hermaphroditic creatures.

Common belief has it that hyenas are scavengers pure and simple, but I shot one attacking a woman on the outskirts of a jungle village in India, destroyed three more that were running amuck in a flock of sheep, killing out of blood lust, and I have watched a pack of fifteen drive a lion from its kill of an antelope with the sheer persistence of darting in and risking death, until that harassed animal gave up.

But mainly hyenas exist by eating the dead and scavenging the land. Naturalists say they move mostly at night, but I have seen them sit in the broad daylight and watch sky-wheeling vultures, then, when the birds discovered carrion and dove down on it, the hyenas would trot over, drive the graveyard birds off, and demolish the carcass.

The horrible tribe contains two genera, the striped and brown, and the spotted. The brown and the spotted are found only in Africa, the brown mostly in South Africa; the striped hyena inhabits peninsular India, extending its range westward through Asia Minor into North and East Africa. Naturalists believe that Africa was the original home of the hyena and that a paradoxical nature created them eons ago. Both spotted and striped hyenas have been found fossilized from the Pliocene period.

About the size of a wolf or a large police dog, the hyena has a massive head with large, batlike, upright ears, and a strong forebody with weak, drooping hindquarters supported on short, knock-kneed hind legs. He has a dorsal crest of long hair, a mane, sharply defined from the rest of his body, that varies from cream or buff to a gray or dirty white in the summer. His stripes are transverse and as well defined as his spots. The hyena has a strange gait, a shuffling lope caused by walking on his toes. There are four short, blunt, non-retractable claws without protective sheaths on each foot. The adult male is 5 feet in length, stands about 3 feet in height, and weighs 80 pounds. They have a keen sense of smell and a remarkable facility for locating the dead.

Hyenas like bare, open plains, desert, rocky scrub-covered hills and *nullahs,* high grass, and relatively open jungle. They seem to avoid the interior of heavy forests and often bold packs of them will live near Indian and African villages, harassing the people and smaller livestock. They find shelter from the heat of the day in caves, in the shade cast by huge rocks, in holes which they sometimes dig or confiscate from another smaller creature, often a porcupine. They grow a thick winter coat, soft and full and softened with a heavy underwool. The summer coat is scant and straggly.

They give a variety of cries, including the famous "laugh" which is actually a chattering cry likened to that of a person suddenly bereft of his senses. This sound is made when they are extremely agitated and when their patience is exhausted, such as in waiting for lions or leopards to leave a carcass. They also laugh in rage when fighting with one another, moan like a person in pain, and their wailing howl, something like the eerie call of the coyote, always brings nostalgia to the African or Indian big game hunter, recalling far away campfires and hours forever gone.

Naturalists tell me that other animals are alert to the so-called laugh of the hyena because it often is a signal that they are fighting over a fresh kill. Personally, I have not heard the laugh often, but their moans, sighs, screams, and wailing have disturbed many a soft Indian night for me.

Actually the untouchables of the animal world, hyenas are shunned and despised by even such low-rung creatures as vultures and jackals. Lions will go out of their way to kill them, and I have seen hyenas dead beside the finished kill of the true king of beasts, the Indian tiger. Wild boar will gang up and attack hyenas and are one of the few animals that have nerve and strength enough to face up to several hyenas. Most animals do fear them.

Living on what is left of a carcass after the lordly lions, tigers, and leopards have left it, the hyena's share is mostly bones and coarse remains. In order to handle these, the animal is endowed with some of the most powerful jaws of any creature. His jaws and teeth are created as bone crushers, with the entire shape of his head changed to provide good attachment for the powerful muscles which work the jaws and teeth. His canine teeth, weapons of attack in most beasts of prey, are small. But the distinctiveness of the hyena's teeth is in the great size and strength of his molars and the massive conical crowns of his second and third premolars in both jaws. These teeth have a large basal ridge, an effective guard that protects the gums when bones are being crushed.

Other animals apparently know of this astonishing jaw power and respect it. Vultures and jackals leave in terror when the hyena approaches, and I have seen two striped hyenas drive a leopard from its kill. The big male leopard had killed a blue bull calf in a meadow on the edge of a bamboo forest in the province of Madhya Pradesh. As I was interested in studying this fascinating cat, I sat quietly and watched through binoculars from a distance of a quarter mile. I had been told that hyenas have an uncanny sense, detecting dead animals from many miles. These two came out of the bamboo in their rocking gait, tongues rolling. They kept moving in a short, eccentric circle around the leopard, uttering their maniac chuckle.

The leopard stopped eating, rolling his head in a graceful movement to watch as they circled and screamed. The hyenas kept narrowing the circle, closing it in. Now the leopard gave up his meal completely, directing full attention to his attackers. It looked like these animals noted mostly for their cowardice, scavenging, and murder of the weak, were going to face up to the most dangerous animal in the jungle.

There was a hideous greed, a frightening persistence in the way the hyenas kept closing that circle with their peculiar lope, their knock-kneed rear legs trembling in terror or anticipation. Finally, snarling and spitting, the leopard made a great bound in the opposite direction, stood on the edge of the jungle for an instant, watching as the hyenas tore flesh and hide from his practically untouched meal. It was an astounding sight, one that I would never have believed unless I had sat and watched it. I will confess that I didn't observe the scene that followed. But I did return in five hours: all that remained of that husky blue bull was blood splatters.

I've noted that wherever game is plentiful, so are the hyenas—with one exception. Where the lion population is high, the hyenas are scarce, for one of their preferred delicacies is lion cub. They lie in high grass and wait until the lioness goes off hunting food; then they enter the den and carry off the cubs. Consequently, where hyenas are numerous, it is an indication that the lion population is falling off. When this occurs, the hyenas take over that part of the country, and because of their numbers, they find food hard to get. Then packs of them take to killing and pulling down animals, including wildebeest and kongoni—in India they even attack buffaloes. But even when they are in power and a force to be reckoned with they seem to prefer to seek out the injured, the weak, and the sick and have many champions among naturalists and biologists and some hunters who claim that the hyena is an asset necessary for biological balance.

But the hyena himself sometimes destroys this character whitewashing. Once when I was in Africa there was an uproar in Blantyre, Nyasaland, almost a social emergency. The government dispatched a team of forty hunters into the Michesi Mountains in the southeast in a concerted effort to wipe out a band of three hundred killer hyenas. The hunters had instructions to use poison gas and high explosives if necessary to wipe out the horde that had taken to entering the villages and carrying off children. Some on-the-spot investigation brought forth the fact that at least a dozen children had vanished—one was actually seen carried off in the jaws of a large hyena.

I wasn't around long enough to find out how the forty hunters made out, but their job wouldn't be an easy one. Hyenas are not stupid. I saw one attacked by eight dogs suddenly fall to the ground as if dead. The dogs worried it for awhile, then, the fun gone out of the sport, they dashed off for something livelier. It took the big, striped hyena exactly ten minutes to come to life. Then he got slowly to his feet, shook, and loped away, apparently perfectly fit. An opossum never did this trick more artfully.

Anthony Cullen, a long-time African observer, claims that the hyena is so clever that he won't touch a carcass of any animal that has been stricken with rinderpest. Most of the rest of the scavengers will, but not the hyena. Apparently, this fellow whose dining habits would spoil the appetite of a crocodile has only one other objection to food: He will not touch anything that has been killed by a poisoned arrow.

And although the hyena is one of the most hated animals

in the jungles and forests of India and Africa, the noble African Masai tribesmen look to him for a service that he never fails to supply. The tall, handsome Masai, experts with the spear, the only natives who can best an enraged lion with a simple spear and shield, are proud of their physical and mental independence: their women work hard physically, building huts, and carrying wood until they are in their seventies and completely worn out; their men are erect, warlike, and proud until they can no longer walk. When this happens, the old people are simply carried into the jungle for the reliable hyenas to "bury."

Others also respect the "untouchable." Aboriginals in central India begged me to kill hyenas for them so they could collect the tongue and fat: the tongue to reduce tumors and swellings, the fat as a salve for rheumatism. And I have seen fellaheen in the Nile Valley in Egypt broil and eat the heart of the hyena, believing that that animal's courage would be transferred to them. I asked them what courage they were referring to, and one old man answered, "The heart to stand up to the lion and the leopard and to prowl in the dark of the angry night." He also pulled the hyena's whiskers and wore them as a charm against the dark and evil.

The natives of both India and Africa believe that these incredible creatures have the ability to change sex at will. While I was in Kruger National Park in South Africa, I did observe a male hyena suckling its young, and I am told that this is common. Donald Ker, senior partner of Ker and Downey, famed African safari organization, mentions in his book, *African Adventure,* that he has also seen both male and female hyenas suckle their young. He reproduced a letter from one of the most respected hunters and collectors of wild animals in the world to back up the belief that these animals are hermaphroditic. The hunter, still at the top of his profession, is Carr Hartley. Here is his letter:

CARR HARTLEY'S BIG GAME FARM, P.O. Box 13,
Rumuruti, Africa

Donald Ker, Esquire
Messrs. Ker & Downey Safaris, Ltd., Nairobi
Dear Donald,

With reference to our conversation regarding my hyena Willy,
herewith some details about him/her: This hyena was bred by me
on this farm six years ago, and to my certain knowledge has been
male three times and female three times. Willy has served hyena
who have produced pups, and has in turn, when I have been
short of pens and put him in with other hyena, produced three
lots of pups himself.

Willy is a born film star and has featured in four or five se-
quences in African films. "She" is at the moment a very buxom
female and rather anxious to be mated, but whenever put in
with other much more poorly hyena, knocks hell out of them.
Incidentally, the name changes from Willy to Wilhelmina according to sex at any time.

Anthony Cullen in his book *Downey's Africa,* corrobo-
rates Hartley: "It sounds remarkable, but evidence has clearly
established that at least some hyena, in captivity, can behave
as hermaphrodites." As Downey, Ker, Cullen, and Hartley
are among the most respected of big game hunters and animal specialists in Africa, I consider this observation valuable.

This contradictory animal has tangled the facts of the
best naturalists. "A coward," says one well-known biologist. But I saw two drive a leopard from its kill. "Sneaking,
spineless, harmless scavengers," say most big game hunters.
But I killed one attacking an old woman in India, and those
three hundred banded in Africa specialized in attacks on
children.

S. H. Prater, O. B. E., C. M. Z. S., a noted naturalist, writing for the Bombay Natural History Society, says that little
is known of the hyena's family life. We do not know whether

they breed in any particular month of the year or whether there is a restricted breeding season. Nor do we know how the male and female live together. He says that the animals are often seen prowling in pairs, but in the few recorded instances where pups were found, the mother appeared to be the sole protector.

The pups, two to four in a litter, are born in a cave or a hole and are covered with silky white hair and have either spots or stripes but no mane. Their life span is from twelve to twenty-four years; the average age is sixteen.

Although most adults seem to have a mangy look, with a scarred, unkept body, smell like death, and usually avoid humans, at Kruger Park my wife and I got within ten yards of an unsophisticated, spotted hyena, apparently recently weaned and most naïve. He was quite attractive, with a fuzzy, beige undercoat covered with chocolate spots. We were getting even closer when suddenly the mother, a smelly, hair-tangled menace, came tearing out of the underbrush with a crazy scream, frightening both her offspring and us, scattering us in several directions.

The picture turned out well, however, the young hyena standing there placidly staring at us as we set the F-stop and clicked at him several times. He looked more like a fluffy child's toy than the hated, mysterious grave robber that he would be in a few months, an animal that would grow into a nightmare creature that relishes the dead, attacks the old, the feeble, and the injured, carries off children, makes maniac sounds in the dead of night, changes sex, and has eating habits that would disgust a vulture.

But although the words horrid and hyena seem synonymous to me, any profile would be out of focus if it didn't point up that the hyena gives a delicate and necessary balance to nature. He aids the animal world by weeding out the weak, preying on the unfit and the injured—and he burys the dead. He is a horror, but he is helpful.

7

HUSHWING THE HATED

The Owl

An ancient Persian seer claimed that in every man there is an owl, a goose, a parrot, a lion, and a hyena. He explained the differences in human character by the ascendancy of one or more of these creatures. I was reminded of this as I stood looking at a man in the grip of emotion, watching an animal characteristic rise to the surface. He was grimacing; his irregular teeth were brownish-white; he thrust his head forward like a striped hyena approaching a carcass. He was snarling.

And he was frightening. Small, intense, he had a shiny bald head and dead blue eyes that thick eyeglasses magnified into a glare, and he was as charged as a dope addict. "I'll kill them all!" he said, shaking a fist. "See this?" He pointed to a large steel trap on the ground. "Put 'em on posts and in small trees. That gets 'em!"

"He's killed nearly a thousand owls already," said the owner of the game preserve. "He's goin' peel a few from our acres while he's here." He added proudly, "Guess he's the champ horned owl killer of the country!"

This dialogue took place one winter on a shooting preserve in Georgia, where I had gone to spend a few days hunting quail. The owner had told me about the owl hater from Florida who was due to visit him the morning of my departure. He said that the fellow haunted shooting preserves and poultry and game farms, asking for the exclusive right to rid their acreage of great horned owls. "I'm right glad to get him up here," he said. "Don't think owls have been bothering me much, but it's a good idea not to give them the chance."

The owl killer was a true fanatic. He had been a teacher of wood lathing in a vocational school in New York City, quit his job, and moved to Florida. Shortly after he arrived, a horned owl killed some chickens on a friend's farm, and the hunt and the hatred began. He admitted that when he saw his first horned owl sitting in a tree glaring at him he had been afraid.

"Some people call them 'Tiger of the Air,' " he told me. "They're bloodthirsty killers, and I'm making it my business to wipe out as many as I can!"

When I asked him why, he stared and said, "What's the matter with you, Mister? Soft in the head? *Because,* that's why. *Because.*"

And he couldn't come up with a much better answer except that he had appointed himself father protector of birds and poultry. "Defender of the little ones against this monster," he said pompously.

I then told the two men that story about the leopards of Africa. In a way, they were something like the horned owl. They sometimes killed domestic cattle and goats, even poultry and dogs. Unfortunately for them, because their coats were so beautiful, most of the cats in Kenya were trapped out in two years. Direct famine resulted. The "natural" food of the leopard, wild pigs and baboons, soon multiplied to the extent that they finished all the food supply in the wild places and began invading the cultivated areas, destroying crops and causing a very real famine that lasted for a long time.

"Aw, mister," the owl annihilator said, "You're stretching things. What's those leopards got to do with owls?"

It was hopeless, but I tried something else. "How do you feel about other owls?"

None of them was any good.

"I agree that the great horned owl can be a pretty bad actor, but he also does a lot of good," I said. "Do you have any idea of the damage mice and rodents of all kinds do every year?"

Going on to tell him that 1,300 harmful types of rodents destroy almost everything that isn't metallic, killing wild and domestic birds, undermining dams and foundations, doing more that $700 million damage to crops and grain supplies every year, I tried to explain a thing called the balance of nature. It was hopeless.

"Have you got any idea how many mice and rats you have turned loose upon the country by killing one thousand horned owls?"

He snorted. "How about the chickens, the game birds, and the song birds I saved?"

"Look," I said, beginning to lose my temper, "I carefully

watched a great horned owl in my area for over a year. Do
you know what I found in its nest the last time I examined
it?"

He smirked.

"A mouse, a young muskrat, two eels, four bullheads, a
woodcock, two grouse, one rabbit, and eleven rats. Work
that out percentagewise and you'll see that you're the one
doing the damage. Not the horned owl."

It was a waste of time. If people hate owls, there is no
talking them out of it. This dedicated owl killer figured that
I was a confused citizen and, undeterred, went about the
destruction of the enemies he hated "because."

In fear of getting the steel trap over my head, I didn't
tell this immovable object that I had once had a great
horned owl as a pet. Some farm boys had killed the adult
owls in a nest two miles from my house, leaving a five-week-
old youngster starving. I wrapped him up, took him home,
and kept him in an empty chicken house.

I called him Buster and finally began letting him out. He
didn't seem to mind captivity and stayed around like a tame
pigeon. He was at least three months old when I measured
him: 2 feet tall, a wingspread of 4 feet, and 1-inch talons.
He ate anything: cookies, ground meat, boiled eggs, or cold
leftover roast, and he thrived. Buster would walk around the
place like the landlord, and seldom flew, except occasionally
to get up on a branch and nap. The only thing I ever saw
him kill was a night-prowling cat and some skunks.

He stayed with me for almost a year and was one of the
most interesting creatures I have ever studied. He hated
skunks but had a disconcerting habit of killing them and
depositing them on the front porch. To my sorrow, someone finally shot Buster.

This so-called monster, the lord high executioner, the
great horned owl, despite his evil reputation, made an

amusing, unaggressive, fascinating pet. But regardless of what you prove about this bird, from a balance of nature or help-to-man viewpoint, the owl often comes out as a villain.

Of all America's birds owls (and hawks) are the least understood. These silent benefactors are misunderstood because they are not seen often and are shy and secretive. Most species are hidden during the day, hunting only at night or in the dim light of early morning or evening. A few owls do prey during the day: the short-eared and the large owls of the north, the snowy, the great gray, and the hawk owl. But in addition to dwelling in sparsely inhabited areas, they are so silent, so swift, and so skillful that they are seldom seen.

For all of their mysterious habits, owls are the most sophisticated of birds and are found in just about every section of the world—ranging from the 33-inch great gray owl of Hudson Bay to the elf owl (the size of a sparrow) that lives in woodpecker holes in the giant saguaro cacti of Arizona. Of the five hundred different kinds of owls, forty-five species inhabit North America. The most important of these are the great horned, the snowy, the barred, the barn, the screech, the hawk, the short-eared, the saw-whet, the burrowing, and the pygmy owls.

Centuries ago the owl learned that men, rats, mice, and other rodents live together, so they moved in to dwell in old barns, church belfries, chimney tops, even in trees along highways. From here they make their nightly forays to hunt the real enemies of man. Yet, ironically, man remains their greatest menace.

Since we have been able to communicate, there have been owl superstititions and legends. Their weird, often frightening, night hootings and screams were and still are believed to predict death or disaster. They have always been thought to be the companions of witches, hobgoblins, ghosts, sorcerers, and even of Satan.

I have a relative in Georgia who gets out of bed and turns

his left shoe over when a screech owl screams. In the South they are called "shivering" owls, and many superstitious people actually do shiver when the owl calls; they throw a nail or some other metal object into the fire to ward off the evil spirit.

Yet some of the ancients, notably the Greeks and the Romans, revered the owl as a symbol of intelligence, believing that it was the constant companion of their goddess of wisdom.

The old belief that owls can't see in the daylight is not true. All owls see during daylight hours, but most of them do better at night because their eyes, especially adapted for night hunting, are sensitive to light, the iris almost closing in harsh light. Some scientists believe they are particularly sensitive to green, yellow, orange, red, and the infrared rays that are invisible to man.

The most perfect organ of vision of any creature, the eye of the owl is one hundred times as acute as that of the human and can be instantly focused to see near or far. One owl was tested, and it captured its prey in such dim light that it was only equal to that of a candle burning 2,582 feet away.

The owl's eyes, set in the front of his skull, are immovable (cannot be rolled from side to side), which gives the bird a fierce, staring expression. But to make up for this deficiency, he can rotate his head 180 degrees in either direction, so that he can even stare back over his shoulders. I remember several of us, with age ten cruel curiosity, would try to make a tame barn owl wring its head off by walking around it.

A human eye has both "cones" which are used to distinguish colors and "rod" cells which gather light. The eye of the owl is a mass of rod cells which contain a chemical, visual purple, a converter which takes even the faintest touch of light and gives a chemical signal that immediately gives the owl a sight impression. The human eye, with its mixture of cells, can only get an awareness of light.

Bird men have had trouble trying to explain how an owl can operate when there is complete absence of light. Robert Payne, a graduate student at Cornell, decided to find out. He sealed a room, covered the floor with leaves, and turned a barn owl and a live mouse free. The mouse made a rustling noise in the leaves, and the owl left his perch. When Payne turned on the lights, the owl had the mouse. Then tests were tried to determine if the owl was depending upon its excellent sense of smell or the sort of invisible heat waves that rattlesnakes use. Result proved nothing. Payne then plugged one of the barn owl's ears. Next time the lights were doused and a mouse was released, the owl missed.

Nature has done a marvelous thing in clothing the owl, covering his body with such soft feathers, almost down, that they seem to destroy sound. His "silent" flight is further aided with fuzzy flight feathers that deaden the usual whirring noise all other birds make. The bird's face is surrounded with a stiff curve of feathers that throws sound waves into his eardrums, the largest of any bird—on some owls so large that they cover the entire side of his head.

Nesting in late April or early May, wherever it is convenient—church towers, barns, trees, cavities of gullies, or rocky cliffs—our most common owl, the barn owl, doesn't do anything fancy for her offspring. She simply lines the nest with a sprinkle of feathers plus anything else she can collect without much trouble. Usually, from four to seven dull white eggs are laid, but I have found ten in one barn owl's nest. The period of incubation is from three to three-and-a-half weeks, the bird beginning to set soon after the first egg is laid. As eggs are laid on alternate days, the last one may not hatch until two weeks after the first. Both parents hover the eggs.

Although they may not be great home builders, they are devoted parents. I once watched an energetic mother and father bring food to their nest fourteen times in half an hour. The food each time was a mouse.

Owl sounds are quite wonderful. Once, when I approached a nest, the mother started making the sounds of a catfight; then she left her nest and hid in the trees, making the dreadful moan of a rabbit being killed. This versatile ventriloquist even barked like a dog to distract and lure me away from the nest. All species are courageous and will attack any man or beast that tries to molest their nests.

To locate and attract mates, they also use sound, anything from a cough to a shriek. The great horned owl perfectly duplicates the call of the cougar; the barred owl makes an insane laugh; the screech owl sounds like a woman being strangled. They hoot, scream, gobble, groan, and hiss; one even sounds like a rattlesnake.

But, as the most successful of all winged hunters, they make no sound as they glide through the night searching for prey. They swallow their prey whole, like the hawk, always eating the head first, then making the big swallow. The indigestible portions, fur, feathers, bones, are rolled up by stomach action into "pellets" which are discharged from the mouth. The pellets, amazingly, are clean and dry and without smell. I always locate a nest by these telltale droppings piled under it.

Thus, the owl's eating habits are neatly wrapped up in capsule form. An examination of these pellets is definitive proof that all species are beneficial to man.

One study proved that in one section owls took nearly 25,000 rodents for each square mile. The smaller owls eat mice, grasshoppers, beetles, and other insects almost exclusively. Of 255 stomachs (some containing more than one foodstuff) of screech owls studied by Dr. Fisher for the Department of Agriculture, 100 contained insects; 91, mice; 38, small birds; 11, mammals other than mice; 9, crawfish;

7, miscellaneous food; 5, spiders; 4, batrachians; 2, lizards; 2, scorpions; 2, earthworms; 1, poultry; 1, fish; 43, empty.

There are numerous reports of scientific examinations of the pellets of all species of owls and, in every case, they conclusively prove that owls are a major control in keeping the rodent hordes in check. Yet only fourteen of our states legally protect owls.

There is hardly a hunter who doesn't take a shot at an owl any time he sees one. And remember our fanatical little friend with his traps and his kill of one thousand horned owls?

People need education on this subject—and fast. One of man's best friends is being stupidly shot, trapped, and driven from the earth. If something isn't done soon that old question, "Are we men or mice?" may finally be answered—by the mice.

8

KING OF THE ICE

The Polar Bear

I was aboard the Norwegian diesel ketch *Havella* cruising the Arctic Ocean in the late summer of 1960 when I spotted a queer wave making a V far off to our left. Watching for awhile, I decided that it was something alive swimming far out in this roughest sea in existence. Alf Olsen, the ship's mate, came out of the pilot house, and I pointed.

"It's a polar bear!" he said, going inside to direct the captain. It was hard to believe that a bear, a land animal, could be this many miles out in this open, frigid ocean. We were so far from land that we no longer could see the distant outlines of the islands in the Svalbard archipelago, far above the Arctic Circle.

Within minutes we overtook an enormous bear. An old one, Alf said, with black spots showing through his ivory-yellow hide, and he was swimming gracefully, using only his front feet, his rear legs hanging straight out like a rudder. He swung his head in a menacing gesture as we pestered, pacing him, photographing his movements. We followed for two hours, estimating from the boat speed that he was consistently making three miles per hour. Captain Godtliebsen said the bear was making for C. Mary Harnsworth, part of Russian-owned Franz Josef Land, so when the misty outline of the taboo island showed against the flat horizon, we left, the bear still swimming powerfully toward land.

I remarked redundantly that it was amazing to see a bear out that far. "A seal or walrus, yes. But a *bear*. . . ."

Alf Olsen smiled. "That isn't far for *Is Bjorn* [ice bear]," he said. "Two years ago, when I was sealing, I saw an old she-bear and two half-grown cubs in open water almost two hundred miles north of Greenland. They were heading farther north for the ice pack which was at least another hundred miles."

An explorer-scientist with the United States Air Force 1952 "T-3" arctic expedition saw one bear with two yearling cubs in open water one hundred miles north of Alaska. They were swimming northward toward the edge of pack ice, which at that time was one hundred miles farther north.

Zoologists in the Department of Mammology of the Museum of Natural History told me that there are many cases in which polar bears have been seen more than two hundred miles in open sea. They claim the bear, also known as the sea bear, water bear, Greenland bear, ice bear, ice tiger, ice king, and the Eskimo *nahnook,* is really more of a marine mammal than a land mammal, that he spends so much time in water that he now swims like a seal or a penguin without using his back legs. They also suggest that he is ten million years old, probably older, citing that bears were part of the Pleistocene period and that the polar bear is a natural offshoot of that Ice Age.

Although there is current controversy about which is the larger bear, the polar or the Alaskan brown, there is no doubt that the white bear is the largest carnivorous one. All other bears are omnivorous.

One of the three hundred species of Carnivora, the polar bear, *Thalarctos maritimus,* falls into the suborder *Arctoidea,* comprising bears, dogs, raccoons, weasels, and their allies. Of the sixteen kinds of bears and the five principle generic groups of American bears, he departs most widely from ordinary type.

He can see at least a mile, farther than any other bear. For short spurts, he can make twenty-five miles per hour across ice, has been clocked at six miles per hour in the water, and can make sudden forward plunges of 15 feet while swimming.

An English explorer named Brown told Ernest Thompson Seton, "I have chased it in open water with a picked crew of eight husky whalemen, and yet the bear managed to distance us in the race for the icefield."

Most land animals have to paddle vigorously to stay afloat, but the bear lies motionless for long periods with the greatest of ease. Air spaces in his fur, oil glands in his skin, and a thick layer of fat help him perform his floating miracle. His legs are jointed so they can swing in a wide circle, an aid in swimming and maneuverability. He has special arctic sunglasses, a nictitating membrane which protects his eyes from ice glare and from snow blindness; his toes are partially webbed, and he is the only bear with hair on the bottom of his feet, making them into combination snowshoe-paddles. His unretractable claws, kept cat sharp by constant honing on ice as he walks, are precision instruments used for hooking seals out of their air holes in the ice.

With his elongated body weighing from 800 to 1,600 pounds; his snaky, pointed head; and his slender limbs, long neck, short ears, and creamy-white coat, he is physically un-like any other animal. Although he is extraordinarily grace-ful, his rump, rising higher than his shoulders, makes him look awkward in movement. He hisses like a cat when annoyed and will roar when wounded, but he is usually as silent as the surrounding snow. He moves across the ice as confidently as an Olympic figure skater. Eyewitnesses say that this half-ton animal can easily make his way across ice unsafe for a man. I had one get within 15 yards of me over young ice before I knew he was there. And I was standing in a boat, carefully watching for him. He appeared as silently as arctic mist. I spotted him by his black nose.

Knowing this is a telltale mark, the polar bear usually hides his nose when awaiting game or stalking. F. J. De Gisbert, a noted arctic hunter who has caught 416 polar bears, 62 of them alive for zoos, says that he once saw two bears sit down on ice near the sea. Like old people protect-ing themselves from the cold, they covered their black noses with their paws and sat patiently waiting. Presently a bearded seal popped out of the water. One bear put his paw under it as you might pick up a lump of sugar, flipping the 500 pounds of flesh out on the ice.

While anchored in a quiet fjord, I saw another example of the white bear cleverly hiding his nose. I watched through glasses as one approached a flock of eider ducks, among the most talented divers in feathers. He swam slowly, scarcely rippling the surface, his nose buried in the water, only the top of his head visible, moving like a chunk of floating floe ice. Suddenly, he was among them, and they dove; so did he.

Finally, after what seemed like ten minutes, he came surging to the top, a flapping eider in his mouth. These alert birds didn't even know he was around until he appeared in their midst. The duck hunter, meal in mouth, didn't head back toward shore but swam to a floe five miles away.

The polar bear's stamina and strength are unbelievable. De Gisbert roped one in the water, but somehow, even with five men in the boat pulling against it, the animal got up on an ice floe. With the five in the extremely heavy whaling boat pushing with oars and *hakepiken,* attempting to shove the boat back, the bear dragged boat and men 600 yards across the floe. "This is an animal of physical perfection," De Gisbert wrote. "All senses except hearing are exemplary."

Many animals have a certain sense developed to a high degree: a pointer dog scents quail farther than he can see; foxes detect partridge at more than 200 yards; wolves pick up the odor of a wounded moose at over a mile. Sometimes to his detriment, the polar bear scents seal blubber at twenty miles. Hunters often entice him to his death by burning it. A rope with a bell is tied to a piece of blubber or seal meat and hung outside a cabin. When the bear removes the bait the bell sounds and the hunter fires through a small hole in the door.

Alf Olsen told me of the party that had gone out just before us last summer to photograph polar bears. They anchored the *Havella* by staking it against an ice floe and burned some seal blubber to see if they could attract a bear. They were in a position where they could see for many miles with binoculars. After about an hour they saw a speck in the water: a bear swimming toward them. Finally, he got out of the water, approaching cautiously. He walked up to the anchor rope and, using his paws like hands, pulled the boat closer to the floe.

Olsen said they decided to play with him and give the

clients some unusual pictures (I have seen his movies of this and later was to have the same experience). They placed strips of seal blubber on a long stick, holding it over the edge of the boat. The bear understood immediately when the first strip was proffered. He stood up like a man (Alf said that he was over 10 feet tall), reached over, and hooked the blubber off the stick into his mouth. This went on for a half hour until everyone had enough of the spectacle on film. But when the blubber stopped coming the bear became annoyed and again pulled the boat closer with the anchor rope. When it was close enough, he crouched for a spring. "In a second," Alf said, "we would have had more than a thousand pounds of anger aboard. We didn't want to but we had to shoot him just as he left in a leap."

Would the bear have tried to kill them? Alf said he would have attacked, and he has seen almost as many bears as people during his career in the cruising diesel ketch. This is controversial. Some say that the polar bear won't attack, but many of the experienced claim that the polar bear not only will but is the only animal that normally stalks and eats man.

Sally Carrighar, writer-naturalist, who has spent more than ten years in the arctic, feels bears are a staggered menace in their relationship to men. Black bears usually can be bluffed away, grizzlies will attack if startled or angry, the big brown Kodiak bears will sometimes kill a man without provocation and maul his body. But polar bears kill a man and eat him. Miss Carrighar reasons that perhaps in the case of Eskimos polar bears think they are eating seals because their clothing smells of seal oil. Yet polar bears have killed white men. Many sportsmen have thought that they were hunting a polar bear when they looked behind and found that he was hunting them.

A friend, Richard Pistell, and his photographer Sam Shulman, were in the Norwegian north several years ago doing a film on polar bears. They were on ice with the camera set up in action on a bear hundreds of yards away. Suddenly, they heard a slight sound, wheeled, and found a bear advancing. Pistell had a revolver, and he fired, splintering ice, driving the bear back, and alerting his guides and another friend, Bill Howe.

I was out in a small outboard near the same area, Nordaustlandet, an island in the Svalbard group, one August when we sighted a bear swimming. They are curious critters, and we sat and let this one get within 20 yards before we revved up and got back to our anchored mother ship. Would he have attacked? We didn't wait to find out.

De Gisbert, the man who liked to capture bears alive, told of one swimming up to his whale boat, putting his paws on the stern, then trying to use his enormous strength to tip it over.

He had another experience trying to lasso one. He and his crew were moving through ice floes when they saw a bear. "He soon caught sight of us and came along at a lively gait to meet us. Our intention was to get him into water but unfortunately our boat got jammed between two floes and before we could release it he charged.

"I have never seen a bear charge so rapidly. I was in the bow ready with the rope when our boat struck, and he was about 15 yards away. He covered that distance giving me scarcely time to drop the rope, pick up the rifle, shove the muzzle against his head, and fire. Next moment I found myself pinned to my seat by the weight of a single paw."

Later they skinned and examined the bear, finding that he had just eaten the skin and blubber of a seal. (Unless there is more than one bear at the kill, they eat only blubber, leaving the rest for the arctic foxes, their constant winter retinue.) "Therefore," a puzzled De Gisbert recorded, "it was not hunger that prompted him to charge."

C. V. A. Peel, F. Z. S., F. R. G. S., believes that the polar bear stalks man when there is no wind, or what little wind there is blows from bear to man. When these conditions exist, according to Peel, the bear will charge with the intent to kill for food, thinking that man is a seal. Dr. George Goodwin, former mammalogist and zoologist of the Museum of Natural History was in agreement. Many arctic explorers are not.

Kaare Rodahl, a Fellow of the Norwegian Polar Institute of Oslo University who, for many years, has accompanied Swedish, Danish, and American expeditions to the far north, feels that the polar bear is completely unpredictable. At times he will attack man; at others he will flee at the slightest scent. Rodahl tells of one companion being stalked. He was carrying a log on his shoulder when the bear leaped from behind and hit the log. Both were confused, but the man recovered first, cocked his rifle, and fired without aiming as the bear charged. He missed, and as he ran, he cocked his rifle again, but the discharged cartridge stuck. Getting down behind a large block of ice, he was trying to remove it with a knife when the bear suddenly reappeared. Quickly, Rodahl's friend grabbed his rifle by the barrel, struck the bear over the head, and ran for his cabin (which he reached safely).

Authorities I questioned stated that there are only two bears that have regarded man as an article of food, the polar bear and the Great Cave Bear of Europe, now extinct. Fridtjof Nansen, the famed arctic explorer who spent three years isolated on the ice, agreed and made notations in his diary of polar bears attacking members of his expedition. One stalked his closest friend, Johansen, knocked him down, and was about to pounce when Nansen shot it. It was a female, and Nansen wrote, "After I killed the bear two heads peered over a nearby ice hummock, her cubs, waiting to see what the prospects for a meal were." The harrowing episode ended with the two men laughing at the curious cubs.

Polar bears often inspire laughter instead of fear. I saw a big one swim up to a ringed seal sunning itself on a floe, hurl himself out of the water, taking a swipe at the seal as it escaped. He then stood upright on the floe, picked up pieces of ice, and hurled them in rage. Then he flopped down, sulking.

One explorer tells of seeing a full-grown bear sitting in the snow of a narrow fjord in northeast Greenland, trying to catch low-flying snow buntings with his front paws. As the birds dodged by, he would clap his paws together and look very disappointed when he opened them and discovered that they were empty.

On our arctic cruise we hove to just off the ice-covered island of Kvitoya to watch through our glasses several polar bears moving along the shore line. They shambled aimlessly for awhile, then one went up a small icy knoll, turned around, sat down, and slid to the bottom like a child on a playground slide. Two others followed the fun.

But the polar bear is neither a clown nor a villain. He is a dedicated hunter, killing only for food. In the harsh winter of his barren land anything that moves is fair game. Living on sea ice that covers 17 percent of the globe's surface, the bear follows the sun. During the fall he comes southward; in the spring he starts north again, staying on the ice belt along the arctic coast where seal are plentiful. His migrations (and he is constantly on the move, often traveling seventy-five miles a day) are influenced by food and ice movement. He travels circumpolarly from Franz Josef Land and Spitsbergen south along Greenland, west and north through the Canadian Arctic Archipelago, through the Beaufort Sea north of Alaska, and along the northern edge of Siberia back to Spitsbergen.

Although most white bears spend their average life span of forty years on moving ice, never seeing a blade of grass, there are exceptions. One was seen northeast of Great Slave

Lake, seventy-five miles from the nearest sea. Another made his way up the MacKenzie River to Fort MacPherson, 150 miles from salt water. Riding floes down the Labrador Coast to Newfoundland, several have passed through the Strait of Belle Isle, between Newfoundland and Quebec, one hundred miles up the Saguenay River from the gulf.

The chain of life in their arctic world is linked to tiny, shrimplike sea organisms, "krill," that swarm in waters of low salinity. They seek spots where icebergs are melting, diluting sea water. Here fish feed on krill, seals eat fish, and bears hunt seals.

The polar bear likes to prowl lightly frozen cracks in the ice. Formed by storms, tidal currents break 2-foot cracks running for miles in even the heaviest ice. These tide cracks freeze quickly and are soon covered with snow which slows freezing. Seals use these areas as breathing spots, finding it easy to pop their heads up through the new ice. Most arctic seals, the hair, harp, ringed, and bearded, remain underwater for 9 minutes, then surface for 45 seconds to breathe. When the seal surfaces for new air, the waiting bear, almost always using his left paw, flips it out on the ice, killing it with one bite.

Often, if there aren't tidal cracks, seals will sun beside a blowhole that they have kept open during the winter. Their routine of sunbathing for 3 minutes, then lifting their heads and looking for danger every 15 seconds, often is their downfall. The polar bear's timing, taught from cub days, is superb. When he sees a seal, he makes his approach slowly; using his chest and front legs as runners, he slides forward on the ice almost like a sled, moving only when the seal lowers his head.

Through glasses I watched one bear take a ringed seal in this manner. Although the distance couldn't have been more than 100 yards, the patient bear took almost an hour to finally spring up and grab the unsuspecting seal.

The white bear knows that the seal's blowhole is only big enough to admit one seal at a time. So when he sees three or four sunning near a hole, he abandons customary caution and races in, knowing that he will get at least one of the clumsy animals as they rush to escape.

The only living thing (other than the killer whale, known to catch a bear in the water) the polar bear fears is the walrus. Three times the bear's size, he has long, sharp tusks, a hide that is almost impossible to penetrate, and he can outswim and drown the bear. But the walrus is stupid and the bear is not. Major L. T. Burwash of Ottawa states that he has talked with Eskimos who have seen a polar bear sneak up on a snoozing walrus and kill it by bashing its head with a block of ice.

Hansen, the engineer on our ketch, believes the polar bear is the smartest of all animals. He told me of watching a seal lying near a hole on a big floe and of a polar bear 300 yards away making his approach. There were several small floes between them, and every time the bear had to cross an open space he did it underwater. When he reached the big floe he got onto the ice foot, and stood up to make sure the seal was still there. Hansen said the bear remained standing for 5 minutes as if thinking, then slid backward off the ice, vanishing underwater. The next thing he saw was the bear's head and shoulders appearing out of the hole beside the seal.

"Seals sun beside holes just large enough to admit themselves," Hansen said. "This one made a fatal mistake. But how did the bear know that the hole was his size?"

This timing, patience, and judgment is taught to bear cubs by their mothers, among the most devoted parents in the animal kingdom. Mating in midsummer at the age of five, the female bear digs her lair for the January birth of one or two cubs in pressure ice hummocks or deep snow. Soon the entrance is blocked with snow and the temperature rises, as it does in an Eskimo igloo, where it often reaches 86 degrees Fahrenheit. Unlike other bears, they do not hibernate, although the female does stay in her den until late March or early April, feeding her cubs throughout the winter, cuddling them into the warm fur of her abdomen.

She keeps the cubs for two years, not mating again during this time, patiently teaching them the hunting arts. Protecting them carefully, she places herself before them when there is danger and often takes to the water with them clinging to her back. If there is no danger, she makes them swim alone, cuffing them or ducking them under water to make them obey.

Vilhjalmur Stefansson has watched a polar bear mother stalk a seal with two cubs sitting on the sidelines observing her technique. The mother did everything slowly, exaggerating her movement so the cubs would understand the lesson.

Jan Vlasak, veterinary surgeon and superintendent of the Prague Zoo, raised a polar bear cub in his apartment during the German occupation and kept a careful record of the experience. This was the first time a young polar bear had been under constant observation by an expert.

His cub, a female, weighed 1½ pounds at birth (the mother weighed 800 pounds) and was a foot long. In seven weeks she tipped the scales at 9½ pounds and grew another 9 inches. The cub's eyes were open in the fifth week, but for another fortnight they remained dull with a bluish, misty look and a strangely dead expression. At this time she moulted the dull baby hair, growing a thick, soft fur, the moult lasting for sixteen weeks. After the forty-seventh day the cub's eyes began to acquire a luster and life; her hearing was poor until the sixty-ninth day, then she would respond to her name at 100 yards. Her greatest sense, smell, developed on the fiftieth day and quickly became incredibly sharp and delicate. She walked erectly on the sixty-eighth day, becoming agile in another ten days.

When the five-month-old cub weighed 50 pounds and measured a yard from tip of snout to root of tail, Dr. Vlasak returned her to the zoo where she was born. The cub had never seen more than a bathtub of water, but when released near the zoo pool she immediately dove in and swam skillfully.

Authorities at the Bronx Zoo tell me that the savage white bear takes to captivity and summer heat better than most of our temperate zone animals. Because of his unusual appearance, his amusing antics, and his Olympic prowess in water, he is one of the favorites of the zoo goers, and he knows it. A pair of bears in a Quebec zoo with a diving board at their pool never do the high jinx act unless there is an audience. Another bear in the London zoo sits erect like a proud old gentleman only when a person with a camera approaches.

Dr. Vlasak thinks that polar bears are like people. "It may seem drastic to compare a bear with a child," he says. "But there are many things in which the two show a striking resemblance. Moreover, it is the opinion of those who have had the opportunity of studying polar bears in the wild state, as well as those who have kept them in captivity, that they do behave very much like human beings."

Eskimos agree. They are deeply impressed by resemblances. Many of them say that there are three kinds of people: Eskimos, white men, and bears. Claiming that the polar bear can stand and walk upright, that he has hands and can take hold of things, that when the skin is off the body is like theirs, Eskimos also believe that bears understand what people say.

Robert Peary's daughter, Marie Ahnighito, once asked an Eskimo his idea of complete happiness. The man answered: "To run across fresh polar bear tracks and to be ahead of the other sledges." Another, Kood-Look-too, told her that the constellation Polaris was the spirit of a huge polar bear which in ancient times had escaped hunters by rising into the sky in the form of stars.

Eskimos (and northern explorers who have become ill, with skin peeling from their bodies) believe that polar bear liver holds an evil spell, that it will bring death and madness. They bury it when they kill a bear or hang it high so their dogs won't get it.

I once saw a flock of herring gulls, ravenous birds that will normally eat anything, ignore a fresh bear liver. But now the mystery has been solved. Studies conducted by Drs. Moore and Rodahl at the Dunn Nutritional Laboratories in Cambridge proved that two ounces of polar bear liver contain enough vitamin A to supply the normal requirements of a man for a full year. Thus if a person eats too much he develops hypervitaminosis A.

Although 50 percent of all the polar bears the doctors examined were found to have trichinella infection, similar to that in pork, they discovered that bear meat was safe if cooked thoroughly so the trichinella larvae were killed. Examinations of bodies of lost explorers, frozen and intact after many years, had proved that many died of trichinosis, contacted when they ate undercooked bear, the only food they could find.

Polar bears are not killed only by starving explorers, Eskimos, and big-game hunters who consider them the world's Number 1 trophy. For centuries, it has been the custom of anyone traveling the arctic to kill any bear he sees. One exploring party killed 250, recovering only a dozen. Norwegians seem to be the worst offenders. One trapper, Henry Rudl, with 700 to his "credit," is the king of the polar bear killers.

When I was in Norway a few years ago, a front-page news item in an Oslo paper proudly proclaimed that two trappers had killed fifty-seven bears in two months. A cod fisherman from the trawler *Brandel* anchored at King's Bay, Spitsbergen, offered to sell me a bear hide for $15 and showed me a half-dozen bloody skulls in the stern. Everybody seems to be in on the slaughter: sealers, cod fishermen, trappers, and sportsmen.

Residents of Norway, Sweden, and Greenland can kill without limit. The Scandinavians claim that they don't protect the polar bear because he is ruining an industry—sealing. But there is another reason: live cubs bring $500 in the zoo market and skins sell from $25 to $50 to taxidermists who then sell them to tourists for $200. In Tromso, I saw one bear rug with a hi-fi unit in the head price tagged at $800.

The white bear has been sought, dead or alive, since the ninth century, when the princes of Europe considered them their most prized possession and paid lavishly for live bears. Ingimundr the Old sent two cubs to King Harold the Fairheaded of Norway and was rewarded with an ocean-going vessel loaded with timber. When the Icelander Isleifr was seeking to establish a bishopric, he presented a polar bear to Emperor Henry III. Soon he became Iceland's first Bishop of Skalholt.

Both Henry III of England and Emperor Frederick II had polar bears. Writs are still in existence directing the sheriffs of London "to furnish six pence a day to support our white bear in our Tower of London and to provide a muzzle and iron chain to hold him when out of the water and a long, strong rope to hold him when he is fishing in the Thames."

During the thirteenth and fourteenth centuries, every church in the north countries had at least one polar-bear rug. Priests used them on the altar in cold weather, and penitents who stood barefoot before the church door were often loaned a bear rug.

The trading, trapping, and shooting of bears became such a thing that in the sixteenth century the king of Iceland decreed that polar-bear pelts acquired in Iceland must be offered for sale to royal officials, and only with their permission to others.

But because of his inaccessability, the polar bear has survived. Now, with the advent of the airplane, fast boats, and high-powered rifles, the strange white bear of the Ice Age is in danger of extinction. Experts give me an educated guess that the total bear population is about twenty-five thousand.

The problem in protection lies in the fact that he is an international animal, and each country bordering the Arctic Ocean has its own laws. Hunters also take advantage of the fact that the bear is unprotected beyond the three-mile limit. It is clear that new laws are needed. Alaska allows sportsmen only one bear, so does Norway—but this applies to nonresidents only. Russia permits no shooting of bears, and Canada, claiming that the polar bear is conserving a valuable fur supply, the arctic fox, protects them.

Concerned with the plight of our most unusual animal, the United States Fish and Wildlife Service has declared: "Until more is known about polar bear population; until more is known about the number of cubs born every year and the number which become adults under their normal conditions; in fact, until there is a considerable amount added to the current skimpy knowledge of the biology of the polar bear, no one can say what rate of kill the species can stand."

E. L. Bartlett of Alaska registered a request with the Department of the Interior shortly before Alaska became a state. Remarking about the terrific increase in polar-bear hunting and that the present rate of kill may lead to virtual extinction, he said, *"Please* save our bear!"

I'd like to see all hunting of the great white bear stopped, especially the American technique of spotting them by plane, then swooping low over them, herding the animal to a place where the plane can land and the "sportsmen" hop out, make the kill, then take off on vulture wings with the body.

We have reached a point in history where the lonely wild ones such as the polar bear need complete protection if they are to survive. If they can live in that unbelievably harsh land confronted with the constant, often hopeless, search for food, we should doff our hats in respect.

9

MONSTER IN YOUR BACKYARD

The Shrew

I first heard of what many biologists call the world's fiercest animal shortly after the natural history museums began using tapes to describe exhibits. I was familiar with the word shrew, a part of our language even before Shakespeare wrote *The Taming of the Shrew*. But the tiny creature that I now saw (a mounted specimen) that looked like it was enclosed in a bubble, was unknown to me. I'm fairly sure that it was at the Natural History Museum in New York that I stood and stared and listened to the tape.

"When the water shrew, a small mouselike animal, first enters the water," the tape intoned, "it has a silvery appearance, caused by water trapped in its fur, so that the animal almost seems to be encased in a bubble.

"After a minute or so, the air is lost, and the fur begins to get wet. This is a serious hazard for the shrew, since heat loss from the cold, wet fur in contact with the skin can cause the animal's death in a very few minutes. Thus, the shrew's diving and swimming periods are of brief duration, and as soon as he emerges from the water he dries his fur by vigorous grooming with his hind feet. This interesting animal is closely related to the short-tailed shrew, his terrifying cousin that lives by murder."

That terrifying cousin was the first shrew I met in the wild. The wild place was my backyard. I own a few acres of land in rural Connecticut and was sitting out on my terrace one evening just before dusk. Movement in an open area near my garage, in a small glade about 10 yards from the woods, attracted my attention. As I watched, a mouse minced carefully out into the open, a cream-and-tan white-footed mouse. As he stood there, his head raised, listening, a blur of motion came from the woods accompanied by a shrill, twittering sound, sort of a mad bird call that I couldn't identify. Then I saw that the mouse had a small creature on its back. In milliseconds the mouse was down, and the small gray creature ate it alive. When I got to the scene all that was left of the white-footed mouse was its tail, and I could hear a crazy scamper on the leaves in the woods.

I had just witnessed a killing by the short-tailed shrew. Victor H. Cahalane, former chief biologist of our National Parks, said of this tiny horror: "This is probably the fiercest animal in existence. Anything smaller than a mink that runs, crawls, or flies is tempting to this insatiable little assassin."

Other experts say, "This is a true monster. Most of its victims do not have a chance . . . If this animal were the size of a leopard, mankind would be in danger of extinction."

Since the day I saw that savage sight, I have made it a point to look for shrews. You see them at night, streaking across the road before your headlights, and if you are patient and quiet, you can watch them stalk your meadow like a tiger in the grass. There are millions of them, and they are just about everywhere. It might take you a while to learn the knack of finding the mythlike mite weighing $\frac{1}{15}$ of an ounce, even the largest never more than $\frac{4}{5}$ of an ounce. I have seen short-tailed shrews in the state of Washington, so many that they covered the ground like a living blanket. They were in a grove of Douglas firs, dining on the seeds that dropped, rushing from seed to seed as if they were starving.

This abnormal appetite is what drives the little killer. He has such a rapid metabolic process that he would starve if he didn't eat every two hours. The shrew's digestive system is such that he can consume his own weight every three hours.

They'll eat anything they can handle. I understand that they rarely work in teams, like the jungle animals, the tigers and leopards. But I did see two tackle an animal several times their size.

True, the animal was blind. But it was big and strong and a fighter. It was a mole, a large one, five times the size of the shrews that appeared out of the brush in front of my house and, moving like a ray of light, each attached itself to opposite sides of the mole. The animal never had a chance. The shrew is the fastest thing in the animal world, moving so quickly that few of its natural enemies, such as cats, dogs, or foxes, can catch it, unless it is in a weakened condition from old age or lack of food. The pair of shrews that were on the mole then started their grisly process of eating the animal alive, meeting nose to nose when they were finished. I wouldn't have been surprised to see them start nibbling at each other. But they didn't. As soon as the mole was demolished, they vanished as swiftly as they had appeared—little brown ghosts disappearing into the woodland.

Personal experience taught me about their poison. Once my dog brought me one of the creatures, about two inches long. The dog is a retriever, and he dumped the shrew in my hand. I thought the shrew was dead, but suddenly he came alive—fiercely, biting. It was like the sting of a bee, the swelling was slight, but where I was bitten by the tiny jaws the area was inflamed and painful. The next morning I felt like I had had a three-day bout with bourbon, a sickly, dehydrated, hang-over feeling that lasted all day.

"No wonder," said a biologist friend of mine. "The bite of a shrew is somewhat like that of a cobra. In a recent experiment, 6 milligrams of pulverized salivary gland of the short-tailed shrew killed a mouse weighing 20 grams. The glands of that one shrew contained enough poison to kill more than 200 mice."

Secretion from the salivary glands flows when the shrew fangs its victims with lower incisor, needlelike teeth, slowing the heart action and the breathing of the attacked animal. Then all the shrew has to do is tear the victim apart, eating skin, bones, everything. I understand the shrews I observed must have been of the finicky variety; few even leave the tail.

Most of us have heard women of a vicious or nagging nature called "shrews"; the name used in a derogatory manner is old in the history of literature. A few centuries ago it was firmly believed that the shrew could paralyze any animal or person, could "cast a strange spell" merely by running over the body. An old dictionary defines the words "shrew-struck," "shrew-run," and "shrew-afflicted," as meaning "a person who suddenly has had the use of his arms and legs taken from him."

You can identify the short-tailed shrew primarily by his size, which is much smaller than that of a mouse. In fact, you could call him a miniature funnel-nosed mouse with half his tail gone. The one that bit me measured just over two inches, was covered with lustrous, rather dense fur, slate-gray on back and creamy underside. At first I didn't think he had ears, but finally I located them, two tiny openings lost in the thick fur. The paws were snow white; the delicate little things reminded you of hands. There were thirty-two teeth. It seemed fantastic to believe that nature had endowed such a minuscule creature with the poison and the power to strike terror in animals many times his size.

But, apparently, nature's scheme is wise—the shrew actually is beneficial. He doesn't destroy property or invade and infest your house as mice do and, technically, the animal is classified as an insectivore. Unless he can get a juicier meal immediately, the shrew dines largely on insects of all kinds, even on insect larvae and earthworms.

Last summer we had a gypsy moth invasion. It was an education to watch how nature combatted the freak attack. The larvae, the caterpillars, came in hordes, climbing the trees, and turning the tree trunks into fantastic, furred horrors. They destroyed the leaves, overnight leaving some oaks and maples bare. Then the big green caterpillar beetles came, shining like jewels, some the size of a half dollar; they lumbered into the trees and attacked the caterpillars. Then the shrews appeared like a combat battalion. At one time my wife and I counted thirty of them killing. It was sheer butchery; but it was beneficial.

Because we were aware of shrews and their habits, it gave us the opportunity of a lifetime to see the mighty mites at their best—or their worst, depending upon your point of view. They came into the open unafraid and uncautious, which is not their custom. They showed themselves in clear sunlight, which is also unusual.

They whipped across our land like wind dressed in gray fur, leaving dead and dying caterpillars behind, eating what they wanted, then retiring to their woodland.

It is rare, however, for shrews to appear together in this fashion. They are loners, nervous, nasty tempered, and they do no one a favor, especially one another, if they can help it. When not on the almost never-ending ravening hunt for food, they fight among themselves, killing and devouring one another. I once found one dying in the meadow before my house, scarred, fur torn, and one leg missing. Why his adversary didn't finish him off is a mystery. And whether they have immunity against their own poison is also a mystery.

An experiment conducted by Dr. Hart Merriam gives an excellent idea of what kind of horror the shrew is. The doctor put three short-tailed shrews under a glass tumbler to observe their demeanor together when captured.

"Almost immediately they started fighting," the doctor says. "In a few minutes one was killed and eaten by the other two. . . . One of these then killed and ate his surviving companion."

The only other animal the shrew tolerates is his mate, often living with her before and after the mating season. The family is born in a grass nest under a log, in a stump, or in a narrow burrow near the surface of the earth. The ball-shaped nest often contains from three to seven young. The size of a housefly when born, they begin getting fur in a week. At the end of the second week, they are well furred, their ears open, and their teeth start appearing; in a month their eyes open. The mother throws the father out before the nest is finished; she pushes her offspring out into the fierce, competitive world as soon as their eyes open. They are on their own for the rest of their lives. They live purely by instinct and are not taught how to hunt by the parents. They start on insects, flies, moths, butterflies, grasshoppers, berries, and nuts. With their incisor teeth, even the very young can bite open a tough snail shell. Lizards and young mice are attacked and eaten—if the young shrew is fast enough.

Ernest P. Walker, assistant director of the National Zoological Park, had a pair produce sixty-six young in less than twelve months. His calendar showed the shrew's gestation period as never more than sixteen days, often twelve days. Four times one of his captive shrews gave birth, raised her young, and had another litter—in twenty-four days. He also found that they often had first litters when they were three months old.

There is little doubt that shrews keep our mouse population in balance. Robert Eadie, a professor of zoology at Cornell University, discovered in 56 percent of the nests he examined that the residents had been dining exclusively on field mice.

Shrews do have natural enemies: hawks, owls, shrikes, foxes, bobcats, weasels, coyotes, and even snakes hunt them. But even here nature has come to the shrew's aid. A gland in each flank throws off such a strong musk that most of the predators, except for the hawks and owls and snakes, prefer another type of meal and will stalk shrews only if extremely hungry.

The shrew is so busy eating and reproducing that he has no time to hibernate; it is rare that he lives longer than sixteen months.

Shrews inhabit most of North America and are classified in five groups (of a dozen different kinds): (1) the common long-tailed shrew; (2) the tiny water or pigmy shrew; (3) the "little" shrew; (4) the short-tailed shrew; and (5) the Crawford or gray shrew. The long-tailed shrew also poisons his victims, but he doesn't have the potency of the short-tailed shrew.

Other than the short-tailed shrew, I think the most interesting are one species of water shrew which holds air bubbles in his feet and actually walks across water; the elephant shrew, a timid animal, 4 inches long with a long trunklike snout, which makes it resemble an elephant; and the pygmy, weighing $\frac{1}{14}$ ounce. The clown of the clan is the Crawford, which also has a short tail and enormous batlike ears.

Hunters and fishermen stand the best chance of seeing and observing one of our most interesting animals in action. I was in the Adirondack Mountains one fall when I had the opportunity to explain what a short-tailed shrew was to my companions.

I had noted there were shrews flashing about the woods. Once one came right up to my foot, nose twitching, body twisting. Apparently, the leather of the boot had no appeal for he moved on. But a friend a few hundred yards away had rubbed his boots with some type of animal fat, and one inquisitive shrew ran up the boot, then went farther, ending up biting him on the leg. Now I actually saw modern man "shrew-struck."

I heard him shout and went over. He was holding his thigh, his face was red, and he was agitated.

"A mouse bit me!" he said.

"A mouse! What did it look like?"

He hadn't killed it. It was too fast. And he described the short-tailed shrew perfectly. I looked at his thigh. The little monster hadn't bitten him once, but four times, and the area was inflamed and swelling. I didn't know what kind of first aid to give, but I remembered my own experience of a single bite. This apparently had been a hungry shrew, but he had tackled something that was just a little too big. I shuddered to think what could happen if fifty shrews worked together.

My friend limped back to camp, went to bed, and was sick for two days. He couldn't eat and got little sleep.

I'm not so sure that all this ancient business about shrews is sheer superstition. They're incredible little creatures.

10

THE BLACK BRAIN

The Crow

It was several years ago when I decided to give up that useless, inane, and even cruel sport of crow shooting. I had been led to believe that every time I downed one of the black ones the farmers of America breathed their gratitude. But I am selfish about it now. My sport has changed from shooting to watching—and respecting.

The decision was reached several summers ago, after I had made one of the best, or luckiest, shots of my life with a

scoped .243 Winchester. Standing on the terrace of my
home in the wilds of Connecticut (what wilds there are left),
I saw a crow sail in, feathers satiny black in the midday sun,
and light in a big oak, perhaps 200 yards away. I got my rifle,
leaned against the house steadying myself, exhaled, then
slowly squeezed off a shot. The bird fell, caught in the
branches. Then as he started the branch-to-branch fall to
the ground his black brethren began arriving, cawing, swooping close to him. In ten minutes there were fifty crows trying
to lift him, pushing with their beaks, attempting to clasp
him with their wings. They set up the most unforgettable
funeral dirge I have heard: a series of startling but mourn-
ful cries, hovering over the dead one for ten minutes, until
they realized that they could be of no help. They then
climbed into the sky, a long, black funeral parade, still
loudly mourning the departed. It was such a display of
affection, loyalty, and bravery, that I felt guilty for days for
killing a bird of a clan that obviously had such high intelligence and rare camaraderie. This is seldom seen in the wild
—or in the supposedly civilized world of man either: last
summer on Eighth Avenue in New York City a man lay
dead on the sidewalk for three hours before anyone had
enough interest to roll him over.

And I held to my new-found belief, that crows are not
put on earth for man to shoot, but to watch and perhaps
even admire, joining a club that is rapidly adding members.
My belief held even after fifteen of the rascals came barrel-
ing in one day, almost scaring the hair off my Siamese cat,
buzzing her in such savage swoops that I am certain they
would have finished her off if I hadn't come to the rescue.

Actually, the crow is a celebrity, the best-known bird in
North America, probably the world. People who can't identify more than three birds always name him first when they
start exhibiting their knowledge of natural history. But
there is much that we haven't bothered to learn about this

tar-feathered character—a bird of such talent and fascination that even those who think they hate him admit that he is smarter than they.

Largest of the perching birds, he is technically a songbird with the syrinx of the singer. He can make soft, melodious calls, cry like a baby, crow like a rooster, coo like a dove, and imitate many sounds. He belongs to a complicated family, *Corvidae,* which has upward of two hundred species, including crows, ravens, daws, rooks, jays, nutcrackers, and magpies. The family is further split into the *Corvinae* dominated by the crow and the raven. The raven is the largest member of this grouping, usually identified by long, pointed wings which exceed his tail in length. The bird we are interested in is of the genus *Corvus,* more particularly *C. brachyrhynchos,* known as the common American crow, which with several slight differences is at home throughout the North American continent. Smaller types are the Southern, Eastern, Western, and the Fish crow—but the whole tribe are birds with brains and personalities often praised by the more sensitive and observing.

"There are few things more melodious than his caw of a clear winter morning as it drops to you filtered through 500 fathoms of crisp blue air," wrote James Russell Lowell.

Thoreau said, "This bird sees the white man come and the Indian go, but it withdraws not. Its untamed voice is still heard above the tinkling of the forge. It sees a race pass away, but it passes not away. It remains to remind us of aboriginal nature."

Actually, there are more crows in the United States now than before the white man came here, upward of three billion in North America. They have survived and prospered under the all-out attack of civilization, where everything from fire, bombs, poison, mass slaughter, and electronic execution have been used to exterminate them. Hunters make crows their constant target; farmers have been feuding with them for generations. Ingenious but insipient murderers have been after them for years.

A group of these "sportsmen" found a large crow roost not far from Harrisburg, Illinois, crept in during the daylight hours when the crows were off hunting for food, and hung sticks of dynamite in cans which were also filled with pieces of scrap iron. They linked about one thousand of the cans, hung in nests and trees, to an electric line. Then they waited until night, were patient until they assumed that the crows had been there long enough to drop off to sleep, then exploded all of the cans with one pull of a switch. They counted one hundred thousand dead crows the next morning.

The newest "kill-the-crow" gimmick is the recorded call, where the assembly and alarm calls (crows respond to both; assembly from tribal habit, the alarm call to be around in case help is needed) are taped and then pressed into a record or run off directly from the tape recorder. The sportsman then hides, turns the machine on to full volume, and waits. A year ago I sat with a man who *used to be* a friend of mine and watched this "machine gunning."

The machine was turned on full blast to an assembly call that some sneak had taped and pressed into records that were sold for $3 apiece. In minutes the crows responded, coming in from every direction, loyally answering the call that had kept them together for thousands of years. When they were within range my former friend, with three shotguns at his side and all automatics loaded with five shots, began blasting. Of course, even though they were being murdered by the dozen, the crows didn't spook and flee. For the electronic electrocutioner wasn't through. Now, the alarm call was quickly substituted, rallying the black birds to the aid of besieged friends. Mourning at the dead ones falling, some going to the ground and trying to help the wounded fly, others darting in to attack their still unseen foe, the crows kept coming—and dying. Finally, I could stand the slaughter no longer, and switched off the death box. When the sound ceased, the crows, some wounded, made a circle in the sky and left. The whole thing lasted less than a half hour. The jubilant gunner counted fifty dead birds on the ground. He picked up his murder box and went—the crows lay on the ground where he left them, seeming to me still defiant in death, the sun picking up little purplish iridescent spots on necks and breasts. My remark just before I told this delighted gunner what I thought of him: "Wouldn't clay birds have been as much fun and less bloody?" He gave me a long diatribe about how he was helping farmers and benefiting humanity with his electronic crusade against crows.

What is there about the crow that has put him on the bounty and hate list along with other creatures undeserving of the branding like the wolf and the fox? Just what are the crimes he has committed? It is true that from May until late June crows are destructive in cornfields, digging up newly planted corn, often even yanking up the roots of those that have begun to grow. But there is an inexpensive solution which when sprinkled on the grains of corn to be planted will keep the crows away. I have used it myself. It is no trouble to apply, costs little, and is effective. But even now, in the day of the pesticide and the spray, few planters take this precaution. They prefer to curse and persecute the crow as a criminal. What about the harmful insects he kills: the caterpillars, grubs, beetles, mice, and worms? Few give him credit for good deeds.

Summing up man's feeling for the crow, Alvin Johnson said, "This is the least beloved of our land birds, having neither melody of song, beauty of plumage, excellence of flesh, nor civility of manners to recommend him."

I disagree. That plumage gleams in winter sun like rarest sable touched with violet and shimmering emerald, and his walk is as dignified as that of any judge entering a courtroom. That long, drifting flight at dusk as the crow flies against an arching blue-gray sky toward his roost in forest of white pine is as graceful as the stroke of an artist. And in deep winter when his confident caw comes in early morning it seems to me a warmly reassuring note that I am not alone in a bleak world. And did any of his detractors ever see a pair of crows in a meadow, the sun shining them up like handsome oriental ebony figures in postures of tender love and devotion?

On the less poetic side, farmer Gardiner Hammond of Martha's Vineyard learned that the crow was handy to have around. Believing that crows were killing his new-born lambs, Hammond declared all-out war, offering a bounty for dead crows. This went on for two years until one day he noticed that all of his grazing grass was being steadily destroyed. Investigating, he discovered that white grubs were cutting the grass off at the roots. Prior to his putting the bounty on crows, they had eaten the grubs and saved the grass. Trying an experiment, Hammond now stopped the shooting of crows and did what he could to entice them back. They got the message. Within a few weeks they returned, and the grubs were routed.

Crows also do an effective but unappreciated job of tidying up areas of carrion, a skillful sanitation corps that keeps our highways clear of dead birds and animals. And no less an authority than Richard Pough, a member of the scientific staff of the Audubon Society, said that crows eat not only white grubs, but harmful grasshoppers and army worms, insects that few other birds touch. In answering hunters who claim that crows often eat duck eggs, he argued that the black birds actually serve a useful purpose when they destroy a clutch of duck eggs. Pointing out that ducks of one species all lay at nearly the same time, he claimed that crows benefited the entire natural function. If bad weather arrives just after the eggs are laid, it often wipes out the current crop of pintails, mallards, or blacks. But by sometimes destroying eggs, crows force ducks to lay again, often doubling the chances of a successful hatch.

In further defense, the United States Biological Survey claims that crows occupy only one sixth of duck nesting areas. Scientists at the University of South Dakota say that crows prevented a grasshopper plague in that state, that in areas where crows were driven out wire worms were wiping out cabbage farms, green worms were invading tomato fields, and pastures were being destroyed by white grubs.

Aldo Leopold, one of our most widely respected wildlife experts and naturalists, conducted a study proving that 80 percent of partridge eggs were wiped out by mowing machines, while the crow, that a growing faction was trying to prove was responsible, took only 6 percent.

I'm not trying to paint the crow white, nor make a hero out of him, but I feel that it is only right that the facts regarding our most maligned bird be brought into focus. I also think it is wrong for sportsmen to massacre crows by unfair means while hypocritically claiming to carry on a holy war against one of the great enemies of mankind. The crow is not that. He is a wary adversary, yes—even a good game bird. It takes an expert with a crow call to pipe the clever bird in, and no novice at shooting or camouflage will ever get far.

Even the experts have trouble. When Alfred Hitchcock was making his picture *The Birds,* his technical advisors had plenty of trouble catching the crows and ravens to star in the movie. They finally solved the problem by dressing in black, blacking their faces, and creeping into the crow roosts on moonless nights with long-handled nets. When the picture was completed, the unanimous opinion was that the crows were the big brains among birds, the easiest to train, the most difficult to catch, the ones with the most personality.

They were even trained to attack an object on command. As a matter of interest, it was discovered that the "meanest" and most stupid bird was the sea gull.

Catching a crow alive has never been easy. Some use the clap nets familiar to falconers; baited with a live crow, even a stuffed owl, the net collapsing and imprisoning the crow that flies into it. Some trap them by forming a strong piece of paper into a hollow cone, heavily smearing the inside with birdlime. This is placed in a crow area; corn is dropped inside. When the crow tries to get the corn, he is hooded, trapped. The best method is the one the Hollywood experts used: find the roosting areas and approach at night and try to get nesting birds. As their arch enemy, the great horned owl, has discovered, crows are largely helpless in the dark. They usually roost in thick pine or evergreen groves or in trees in the midst of a swamp, nearly always in hidden places as far from man as they can get. It isn't unusual for them to assemble from a forty-mile area to their roosting place.

But sometimes they are caught off guard in open places. Once, walking by a sunlit meadow, I saw a pair (their usual alertness dulled by love) in a romantic mood. The larger bird, obviously the male, was facing the female, fluffed feathers sparkling in the sun, wings outstretched, he was making a series of courtly bows and a sound like a baby's rattle being vigorously shaken.

The normal aftermath of this courtship is the nest which is built by both, the male bringing the material, the female putting it together. Nine inches deep, with an outer layer of quarter-inch twigs, it is usually built close to the trunk in a high tree. The inner nest is cleverly woven with a mixture of fine twigs, wet moss, bark, and earth, then softened for the youngsters with cow hair, horse hair, or wool—any soft material they can find. The eggs, from four to six, are bluish to olive green, often flecked with brown or gray. It is not uncommon for females to share a nest, taking turns hovering the combination clutch of eight to ten. This has given rise to speculation by some observers that crows practice polyandry, two males accommodating one female, or the reverse, polygamy. Such is not the case, crows are loyal mates and excellent parents. (If two females use one nest, it is probable that one male is hurt or dead.) The male feeds the female well during the eighteen-day incubation period, often covering the eggs himself and always standing guard. The young's eyes open at five days, and from then until they are pushed from the nest at five weeks, they eat half of their own weight in food delivered by the parents each day.

Sentinel duty is extremely important during these weaning days, as it is during the crow's entire life. There isn't a suspicious movement that isn't instantly reported with the "caw-caw" (watch out!) of the bird on guard. There is much speculation about the duties of a sentinel—and his intelligence. Testing it one day, I got within 20 yards of an oak tree in which three crows always lighted and sat in the morning sun, flexing their wings and talking over their plans for the day—actually on guard for a flock which was in a hidden meadow. The second day, carrying a fishing rod in an aluminum case over my shoulder, I got within the same distance; again, the third day. The fourth day I walked out with a gun over my shoulder. This time they gave the alarm call and went howling out of the tree at 60 yards.

Anyone who has walked in the country knows that flocks of crows always post a sentry or two when they are in a meadow feeding. It has been reported that when this sentry doesn't do his job properly he is set upon by the flock and killed. Some nature writers claim that when they get back to the rookery the crow clan have a trial by jury, deciding the fate of the careless sentinel. The noted naturalist John Burroughs handled that myth this way: "A man sees a flock of crows in a tree in some commotion," he wrote. "Now, they all caw, then only one master voice is heard. Presently, two or three fall upon one crow and fell him to the ground. Spectator examines him and finds him dead with eyes picked out. He interprets it as a court of justice; they were trying a criminal and having found him guilty executed him. The curious instinct which often prompts animals to fall upon and destroy a member of the flock that is sick or hurt or blind, is difficult of explanation, but we may be quite sure that, whatever the reason is, the act is not the outcome of a judicial proceeding in which judge, jury, and executioner all play their proper part."

But some of their acts cannot be explained with this aplomb. Freeman B. Currier of Newburyport, Massachusetts, told of seeing a crow fall into the Merrimac River; his feathers apparently were soaked and he couldn't rise out of the water. He flapped and cried, but couldn't make it. In seconds, a flock gathered and, after a caw conference, one dived, grabbed the drowning bird with its claws, and flew shoreward, dragging it across the water. When he tired, another came and pulled the crow to shore. The three stood on the bank until the drenched one dried out, then they went aloft to join the flock which was still waiting.

Another curious side to the complex character of the crow is that although they are among the wariest of all creatures and are highly suspicious of man, when they are captured young they make wonderful pets and are extremely sociable and sophisticated, often remaining with a household all their lives. The Reverend Whitney Dough of West Palm Beach had a crow named Andy who lived with him for twenty-three years. The normal life of a crow in the wild is about five years. Andy said "Hello there!" to delivery people, "Hot dog!" during some of his master's more solemn sermons, could cry like a cat, said "I won't!" at the right time, and had a vocabulary of about a dozen other words. Contrary to general belief, it is not necessary to split a crow's tongue to assist it to talk. In fact, this is cruel and harmful and works in the opposite manner. The trick is to capture the crow young, tame him, feed him well, and make him become dependent, even fond of you.

I had a friend whose pet crow Fred would light on his shoulder at the command "Come!" He could also make the sound of a train whistle, was on the back porch for dinner promptly at six every evening, and would crow like a rooster just after the real chicken made his howl at dawn. One farmer had a crow who learned to call the cows; another called the cat in each evening. I have heard several crows say things like "Come on Jack!" or "Now you've done it!" Simple words like "chow," "mother," and "dad" are easy for crows. Pet crows have learned to laugh like a man, bark like a dog, and one, with a sense of humor, picked up the technique of clucking like a rooster calling his harem. When the hens came running, he hopped about in his tree in glee at their confused milling about looking for their rooster.

Some scientific observers believe that crows can learn just about anything. One picked up the technique of ice fishing in a matter of minutes. It seems that one day ice fishermen in Sweden chopped holes in the ice, dropped in their lines, and attached the tip-up flag which popped up when a fish was on the hook. This crow watched for awhile, until there were a couple of strikes and the fish were hauled in. Then, when he thought the fishermen were gone, he waited until a flag came up, flew to the line, and grabbed it with his beak. Tugging it, he walked backward with the line as fast as he had slack. Then he went back to the hole in the ice, carefully walking on the line, his weight keeping it on the ice so it wouldn't slip back into the water. At the hole, he grabbed the line again and brought it backward across

the ice. Then, like a tightrope artist, he walked the line
back to the hole. He kept this operation up until he had
the fish out of the hole; then he promptly ate it. This documented action of the brainiest of our birds was reported
at length in the *Science News Letter* as an example of avian
intelligence.

Truly, here is a bird with something to crow about.

11

MINISTER OF DEATH

The Vulture

Someone once said that life on earth requires many ministers. The vulture is one. He is the minister of death. I've spent hours in many places, India, Spain, Greece, Mexico, Georgia, Mississippi, even Pennsylvania, watching vultures soar, the beauty of their flight belying their dreadful purpose.

The bird, ugly, even monstrous, in almost every aspect except flight, in all of its varieties has aroused intense interest since the time of Pliny. There are few aware people who haven't watched the graceful undertaker of the skies, playing his funeral dirge in aerial acrobatics rather than sound, and asked themselves the old question: "How does the vulture find his prey, by sight, scent, or some uncanny preknowledge?"

Most naturalists claim it is by sight that the vulture knows when death has come. I have some incidents regarding the matter that probably will add to the confusion.

We found the vulture one of our greatest enemies in hunting the tiger in the Indian jungles. The tiger would kill our live bait, and if we didn't get to it fast and cover it with grass and leaves, shielding it from the sharp eye of the bird, it would soon be reduced to bones, and nothing would remain that would attract our lordly cat back. But one evening, just at dusk, when we had uncovered a free kill of a buffalo that a pair of tigers made, we discovered that maybe it wasn't the vaunted eye of the vulture that brought the carrion birds in.

In five minutes after the body of the buffalo was bare of camouflage, a dozen crows buzzed in, caw-cawing loudly enough to rouse the entire jungle. They lit on the animal and pecked away with gusto, but in ten minutes the vultures started dropping from the sky, hissing the crows away. They all came, the white-faced, the black, the kings, and rose flapping heavily into the sky only after we came down from our tree and drove them off. Twice more we noticed that the crows came first, alerting the vultures.

Once I tried an experiment. I noticed a group of white-backed vultures in a *sal* tree about a mile from our jungle camp, sitting there as solemnly as a convention of undertakers. We had bagged a calf-killing leopard that morning, and I asked the skinner to take the carcass into the shade of a big mango, well across the road from camp, where I could sit and observe. Checking my watch, I figured that the crows made the discovery in 5 minutes, and the death birds in the tree a mile away that were supposed to have some supernatural awareness of the fact that a body was waiting to be demolished, took another half hour to get to the meal—even with the godawful noise the crows were making. I doubt that this is a discovery that will shake the world of natural history. But there was a good breeze that day, and the vultures were sitting downwind. They didn't scent the leopard, obviously, and they didn't see it. They came in to the sound of the crows.

We tried another experiment one day when cat hunting was slow. We hid the remains of a buffalo under some trees, didn't cover it, but just dragged it out of view; the other, a pretty badly decomposed one, we left in the open. This was deep jungle, and there were no crows. But, confusing our newly found theory, the vultures discovered the animal in the open in 2 hours. They never did find the other one.

To complicate the question of sight or scent further, I trailed a wounded Indian wild boar in the deep jungles for 2 hours and finally found him dead, ringed by white-faced and white-backed vultures. How had they arrived so fast? What sounds brought them in? The jungle was so dense that no matter how high they soared or how sharp their eyesight, I don't think it was possible for them to sight the wounded animal.

Another time, closer to home, in Georgia, I came across a runaway cow in a swamp, sunk so deeply in the muck that it would have required a helicopter and a squad of men to extricate her. Sitting in trees all around the doomed animal were fifty silent, staring turkey buzzards—our own species of vulture. How did they find the cow? She was in a dense part of the swamp with trees rising above her like an umbrella.

Robert Hall of Bethlehem, Pennsylvania, sent a report to the Audubon Society saying that while he was playing golf in Florida he killed a snake, a moccasin, he thought. He threw it into the high grass of the rough and continued his game. The next day, playing the same hole, he saw a buzzard flying down the fairway in a peculiar manner. The bird was casting back and forth and was so close to the ground that each time it canted its wingtips they almost swept the ground. Finally, it settled on the ground about 100 feet from where Hall had thrown the snake in the grass. With head lowered and neck extended, the bird ran forward a few paces, stopped, moved its head from side to side, then ran forward again.

On reaching the high grass of the "rough," the bird ran in and soon came out holding the snake. Hall concluded, "He couldn't have seen that bit of carrion until he was right on top of it. If he smelled it, the distance where I first noticed the peculiar flight, at least 150 yards from the snake, indicates that the bird has an extraordinary sense of smell."

Last summer, in Greece, I asked a hunter, a man who had been born in the mountains and knew its wildlife well, what he thought about the vulture. There were two layers floating above us as we talked—twelve soaring at perhaps 2,000 feet; another fifteen or so were up another 2,000 feet.

He said that he also had often thought about how the bird knew where its victims were and had talked with hill people about it. "Only one old man, a shepherd, made any sense," he said. "He had his own theory, and it is good enough for me."

It seems that the shepherd believed that all flock animals when they became ill, or were in some way abnormal from their fellows in the flock, would go off a distance from the rest of the animals. When vultures noticed an animal lying at a distance from the rest, they mark it down as a possibility. They then check on it every day. "When someone feeds on the crumbs from another man's table, he is long suffering and patient," the old shepherd said. So, he reasoned, the vulture who flies so high, often at 10,000 feet, and has eye-sight superior to that of a man with powerful binoculars, spots these "different" animals. If they remain in the same position, the bird comes in for a closer look, watching for motion. If there is none, the patient, feathered ghoul goes aloft again, returns the next day, comes lower, and even flaps to the ground and approaches. If there is death, he's in business; if not, he goes aloft again and checks another prospect.

This doesn't answer all the vulture questions, but it's pretty sound theory.

One day in the remote mountains of Spain I watched a dead goat being reduced to bones and realized that there was such a thing as a vulture society. The big, brown-black birds came in first, maybe fifty. When they had gorged, the little Egyptian vultures or Pharoah's hen and the kites came in. These have slimmer beaks with which they can probe the bones and the joints. The Egyptian vultures then left the kites on the carcass and a lammergeier came in, a big, bearded bird with a feathered head, looking like a giant hawk. His job is to take the big bones, fly into the sky, and drop them on the rocks, smashing them. Then he flies in and eats the marrow. That was it. The whole clean-up job took exactly a half hour.

It was almost the same routine in India, except the crows were first, then the white-headed and white-backed vultures; then the black kings, then the big white kites. I never saw a bearded vulture or a lammergeier.

Many beliefs and legends surround the vulture. The Bushmen of Africa claim that it is useless to cover up a carcass and leave signs of blood around. They say that the vultures spot these signs of slaughter from incredible distances and come flying in to investigate whether the slain animal is still there or not. They never kill the bird, believing that he is an evil god who can do them harm.

The South African hunter Colonel Stevenson-Hamilton tells of making "sight" experiments and bringing vultures in by spreading a blood-red blanket on the ground. He believes the bird is not only color conscious but can tell by the blood if the animal is still living. Natives of the Kenya area told me that the vulture dreams at night of a dead animal lying on the plains. At dawn the next morning the bird is able to fly to the body. This belief makes the vulture good medicine for witchdoctors. They take the bird's heart and brain and mix them with certain roots and herbs, and then they either eat the awful mess or inhale the smoke as the mixture is burned. This gives them the power, so they tell their followers, to forecast events and to look deeply into the future.

In India, a place of much sun, many corpses, and death in various forms, the vulture is protected and respected. In Hindi they call it with some humor but realistically the "Honorable Sanitation Corps," and there is even one open-roofed edifice in Bombay, where human bodies are brought, placed on rock altars, and left for the birds of prey to "bury."

There are so many species, subspecies, and varieties of this graveyard bird that has fascinated, repelled, and puzzled man ever since he crawled out of the primeval ooze, that there is not space to list them here. The condor is the largest, having a wingspread of 10 feet; Pharaoh's hen is the smallest, and the most unusual is the awesome "bone-breaker," the bearded vulture, lammergeier or "lamb eagle."

Actually, the true vultures are confined to the Old World, with the original type, the cinereous vulture (*Vultur monachus*) inhabiting tropical and subtropical areas, but also found from the Straits of Gibraltar to China. And although our American forms are quite distinct from the foreign, we have them in variety. We have the condor, the California vulture (*Gymogyps Californianus*), and the king vulture (*Sarcoramphus papa*), with gaily-colored head, the turkey buzzard or vulture, so-called because of similar coloring (*Cathartes aura*), and the black buzzard. Although the most common, the turkey and black, are seen in abundance in the southern United States, they have also been sighted in Connecticut and Pennsylvania.

The bird we see most often is the turkey buzzard, the adult never exceeding 2½ feet from bill tip to tail tip, but having a wing expanse of 6 feet. Weighing 6½ pounds, he has a heavy coating of brownish-black feathers, a featherless neck of a scaly, repulsive red, and a dead-white hooked bill. His eyes are brown, large, and have a fearful expression. Although an ex-president of the Audubon Society said of the vulture in the sky, "Behold flight in its utmost perfection," on the ground the bird is clumsy and slow. His claws, although curved, are weak and are not designed for protection, fighting, or even as a help in tearing food. The bird protects himself by raising his wings like Dracula and hissing. If this doesn't frighten his enemy, he will then retch and actually throw vomit at his attacker.

This regurgitation is also the feeding system. The male will gorge so heavily on a carcass that he can't fly until some digestion has begun. Then he gets into the air with great effort and returns to his nest where he vomits. The female selects the best of it, the young get the remainder.

Their nesting places are hollow logs and stumps, sinkholes, or caves. Usually, no attempt is made at building a nest—two dull white or yellow eggs, blotched with chocolate coloring, 2¾ inches in length by 2 inches wide are deposited in rotten wood and mixed with leaves that have blown in, not brought by a diligent parent.

The young are covered in a few days with soft, white down. (I saw one baby turkey vulture, naked, without a single feather, eat a 3-foot black snake whose weight was half that of the vulture—the bird digested him in a little over an hour.) The young inhabit the nest for ten weeks before they are pushed out by their parents and urged to go off and find their own dead bodies. They have long lives; some naturalists believe they exceed fifty years.

It is also believed that vultures attack the living young of many kinds of birds, herons, ibis, and even ducks, and that the condor and the bearded vulture attack young lambs and sheep and carry them off. But this has seldom been observed, and both of these birds are extremely rare today and are protected.

We have another moot question about the bird of death. Does he sit and wait for death to come or does he sometimes hasten it along?

Ernest Hemingway claimed that he had seen five hundred assorted vultures leave nothing but the bones of a zebra twenty minutes from the time the wounded animal hit the ground. He also said that vultures will come in on a live man if he is quiet and probably unconscious. He told of an Italian soldier wounded in Ethiopia who, while he lay unconscious, had his eyes removed by vultures and half of his face eaten away. They were pecking at the soldier's clothing to get to his kidneys when the stretcher-bearers arrived.

As for me, I watch vultures writing their curious calligraphy in the sky during the daytime, showing them I'm alive and kicking by rapid motion. When I nap in their country, I do it with a guard at my side or behind closed doors.

12

THE BIRD NOBODY KNOWS

The Hawk

In some of the last writing that Ernest Hemingway did, he mentioned driving over the mountains of Spain to Madrid, stopping and watching two hawks fly above the meadows. "A pair of hawks out working for breakfast," he wrote. "These are birds that always make me feel good."

I have the same reaction, having watched hawks in the Far East and all over Europe. Their flight is poetry. Perhaps Mr. Hemingway and I felt somewhat like the Italian sculpture Alberto Giacometti. He became famed only a few years before he died. Not long after receiving France's *Grand Prix National des Arts,* something every serious artist lives for, he said, "I prefer the sight of a bird living in the sky to any masterpiece of art."

Unfortunately, not many people share these feelings, especially about the hawk. It could be that this is the most hated and least understood bird. No one can argue the fact that he is the most beautiful and is among the most interesting. Why, then, is he the most hated? Because of ignorance, mostly, and also old wives' and farmers' tales about his destructiveness. For shallow reasons, sportsmen think the hawk is cheating them of game and the man out hunting partridge, pheasant, or rabbits has become the worst offender. Biologists believe that 85 percent of our sportsmen instinctively raise their shotguns and shoot when they see a hawk.

Maybe "offender" isn't a strong enough word. Actually, the sportsman or farmer who shoots a hawk is a careless killer of necessary wildlife, doing serious harm, costing our economy millions of dollars and upsetting that important and delicate mechanism known as the balance of nature.

Recently, the United States Fish and Wildlife Service reported that serious outbreaks of rodents have been occurring throughout the nation. Rodents in Texas, Oklahoma, Louisiana, Alabama, and the Pacific Northwest have caused extensive damage amounting to millions of dollars. Ranchers are banding together, insisting that predators be given complete protection and asking that anyone caught shooting a hawk be fined and jailed.

Forty-four states have created laws making it illegal to kill hawks. But too many have negated the benefit by protecting all *except* the goshawk, the Cooper's, and the sharp-shinned, reputed to be bird killers. The weakness of a law protecting the rodent killers and declaring open warfare on this accipitrine species was pointed out by Dr. F. J. Trembley of Lehigh University. At a meeting in the Philadelphia Academy of Natural Sciences, the biologist came out with a plea to protect all hawks. "Few hunters," he said, "can identify hawks in the air. This leads to the destruction of beneficial hawks rather than the fast-flying accipitrines. Also, the so-called game bird depredations of the goshawk are grossly exaggerated."

The "terrible three," as they've been called, are seldom seen, even by hunters. They are shy, cautious birds that hunt by stealth and speed, and even if a hunter did see one on the wing, he'd have to be an exceptional shot to bring him down.

Being fond of squab as a table bird, a few years ago I decided to raise some white king pigeons. I installed a few dozen in a loft behind my house, gave them two months to get used to their surroundings, then opened the door and let them fly. I liked to see them in their morning exercise flights. I watched them closely every day, yet at the end of one month, a dozen were missing, taken I knew by goshawks. Yet, in all that time I never saw a hawk. I use this anecdote to point out that if there is such a thing as a dangerous hawk, he is the one you never see.

The word "hawk" actually has indefinite meaning, but most often it is used to include all birds of prey, except vultures and eagles, although technically the eagle is a hawk. Restricting the word further, it also excludes buzzards, kites, and harriers. Characterized by long legs, sharply clawed feet, short wings, and a bill that curves magnificently from the cere, the hawk is our most distinguished bird. The female is larger than the male and, some experts claim, the better hunter. The largest is the goshawk; the smallest, *Accipiter tinus,* is the size of a song thrush. The family is a complicated one with many species and subspecies. For example, fifteen different hawks are native to the state of Virginia alone. My observations are restricted to those most often seen in the United States. The Buteos, the broad-winged or "mouse" hawks, are the rough-legged, the red-tailed, the red-shouldered, the broad-winged, and the marsh hawks; the falcons (not true hawks), the pointed-winged birds, are the peregrine falcon or duck hawk, the merlin or pigeon hawk, and the sparrow hawk, these titles are misnomers since neither hawk kills the birds it is named for. Then come the short-winged speedsters, the Accipiters, goshawk, Cooper's, and the sharp-shinned.

The harmless, beneficial birds are the broad winged, the ones that soar lazily, the figure-eight skywriters. These are the ones hunters pot shoot; they are easy birds to kill. If you're a sportsman who always shoots when he sees a hawk soaring, thinking that you are conserving game, doing nature a good turn, then a study made by the Fish and Wildlife Service should be carefully read by you, pasted in your hat, and reread at the beginning of every game season.

After examining five thousand hawk stomachs, the Fish and Wildlife Service came up with the facts that all hawks eat many insects; the sparrow hawk's diet is 60 percent insect. All the rest of our hawks also eat rats, mice, snakes, frogs, a few fish, some poultry, and song birds. The most maligned, the Cooper's, was found to dine on game birds only *12 percent* of the time.

Actually, the natural duty of a hawk is to help maintain a healthy wildlife community, taking what is most abundant, the thing that is easiest to obtain. These prey are the fast-breeding creatures—mice, rats, squirrels, rabbits, insects—that, uncontrolled, might inherit the world. Wayne H. Bohl, New Mexico biologist, goes even further. He feels that the three bird-taking hawks seek unhealthy game birds, those that nature has tabbed for destruction. A healthy game bird with proper cover makes it difficult, if not impossible, for even the fastest hawk to make a kill.

Small birds (not game birds), sparrows, chickadees, nuthatches, and literally hundreds of other species are also among the fast-breeding creatures. Without the few hawks created by nature to control their numbers, these birds would not only become a national hazard and a dangerous nuisance but would eventually destroy themselves. So the hawk is really the protector of their species. Nature is constantly kept in balance by birds of prey and other predators; all of them— hawk, owl, fox, coyote—are here for a designed purpose. Every time man disturbs this purpose he creates a massive problem like the one many of our states are having with rodents.

The naturalist Aldo Leopold said it succinctly: "If you love game and hate predators," he said, "it is like cherishing the right hand and cutting off the left."

This doesn't seem like a complicated situation to grasp, but people *still* say, "But hawks kill *song* birds, game birds, and *chickens!*" Sure they do. But this is true of perhaps four of the fifty or more species. And biologists and naturalists who have researched the problem carefully have proved that these hawks have a diet that includes poultry only 10 percent of the time and game birds 7.2 and 12 percent, depending upon the species.

There must be something to the new phrase sweeping the country, "Hawks are harmless; they are the friend of man," when all but six states are making an effort to protect them and the Audubon Society is conducting a national campaign to save all hawks. (Incidentally, if you are interested in learning more about hawks and what they do for man, send 10 cents to the National Audubon Society, 1130 Fifth Avenue, New York 28, N.Y., and ask for their booklet, *A Fair Deal for Our Birds of Prey.*)

The hawk is worth knowing. There is not a more beautiful bird, with his creamy buffs, speckled browns, cathedral grays, and touches of knightly red; his sleek, groomed, almost princely appearance; his swift, graceful flight; his fantastic eyesight, equal to a man's using eight-power binoculars.

Hawks breed and nest like most birds, usually in the

spring, building a sturdy nest of heavy twigs in the highest tree in the densest woods, on a lonely cliff or on the ground in wild marshland, depending on the species. They hatch two, sometimes even three or four, eggs and feed, pamper, and protect their young with great vigor. About the only enemy they have, other than man and the agile raccoon, is the Great Horned Owl who makes a specialty of raiding hawks' nests eating both eggs and young, often killing mature birds.

Hawks are fascinating, not only to watch when they gather for their mass-flight migration, but in their daily hunting maneuvers. They are honorable, selecting hunting territories, then staying to them, seldom intruding on the preserve of another. The Craighead brothers, John and Frank, spent many years in study and then wrote perhaps the only book of its kind, *Hawks, Owls, and Wildlife*. They have made such a minute study of hawks that they can tell almost to the millisecond how long it takes each species to strike down quarry. They claim that the daily hunting ranges of the Red-tailed are 2 miles in extent; Red-shouldered, ½ mile, and Sparrow hawks, 1½ to 2 miles. They describe the range as a series of perches, some representing hunting perches, others temporary stops between hunting grounds.

I spent a month studying the behavior of one Sparrow hawk, discovering it in the same spot on its hunting range in four out of ten checks. In thirty days this bird killed fifty meadow mice on one quarter of an acre, dramatically bolstering my belief that hawks are painstaking craftsmen who stay close to home and mind their business.

Fortunately, I am not alone in my hawk watching. Enlightened bird watchers are beginning to consider hawks a main feature in their outdoor entertainment; everything that comes before the thrilling sight of a hawk in motion is simply preliminary action. Several of the devoted clan I know call hawks "Nature's Airforce."

Most hawks migrate, the majority leaving in September and wintering in our southern states and Central America, the broad-winged and some red-tailed flying on to South America. Those who have seen the flights call them one of the greatest natural spectacles. Last year a friend of mine in Toronto saw four thousand broad-winged hawks in one flight, and this air armada was preceded by several waves of a few hundred at a time of several different species.

These great migrations used to be the scenes of senseless slaughter, especially at Hawk Mountain in Pennsylvania and the beaches of Maine and Cape May, New Jersey. Thousands would gather (just a few years ago) and shotgun as many birds as they had shells to shoot. Hundreds of thousands of hawks were killed, particularly in Pennsylvania, until bird lovers united and Dr. Maurice Broun and an emergency conservation committee pushed through a law. Hawk Mountain, near Hamburg, Pennsylvania, where the greatest flights are seen in this country, is now a sanctuary and a haven for the binocular-band, the bird watchers.

I've watched the hawks there using the elements in their migrations in a manner that requires the least effort, cleverly taking advantage of aeronautical lifts furnished by mountains where a cross wind is bounced upward and there are thermals, drafts of warm air rising from broken or mountainous country. I saw thousands of hawks in five hours during the third week of September at Hawk Mountain, rising on updrafts of air, gaining altitude over the mountain, then gliding as gravity carried them for miles until they were uplifted again by new thermals or "bounced" winds.

No man of spirit and sensitivity who has seen a hawk migration, seemingly precision-planned and regimented, but still a beautifully graceful exodus, could ever raise anything more harmful than a pair of binoculars at these valuable birds.

13

SAILOR OF THE SKIES

The Sea Gull

You can tell he is a sailor by that slight swagger, the roll in his walk, and by the way he favors docks and wharfs and follows ships at sea. Yet to most of us he is much more: he is a symbol of the romance and the vastness of oceans; the cry of loneliness on a dark, wind-swept day; a poem of sand, sea, and sky as he wheels and floats, cutting a graceful calligraphy with his wings, writing a sky language that we all can read. "Come," he seems to say, "there are far places to see. There are strong winds and sea spray. There is a ship sailing into the sunset. . . ."

He is the sea gull, known to us all. Most of us have been caught in his spell—fishermen, duck hunters, boatsmen, swimmers, beach bums, vacationers. Yet, although we think we know the gull, there is much about him that is mysterious: Does he drink salt water? Does he migrate? Is the seashore his only home? How large is his clan? Does he properly care for his young? Is he smart? Is this bird, so graceful in the sky, one of our better feathered creatures?

Actually, the gull is a fraud. That romantic aura surrounds a bird that is greedy, selfish, quarrelsome, and a free loader with an appetite and a digestive system that would shame a shark. This is a bird seemingly with only one motive in life: to eat. Omnivorous, he will eat carrion, fish, insects, berries, worms, just about anything that he can digest. Flowing with juices that can dissolve anything from a bone to a fishing spinner, his 5-foot digestive system is said to work something like an electric mixer. He gobbles, turns on that marvelous motor, and out come those things that even the gull can't handle. I've watched gulls eat live bait flung into the air, catching 8-to-10-inch fish as skillfully as a juggler, swallow them whole, and a short time later spitting the bones down on the deck or dock. I saw one gull brace himself and swallow the head and carcass of a five-pound bluefish without a burp.

This appetite and drive for food make gulls valuable as scavengers, helping us keep harbors and beaches clean. It is also their armor: all gulls are protected by federal law. Killing one is punishable by a $500 fine and six months in jail.

The name "sea gull" is a misnomer; there is no such thing. The gull is a long-winged bird of ocean, lake, or river, ranging in size from 12 inches to over 3 feet, a member of the species *Charadriiformes* and the *Laridae* family.

Twenty-nine of the forty-four species of gulls breed in the northern hemisphere, many carrying names as romantic as their flight: Magellan, Patagonia, Indian and Chinese black-headed, Aden, Mew, Silver, Bonaparte, Swallow-tailed, and Simeon. The one known to us all, almost as familiar as the neighbor's cat, is the herring gull, a big white bird with black wing tips and a pearl-gray mantle when adult or dusky brown when immature. He is seen throughout North America, near the sea, but also on lakes, rivers, even ponds, physically refuting the belief that the gull is found *only* near the sea.

Ten feet from one of the busiest highways in the world, Westchester Parkway, a few miles from New York City, is a small pond which has one big, old battle-scarred herring gull in residence. I drive by often and note that he has been there three years, summer and winter. There are fifty herring gulls living on tiny Lake Zoar new Sandy Hook, Connecticut, miles from the sea. Check any body of water in your area, chances are gulls are there, at least part of the time. One unusual fellow, Franklin's gull, not only migrates across the equator to spend his winters in the south, but he is also noted for his absence from the sea and his penchant for wheat fields and prairies.

The classic case of inland gulls, one that made many of us realize that the bird isn't necessarily a "sea gull," took place in Utah, 600 miles from the sea. Today, in Salt Lake City stands a $40,000 statue of either the ring-billed gull or the herring. This memorial was erected by the Mormons as the result of a dramatic visitation of gulls, one that would make theater audiences wince in disbelief. But it actually happened. The first Mormons planted wheat near the Wasatch Mountains in 1848, a crop that would determine whether they would live or die the following winter. All went well, but as the harvest began to ripen, millions of crickets appeared and began eating the wheat. There was such a horde that the Mormon farmers were helpless. Just as they gave up in despair, a great cloud appeared in the sky, coming from the direction of Great Salt Lake. Thousands of gulls. They dived into the fields and wiped out the crickets.

Studies have been made to determine if gulls migrate and whether their presence on small inland bodies of water are just rest stops. C. C. Ludwig and his sons of East Lansing, Michigan, banded nearly forty thousand gulls over a twenty-five-year period, catching them on their nests on islands in Lakes Erie and Huron. Their conclusions proved that 60 percent of young gulls recovered remained within 300 miles of their island colonies, as had nearly 100 percent of the adults. But 40 percent of those first-year birds did take off, going as far south as Mexico and the West Indies. It also was discovered that few remained in the south after that first winter. In that movement south, and its return north, they stayed to waterways, and not necessarily seacoasts. The Ludwigs believe that this is why gulls are often found on small ponds, lakes and rivers, far inland. As the flight of the young birds goes on every year, perhaps this is an explanation.

Another gull characteristic that must puzzle many of us, at least it does puzzle me everytime I see one take a big gulp of sea water, is how can they take in that much brine and survive? This is supposed to be an impossibility, but gulls can do the impossible: they drink as much salt water as they want without harm. Although the kidneys of most marine birds and animals, even fish, are not equipped to extract and excrete as waste the salt from the blood, the gull has special gear that handles this nicely. A pair of glands above the eyes does this very thing, sending excess salt out through openings in the bill.

Scientists studying the growth of simple organs, those with but a single function, experimented with gulls. Removing the salt glands from several birds, they placed them on salt-free, low-salt, and high-salt diets. They discovered that the glands of the gulls drinking only fresh water grew hardly at all, but those with the high-salt intake quickly developed giant protective glands to flush the salt from their systems.

People who have tried to keep gulls as pets, picking them up on beaches with broken wings, or trying to raise abandoned young, claim that they respond to rescue and care viciously. They peck at the hand that feeds them, and leave as soon as possible. Experts who trained many birds for the Alfred Hitchcock film "The Birds" claimed gulls were the stupidest and the least cooperative (crows and ravens the brightest).

But if they aren't smart enough to make good actors, gulls certainly have enough above the beak to know how to take care of themselves. This was brought out clearly on several occasions when I was blue fishing in the Race in Long Island Sound. We weren't having much luck; then, in mid-afternoon, the gulls appeared, a cloud of them suddenly came, almost darkening the summer sun, and they were in full voice, gurgling and crying and screaming. As they started darting to the surface of the water we suddenly realized that this was more than a spectacle of converging sea birds: this was a slaughter. These were herring gulls doing what they were named for, diving upon a vast school of small herring that had been driven to the surface by marauding bluefish. That was where we came in. The gulls gave the signal, and we responded, moving among them, trolling our lines. We got bluefish immediately.

I have often watched herring gulls drop clams on rocks to open them, but I am told that this is pure instinct, for in experiments the birds dropped wooden eggs, even metal objects.

If their brain isn't overdeveloped, their communications system is surely one of the best in existence. And how it works has been puzzling sailors and science for some time. Run a test yourself. The next time you go bay or ocean fishing, watch the sky. There are no gulls in sight. Start cleaning fish or throwing the remains of lunch overboard and time how long it takes for gulls to appear. I've done this several times. Ten minutes was the longest wait. Some observers claim that like buzzards, vultures, and crows, this marvelous ability to locate a free meal miles at sea is due to amazing eyesight. As far as I have been able to discover, however, science has yet to pinpoint this asset of the gull.

Several years ago I had the opportunity to study gulls at close range. As usual, they had selected a romantic spot to nest, on a cliff behind a little bay in the Far North, in Norwegian Spitsbergen. This was far, far above the arctic circle in the peopleless land of glaciers and icebergs, seals, and polar bears that I was exploring aboard the 57-foot diesel ketch, *Havella*. We were anchored in a little protected bay waiting out rough seas and fog.

At first, it looked like it would be a pleasant interlude. But the gulls quickly took care of that. I have never seen so many birds in one place. There were several species of gulls in this cliff colony, many thousands of them, and they were all in one big squawk most of the time. It sounded as if a giant noise-making toy had been turned on and become stuck —a great, scratchy scream.

Gulls of many ages were there: adults, fledglings, newborn, egg-pipping, immature ones just learning to fly. There were mated couples, nest builders, and wooers.

In two days of watching I learned several things about gulls: they have courage, are good parents, and the female is sexy. Nesting couples did their jobs well, the female covered the eggs while the male stood guard. He also delivered food to his mate, twice in a gruesome way. Gulls jealously guard their nest area and attack anything that crosses this invisible boundary line. Twice baby chicks staggered near the nest

I was watching, and I saw the male quickly kill them and present them to his lady. In another nest I saw a clumsy hen tumble eggs from her nest, breaking them, whereupon she and her mate calmly ate them. But in other nests several times I saw both male and female fight off gulls approaching their fledglings. On the cliff, an old male was patiently trying to teach a youngster to fly, furiously flapping his wings until the earthbound young bird caught on, did the same, and suddenly took off. I saw gulls rise on their nests and scream at a giant skua, a predatory gull, bent on raiding for tasty chicks. At one point, three gulls took to the air and attacked the skua, driving it higher.

I approached one nest on the shore, trying to examine it and perhaps get photos of the mother and young. I didn't. She left her nest in a fury, first attacking an arm I held before my eyes, then zooming up, knocking off my hat and pecking away at my head.

One morning I watched a love affair in its early stage. Apparently, the female is the aggressor. (Most species are indistinguishable plumagewise, the female somewhat smaller than the male.) This one swaggered over and stood by a handsome white-breasted, gray-backed young swain. He stood aloof, ignoring her as she sidled closer and closer until she was pushing against him. He continued to pretend she wasn't there, until she reached up and gave him a lusty peck on the head. That did it. The chase was on, in the air and on the ground. When it was over, such enthusiastic billing and cooing went on that it sounded like an outboard motor with bad spark plugs.

Gulls, especially herring gulls, usually don't mate until the early summer of their fourth year. I am told that some species accelerate this, mating during the second year. The result of this courtship is a nest, a rugged one of seaweed or grass, weeds or sticks, built by both, working as a team, often one lugging the material, the other shaping it into a nest. The nest can be on a cliff, an isolated island, break-waters, sandhills, even bushes and trees. And some gulls have their young far from the sea, but usually return to it when their young can fend for themselves. They mate for life, most species returning to the exact place of their court-ship and first nest until they die.

There are usually three greenish or bluish eggs spotted with brown, black, or purple which the hen incubates for three weeks or a month. (If she loses these eggs, she tries again, the second time laying only two.) From the moment they are pipped into downy chicks, gulls are pampered by both parents. They are fed almost constantly, the mother often regurgitating a whole fish, then pecking it into easily digested pieces for her offspring.

Youngsters can fly at six weeks and in two months use their wings well enough to escape most enemies. Although the normal life span is ten years, gulls have been known to live as long as thirty years. From the ravenous thumb-size nestling, the herring gull grows to an adult in two years, weighing just under three pounds (stomach empty), with a wingspread of 5 feet.

Free loader and beach bum that he is, I can easily forget the unpleasant traits of the gull when he comes miles out to sea to meet my ocean liner, wheeling and crying that land is not far away. When I walk a deserted beach just before dusk, and see him in the sky with his long tapering wings, gracefully using and seeming to control the winds, I can forgive him almost anything. Perhaps we should never look beyond beauty.

14

PROFILE OF A PARADOX

The Porcupine

It was called a river in India, but from where I sat high in
the big *mhowa* tree it looked like one of the creeks that
wind through the southern tier section of upper New York
State, a twisting, happy, humming stream, a big-hearted
run of water that stopped and formed a pool, performed its
ballet twirl, caught its voice, and then ran on along the edge
of the jungle. The pool it left behind held clear Indian sun
like beer in a glass. It was a pool that held my attention

while I listened to the mystic Oriental tune the little river was chanting. As I sat there held in the spell of that singing silence of the Indian wilderness, a peculiar creature came out of the green smear of jungle.

He walked clumsily like a knight in chain armor, made directly for the pool, and drank deeply from that mixture of sun-gold and rock-run liquid. He was *sayal*, the dangerous giant Indian porcupine; his body from head to rump measured 35 inches; his tail with its spines ran another seven inches; and I am told that he weighed as much as 40 pounds, bigger than many cocker spaniels. Porcupines reach their highest development in this animal; his neck and shoulders carry a crown of bristles 12 inches long. He is armored on belly and back with quills; his tail is full of long, white "rattling" spikes. He ranges the Himalayas to Cape Comorin and Ceylon and waddles westward through Iran, Syria, Asia Minor, and even Palestine. But India is his home; here he is found in great numbers; here he is feared as much as the tiger and the leopard. Not only by humans, but by all other animals in the jungle who give him a wide detour of respect.

Now he finished drinking, beads of water glistening on his chin. Suddenly he alerted, bristles stiffening. Coming out of the jungle almost at the same point that the porcupine had was a leopard. He walked toward the pool soundless on his thick pads, did an amusing double-take when he saw the armored knight regarding him with his beady eyes, flicked his long tail, and got out of there. He was a smart cat. There are documented cases of Indian porcupines attacking and killing leopards; tigers have been stabbed to death when they leaped at him.

Rao Naidu, an Indian professional hunter, told me of seeing a tiger tackle an Indian porcupine. "I don't know what was wrong with *sher*, our striped cat that is supposed to have a brain. But I saw him leap upon *sayal*, the speared one. The porcupine was flattened to the ground. Then the tiger roared and went backward as if pushed by some great power. Moaning, he went to his stomach and crawled away into the bushes. It was getting dark, and I feared to go after him. Waiting until morning, I got two men and a shotgun and two buffalo and went to track the tiger. Driving the buffalo before us, we went into the jungle, looking for the blood trail. We soon found it, splashes and specks had been coughed every few feet. The tiger was lying on his side just off the trail under a lip of overhanging rock. He was dead, his lungs and liver full of the long quills. The porcupine? Ah, he must have been all right. He disappeared shortly after the tiger crawled into the jungle."

The method of attack is odd: backward. The porcupine hurls itself back with great speed, smashing its high quarters against its foe, driving erect quills deeply into its victim, with nearly always fatal results. The spear work is done mainly by a compact mass of short strong quills on his rear portion. Such are the weapons that the larger the animal, the more effectively the longer quills come into play. They are not thrown; they are pushed or driven in—like a hammer drives a nail. The force behind that drive is enormous. One naturalist found a leopard with porcupine quills driven completely through the brain. I have seen *sayal* many times in India and always avoided him. Now I was glad that I was high in a tree, waiting for a distant beat to materialize. While I sat motionless, he went back into the jungle, moving heavily under the weight of his portable armory, probably the safest, smuggest animal in the wilds of India.

The porcupine is safe in America too. But he's a puzzle, a paradox; few naturalists have worked out any valid reason for his existence.

My friend, the late Rex Brasher—an ax blade of a man who spent sixty-five of his ninety years in the outdoors, the only artist to paint all of the birds of North America, and whom the National Geographic Society, the Smithsonian Institute, and a former president of the Audubon Society called the best bird painter in the world—claimed that the porcupine was the only woods creature he wasn't wildly enthusiastic about.

"I'd be sitting there in a thicket in the Rockies," he told me, "waiting for three hours for a pileated woodpecker to come out of his hole in a dead oak, when something would nudge my foot. I'd look down, missing the flash exit of the shyest and rarest woodpecker there is, and find a blamed, blasted, stupid, meddling porky gnawing on the leather of my right boot. I'd kick him off, he'd sit, shake his head, then waddle back and start on my left boot. I'd have to get up and leave and find another thicket and another bird. That blamed fool of a quill pig thought I was a tree or something and the salt from my sweat on the leather of my boot was ice cream and honey to him."

Rex Brasher spent more time in the woods, forests, and mountains of North America than any of his contemporaries. He got to know our animals well and often dropped conversational gems. Here are some about the porcupine: "Porky doesn't *throw* any of his 20,000 quills, although I've seen a big male swat his tail and shake loose a few that flew into the air. Most people think the porky a silent, stupid animal. They are kinda stupid at that, but I've sat and listened to them bleat like a moose calf, snort like an old buck deer, moan like a disappointed cat, and cry like a baby with a wet bottom.

"I've seen young 'uns rolling on the ground, looking like these wrestlers on the TV, all the time whining like they was killing one another. Porky is not mean; he stays to himself, minds his own business, and he won't attack a human, no matter what folks tell you. And even the adults are full of fun. I've seen two full-grown quill pigs sashaying around, upright, dancing like two happy youngsters at a barn dance. I guess he does some harm, but I happen to know that when they feed high in a tree they clip off small branches and twigs that deer feed on and look for. . . ."

That was typical of Rex. He didn't care for the porcupine, but closed his conversation saying something good about the animal.

He is the only one I ever heard mention anything good about the strangest resident of our woods, an ugly, clumsy throwback on evolution, probably placed here by nature to prove how fortunate every other living thing is.

The porcupine, *Erethizon Dorsatum* (beast with irritable back), his name taken from the Latin *porcus* (swine) and *spina* (thorn), is also known as the spiny pig, hedgehog, quillet, Urson, and quill pig. He is a rodent (the largest terrestrial rodent in Europe; ours is the beaver), 30 inches long with a 6-inch weapon-tail. Weighing up to 25 pounds, the animal has a blunt, rounded head, fleshy mobile snout, and an ordinary fur coat with an outer covering of guard hairs lavishly sprinkled with barbed quills. I counted 29,000 of the black-tipped, white-based quills on a big male (dead).

The quills or spines are smooth, hollow, tubular, and needle sharp, with barbs starting close to the tip, increasing in number back to the end of the shaft. These, somewhat like fishhooks, are what fasten the quill in the enemy's flesh where, moistened, they expand. As the injured animal moves, the quills penetrate deeper.

No other animal has such protective armor. Not only do the spikes keep his enemies away, frightening and cautioning even wolves and grizzly bears, but the air-filled bristles keep the porcupine afloat in water and cushion his numerous falls from trees. And he can afford to be careless with his barbed lances; new ones quickly grow to replace the lost ones.

Last winter in the Adirondack Mountains (in the interest of science), I annoyed a big, blustery, old male porky, holding a 4-inch hunk of soft pine near his twitchy tail. After putting up with my nonsense for about five minutes, suddenly, in a rapid, graceful movement, not unlike a skilled fencer, he flicked his tail and drove fifteen quills into the wood. He apparently had plenty left. My friend held out a thick deerhide, grease-toughened glove. With the same speed, the little animal sent ten shafts clear through the glove. Then he raised his snout, gave us a cold, disdainful look, and waddled away, the only creature I've ever seen that could waddle with dignity.

When we came back to camp we found him in our car. He had wrecked the upholstery and was starting on the steering wheel when we edged him out with a long stick. Any article that contained salt from human perspiration attracted him. He had also shredded an ax handle before he discovered the open car window.

Porky is piling up a poor reputation everywhere. Donald Schake, a land manager of the Pennsylvania Game Commission, discovered that porcupines had caused destruction to buildings and vehicles belonging to the commission. "They chewed the rubber tires and hydraulic hose right off a tractor left in the forest overnight," he said. "They also gnawed their way into our equipment buildings. The porkies chewed through a 14-inch support post under the barn at the commission school. At least a dozen porcupines have been caught in traps set at the base of this post, which seems to have an attraction for them. It's hard to understand, but on one occasion, two of the slow-moving animals were simultaneously caught in the same trap."

Porcupines aren't smart. Anecdotes of things more stupid than two getting caught in the same trap at the same time have been documented. I threw a stick at one in a pine tree while I was walking in the woods near my camp one fall. He was so befuddled that he stayed up there for three days. Another time, in the forest, I kept one watching a stick

I moved in a circular motion until he became dizzy and fell out of a tree.

The portly old gentleman, waddling through the woods on bowed legs that seem inadequate for his fat body, is never in a hurry, even if he tumbles from a tree and an animal rushes in to take advantage. He protects his nose by sticking his head under a log or stump or stone, brings his feet together, and lays close to the ground, guarding his vulnerable stomach. Then his quills shoot up; he doubles in size, and his spiked tail flips gracefully, powerfully. At this point, most animals depart. But if the attacker continues to molest, or even stay close, the porcupine lashes with his tail and backs into the animal. He can send as many as twenty quills into an adversary with a few quick flicks of his tail—and hundreds more if he makes body contact.

Found in our woodlands nearly everywhere north of the 40th Parallel, he is at the same time our most common and uncommon animal. He doesn't wander much in winter, often staying in a two-acre area. There is one in my forest that spent all last winter in five trees. They feed mostly at night, but they also move during the daylight hours if hunger demands.

With a life span of a dozen years, the porcupine mates in October, shortly after maturing at the age of two. He usually has one offspring, which may weigh as much as a pound. The baby porky's eyes open right away; in less than an hour the many quills, which are soft and hollow at birth, harden and the baby has his protection. Shortly after he is born the porcupine can raise his quills, still wet, and will back up and tail swat anything—except his mother.

There have been some amusing theories about the acrobatics involved in a porcupine mating. An Adirondack guide told me that the female suspends herself upside down from a branch, the male cleverly moving toward her from above. The truth is that they mate normally, like most animals.

But one naturalist claims that he has seen males stabbed to death because the mate forgot to keep her quills down when he came in for a little affection.

I've heard old hunter's saying porcupines are protected in nearly every state because the animal is the only one a wanderer lost in the woods can kill with a blow of a stick. It is true. A friend of mine struck one on his unprotected nose last summer. He died obligingly, and we dressed him for dinner, trying out the "lost in the woods" survival theory. This one did smell appetizing broiling over campfire coals, and the meat turned onto the plate chicken white, tender to the fork. But it was like eating a piece of stringy pine bark. I suppose it could sustain life, but porcupine meat isn't something that will catch on.

And it also isn't true that porcupines are protected. Many states have open season on them. They do much harm besides eating up loggers' and hunters' camps. Many of the lumber companies with huge forest tracts in the west are hiring hunters to kill and trap them. Although the porcupine is essentially a vegetarian, foraging in corn and wheat fields and apple orchards, he also likes the trunks of yellow birch, beech, maple, and hemlock, in fact, about any tree he can waddle up to.

But the porcupine's greatest damage is to pine trees. Sometimes he girdles whole stands, causing the trees to die or making them unsaleable. The United States Forest Service estimates that the bristly ones cause more than $1.5 million damage in the forests of the Pacific Northwest alone. Other estimates place the damage to trees and other property that a single porcupine will cause in his lifetime at $6,000.

Canada is annoyed with the porcupine and has declared open war. Officials there estimate that one porky can destroy up to fifty trees in a year by girdling the main stem of large trees or chewing the tender bark of young ones. Often, they chew out hunks of bark, leaving scars called "catfaces" where insects thrive and help destroy the tree. If the tree does recover and live, the sugar-sap is suppressed from downward passage by the catface. The porcupine returns to the tree later to feast on the sugar-rich bark just above the old scar.

Unfortunately, man himself is largely responsible for the porcupine's harm. We disturbed the balance of nature when we deliberately set about killing the porcupine's natural enemies, fishers,* wolves, bobcats, coyotes, lynxes, hawks, owls—the only creatures brave enough or wise enough to tackle the dangerous quill pig. The birds of prey are too silent and too quick for the thrower-of-darts, and the others, especially the fisher, pounce and roll the porcupine on his back, attacking his unprotected stomach. The fisher is a past master of the art.

New Jersey hasn't seen a quill pig in many years, but now reports are drifting in that the animal is back, and many dogs are returning home sorely defeated by an animal they had not known to exist. Naturalists in that state are in a happy frame of mind about the return. No other state has evinced happiness about the strange quilled waddler in their forests.

The last porcupine I saw was sitting in a tree, feeding itself twigs and wailing like a lost child—or like the lost, misunderstood creature he is. The sound was sad and lonely. I remembered it for a long time.

* See Chapter 16, "The Fascinating Fisher."

15

THE POSSUM ISN'T PLAYING

The Opossum

It was a dark, windy night when I first saw him here in New England, right out of the antediluvian past. For me, he has always been a sly, scaly, nightmare creature. We were in an old farmhouse high in the Green Mountains of Vermont, getting ready to bed down for an early night, hoping the wind would break, at least into an easy, pushing breeze, and that the next morning would be a good one for our trout fishing. Now the rain started slashing against the ancient frame house, hitting the windows in a sound like breaking glass, and the wind was making idiot screams in the eaves. Suddenly, the farmer, our host and guide, knocked his dead pipe out in a tray, the ashes spilling in a silver splash. "Guess I best go out and see that the hen house is closed tight like," he said.

"You would wait 'till it started raining right good," his wife snorted. She was an admirable, attractive woman who cooked like an angel but had the sour tongue of a devil—the prod-and-pray type of which good pioneers are made.

In 10 minutes the farmer was back, wet and shaken, looking like he had seen a ghost roving about out there in the wild night.

His wife stared coldly. "What's the matter, Harold? Did the chickens throw you out?"

He ignored her. "Men," he said. "I just seen the biggest darned rat in the world! Mouth full of teeth, a snarlin' at me. Killed my best rooster and stood there with his naked tail a waggin'!"

This we had to see. "Did you manage to kill it?"

"Yep," he said. "Wouldn't budge off that rooster. Bold as red paint!"

We braved the rain to take a look. When I saw the coarse whitish gray hair, the gray face, the snout, the long, scaly, bare tail, I knew what it was and remembered the words of John Smith, settler of Virginia, when he first saw it: "Hath a head like a swine and a taile [sic] like a rat."

" 'Possum," I said.

"Cain't be!" said the farmer. "He's a *South* animal. He'd freeze to death. What's he doin' way up here in our mountains? Ain't possible!"

The opossum, called by naturalists the most successful of our mammals, has been doing the impossible for at least 110 million years. Back in the Cretaceous period when the world was a mass of steaming earth and impenetrable jun-

gle, when the monstrous *Pterodactyl,* with its 30-foot wingspread was here and the ugly and rapacious trio, *Tricera-
tops, Brontosaurus,* and *Dimetrodon,* were dragging their
60-foot lengths through the ooze, the opossum was present,
lowly, timid, probably venturing out then as now only when
the sun went down so he could find enough shadows to blot
his way. But those seemingly indestructible giants and many
other large, fierce, well-equipped animals have long since
expired. Not the opossum. He, according to educated guesses
by the best of our biologists and naturalists, seems destined
to go on forever.

Exactly, how, why, and when he got out of our South-
land with its warm swamps and mild winters, is still a question being argued in the East and the North.

That next day, while fishing, we talked with a warden
about our chicken-killing opossum. "They don't do that
often," he said. "Leastways around here. But we do get some
trouble from them. People callin' to come and get everything from giant rats to werewolves out of their cellars and
sun porches. We started seeing them about ten years ago."
(This was in 1960.) "They do have some bother from our
winters, freezing their hairless paws and tails, sometimes
their ears. Few coon hunters are usin' 'em for practice. People say they're good to eat," he ended doubtfully. "But I
don't know about that. They look too ratty and spooky to
me. Like something that just crawled out of the grave, that
slimy long bare tail and all."

Southerners assure me that the poky old opossum not
only is a good game animal, exciting hounds into sending
their hair-stiffening music into the dark night, but that
after the hunt a meal of opossum and sweet potatoes is
among the best of all foods of the chase. I remember one
amusing true story Mark Twain told of a time when he
was writing in Elmira, New York, homesick for the South
and its savory food (one of the few observations I violently

argue with Mark Twain) and he wrote and asked a colored employee to come North with a couple of opossums. He went into detail on how an opossum is properly prepared for the pot.

It seems that they are first put in a cage and starved, ostensibly to rid their flesh of any flavor from other unappetizing food they may have eaten. Then, when they are good and empty, they are fed corn, plenty of it, and other wholesome grains and fruits. Mark Twain built mouth-watering pictures of what this was supposed to do. When they are as fat as a force-fed *pâté de foie gras* goose, they are ready for the pan, a slow-roasted, much-basted operation, the animal nested in a circle of sweet potatoes. Well, I was convinced. Twain at a typewriter is nothing if not convincing.

The first opportunity I had (with a brother in Georgia) we had this far-famed dish of the deep South. There was much lip smacking at our table that night, ostentatious proof of the power of Dixie propaganda. At the risk of insulting my Southern friends, I must confess I couldn't even eat the sweet potatoes.

That Vermont warden expressed my feelings succinctly. I've met the opossum informally many times and must admit that, indestructible and historic as he is, he does not rate among my favorite animals—except as a curiosity. Last fall I got home to my Connecticut farm from New York late and was fumbling with the key in the back-door lock when I felt something rub my leg; I turned, looked down, and saw a hissing opossum baring its teeth. It gave me the sensation you would get finding a snake in your bed. I understand many people react this way to the death-gray, bare-tailed creature. But once again the opossum paradox: He really can't be so repulsive if he has enough appeal to emerge as one of the most popular cartoon characters in America. True, it may be Walt Kelly's singular genius and sense of humor that has pushed his opossum Pogo to such astounding success, the favorite of millions of pen-made opossum-philes. Yet, I wonder what many of Pogo's pals would do if they saw an opossum in the raw?

An unlovely lump of gray-furred flesh (but so perfectly designed by nature that he hasn't changed a hair in 15,000 years), he ambles through life living on other animals: mice, toads, lizards, sometimes even tackling rats (he does have sharp teeth, fifty of them, more than any other mammal in North America). Birds and their eggs also appeal to him, and he has been known to take a meal from a hen house; but mainly he feasts on grains, insects, and fruits. Completely omnivorous, carrion and garbage are relished, this appetite giving the opossum a natural advantage over most other animals. Yet, he faints from fright and is so timid that he can be conquered with a push. But with his steady out-pouring of offspring, nothing—flood, famine, enemies, or weather—seems to deter his spectacular stay. Even man, the most dangerous predator of all, who seems determined to destroy all living things, including himself, doesn't often bother the opossum.

Say we arrive and erect a town where the opossum used to live. No bother, the opossum still lives in the town. In Los Angeles they have even been seen in daylight on Sunset Boulevard, a street on which no self-respecting wild animal would be caught dead. They have done so well in this area, among the most populous in the United States, that the Animal Regulation Department of the Los Angeles Police pick up one thousand live opossums a year—usually from people who call in horrified. Hundreds are collected weekly from the highways, run over by the never-ending stream of southern California traffic. But such is their talent for survival that they go merrily on, dodging speeding cars, ignoring agitated development builders, adjusting to the frenzied pace of living in a region which, according to sociologists, is the most frenzied of all. No wonder they had the stuff to outlive the dinosaurs, the hairy mammoths, and the saber-toothed tigers.

Actually, these animals out of a dim past aren't the cowards and scavengers that many people claim they are. They can put up a good battle for a meal. I saw an opossum tackle a 4-foot black snake, whip him into insensibility, and then calmly sit down and eat him from tail to head.

Two years ago, while walking in the woods, I saw an apparition come waddling out of an old woodchuck hole. It looked like a Hindu multigodhead symbol come to earth. It had a dozen heads that turned and blinked at me in the fall sunlight. It was a female opossum with brood riding, hanging on with their curious little prehensile tails and childlike hands while mother went out shopping for a meal. Five young were on one side clutching the fur, three were on top, two on the tail, and two more rode the other side. As the mother swayed along the meadow path they poked their heads around enjoying the scenery like passengers on a sight-seeing bus. They never did see me. (I stood perfectly still. No animal other than the primates can observe a motionless human.) It was quite a sight.

The common opossum (*Didelphis marsupialis*) is a marsupial or pouched animal, belonging to the same family as the kangaroo, the wombat, and the koala bear. The animal we know weighs from 4 to 8 pounds when adult, has a 16-inch body, and a hairless foot-long tail that is almost as facile as a monkey's, enabling the opossum to move in trees as though he had five hands. Those hairless paws actually do resemble hands, fore and hind feet having five digits and a big toe that is a highly specialized opposable, grasping digit. Their tracks in snow are amazingly like a child's. They usually don't start stirring until twilight, moving in a slow, awkward gait, like an old man under a heavy overcoat trudging in slush.

Our opossum has no relatives nearer than Mexico, but

he has at least 150 in Australia. The ordinary Virginia opossum that is becoming familiar as far north as Ontario and Saskatchewan, Canada, has interesting cousins. One of the most remarkable is the parachuting or gliding opossum, a 40-inch animal that lives in eucalyptus trees and has a volplaning membrane that permits him to soar 100 yards from tree to tree, much like a flying squirrel. The largest is the Australian Bobuck or dog-eared opossum, often weighing more than 10 pounds and, to its detriment, possessing a beautiful silver-gray fur that is so valuable that the animals are trapped and shot in large numbers. Smallest is the Murine opossum from South America, a miniature of our opossum, often arriving in this country on banana boats, tucked among his favorite fruit. Rarest is another tiny fellow, the 5-inch Leadbeater's opossum, named after a taxidermist, and believed to have been extinct. He was first discovered in 1867, then declared extinct. Now he is supposed to be around again in typical opossum survival style.

Breeding twice a year with as many as twenty young (although the mother has only thirteen teats, and the young who don't immediately attach to one are brushed off and die of starvation), the opossum has had more misinformation recorded regarding its reproduction than any other mammal. One choice bit, still circulated, is that opossums copulate through the nostrils and, after a period, the tiny fetuses are blown from the nose into the pouch. The birth is unusual, but not fantastic. Lacking placentas like most mammals, the marsupials must nourish their developing young even in the fetal stage by direct contact with the folds of the uterus. Thus, the thirteen-day gestation period is the shortest of any mammal. Birth is rapid. One scientist watched an opossum bear twenty-five young in less than five minutes. Arriving on the life-scene weighing 0.16 grams (170 newborn opossums weigh an ounce; two dozen can nestle in a teaspoon), the young have enough strength in 16½ seconds to crawl through the thick mother-hair to the teats, where they hang on for life.

Growth is slow, the young only opening their eyes and mouths widely after two months. Some may have left the pouch before this time but are still sustained by greatly stretched nipples. The pouch is a natural marvel, containing a sphincter muscle permitting it to be opened and closed at will. At ten weeks the young are able to leave both the pouch and the mother, but they always scamper aboard her back when she leaves the den and continue to do this until they are rat size and weaned at fourteen weeks. Then they are on their own, feeding mostly on insects, for their two-year life span.

Examinations of nearly five hundred opossum stomachs in New York State proved that the opossum is a friend of man: two fifths of the stomachs contained insects, field mice, and shrews; amphibians and worms came from one fourth; and 10 percent were filled with toad remains. This was surprising, for toads are protected with huge toxic parotid glands which repel mammals. But apparently, little repels an opossum.

One of the things that repels them is fright. As everybody knows (the action is part of our language), when the opossum is scared he falls down, pretending he is dead—playing 'possum—until the danger passes, then he staggers to his feet and off he goes, safe again for another 10 million years. But opinion is divided on the action: Is it ruse or real, feigning or fainting?

The backyard experts claim that it is a clever stunt, that foxes, toads, lizards, and even wild dogs do the same thing. They point out the classic example of the spreading adder, a snake that does such a realistic job of duplicating death that it even opens its mouth and stiffens. You can poke it with a stick and it won't move. Neither will an opossum. But biologists claim that the opossum doesn't move because he can't. He is unconscious; the opossum isn't playing.

Dr. Carl Gottfried Hartman, one of the world's foremost opossum authorities (he has written several books on them), believes that the opossum actually passes out with fright, that it is his nervous system that triggers the action, not a cunning brain. He suggests that in the nerve centers there are substances that act as precursors to other substances that paralyze. He says that even the stimulus of a slight touch acts like a blow on a percussion cap, causing impulses to set off a charge—substances stimulate the motor nerve fibers, contracting muscles, causing stiffening. As the paralyzing substances go from the nerve cells, the opossum recovers. In short, he is scared silly, but he soon recovers. After spending more than a decade trying to puzzle out the opossum's personality, Dr. Hartman's word should be considered reliable.

But psychiatrist Hans Lowenback of Duke University confused the issue by testing a number of opossums with electric shock treatments, taking them out of their usual 2-minute, 6-second fright trance in eight seconds. Some of his animals did not freeze at all when alarmed by a buzzer or a flash of light, but came out snarling and fighting. Dr. Lowenback, following the professional pattern, read something alarming in the results. He told the Southern Psychiatric Association "that the opossum's trick of playing dead [we just learned it isn't a trick] may show that the animal is even more beset than the average psychiatric patient by such traits as severe anxiety, neurosis, depression, lack of initiative, and recession into himself."

Dr. William T. James, psychology professor at the University of Georgia, may have the last word on the puzzle of the opossum. He thinks that they are very smart, and he proved it by dropping them in a glass box with a sealed adjoining dining room. Project: Withhold food, lock doors, and see if the opossum can reason his way to his supper. The problem: A pole, set in the floor of the glass box, had to be pushed aside before the door to the food opened. The door was fastened with two latches, set so the lower one had to be lifted first. The opossums did everything right except figure out the sequence of raising latches. But they solved it in time: They broke the latches. It took twelve days for them to learn to do it the right way.

"They change after they have been in the laboratory awhile," Dr. James said. "We are educating them, and this last quarter they have done as well as a lot of students."

In short, the poor old put-upon opossum has a good brain, is adaptable, has a built-in survival unit, no food problem, is a master at procreation, and has the scientists confused.

If you want to see the animal that may outlast man, take a look at the opossum. He isn't pretty, but he's permanent.

16

THE FASCINATING FISHER

A few years ago I heard a game warden relate an experience that is worth repeating. On patrol through the wilderness area in one of our Western states he got off his horse and watched a hunter come down the path carrying a fox-size black animal over his shoulder. The animal's bushy tail sailed behind like a banner.

He stepped out to greet the hunter. "What have you got there?" he asked, after checking the man's license.

"I dunno," the hunter said. "But it looked dangerous, so I took a whack at it."

"Dangerous?" the warden said coldly. "Did he attack you, all 10 pounds of him?"

The hunter fidgeted. "No, but I never seen anything like it before. Isn't a weasel is it? A wolverine?"

"No," said the warden. "Don't you read? We have signs with this animal's picture on it posted all over the woods warning hunters not to shoot it."

"Why?"

"First, because it's your friend. Second, because it is keeping porcupines under control."

"Friend? Porcupines?" The hunter was perplexed.

"Yes," the warden said, "porcupines. Tell me, did you see any porkies?"

"Yeah," the hunter said. "Two."

"Why didn't you shoot *them?* Not dangerous enough?"

"Naw! Pesky things not worth wasting a shell on. Not good for anything."

That conversation in the woods resulted in a fine and the education of a hunter. The next question that the warden threw at the man had him completely bewildered.

"You live in a house?" he said.

The man nodded.

"Made of wood?"

Again the dazed nod.

"Then you might thank the fisher, that animal you just killed because it looked so dangerous."

He went on to tell the stunned hunter that porcupines eat the trunks of yellow birch, beech, maple, hemlock—any tree they can find.*

Then, as he fined the hunter, he told him that the fisher was the only animal that actually preyed on the porcupine,

* See Chapter 14, "The Profile of a Paradox."

the only animal swift and clever enough to persistently take porcupines without harm to itself.

"Every time you kill a fisher," the warden said, as he issued a fine, "you tear down a house."

This experience leads naturally into two observations. First, too many hunters shoot first and then question the wisdom of the act. We lose far too many wildlife friends of man every year by the thoughtless trigger finger.

Second, just what is this fisher, this virtually unknown benefactor of man? Why the name? Is he an animal that naturally preys on fish in addition to porcupines? Is his porcupine-controlling proclivity thrown off beneficial balance by his penchant for prized game fish?

Actually, the fisher's name is a misnomer. Unlike the otter and the mink, the fisher does not have the ability, or seemingly the desire, to catch fish. Naturalists claim that the name evolved from the fact that the fisher became a master at stealing fish from traps baited for other animals. Known scientifically as *Martes pennanti,* the misnamed fisher is also called black cat, pekan, and pennant's marten. The Chippewa Indians, who had a talent for naming animals, called the fisher "tha-cho" or big marten, which still is the most accurate description for this little-known forest mammal.

I became interested as the result of a dramatic encounter several years ago in the Adirondack Mountains. I had pitched a tent by a lake high in that island of mountain and was sitting by my campfire watching the wood turn from rose to gray, caught in the contemplative mood that a dying fire in the wilderness always evokes.

After I had returned from the lake with two bass for supper, I had startled a porcupine as I walked a hundred yards up the shore to scale and clean my fish. The bristly animal stared at me with beady eyes, decided that I was a suspicious character, waddled to a pine, and scooted up. There he was marooned on a limb.

I was preparing to get some lake water and douse my fire for the evening when I saw an animal. I sat still, watching. The approaching animal had head and shoulders silvered with white-tipped hairs, the rest of his body looked almost black in the dusk; he was the size of a gray fox and had about a 15-inch fox's tail and a tapering weasel's head. About two feet in length, he looked like he might weigh 10 pounds. I didn't know what he was.

Now he stopped, sat up on his hind legs like a curious cat, and sniffed the air. Suddenly, he swiveled his head. He had caught the movement of the bristly boob in the tree.

But the porcupine was safe, I told myself. No animal, unless his judgment is blurred with starvation, will attack the armored quill pig and risk the butcher blades in his tail. I was in for a surprise.

Moving as a shadow lengthens, the animal went to the pine tree; as fluid as water, he slid up the tree. In a motion so incredibly fast that I had difficulty following, he flipped the porcupine from the limb, then coming down the tree head first was on him where he lay on his back on the ground, ripping open his unprotected belly. He killed the porcupine so quickly and so neatly that there wasn't evidence of a struggle.

I went over and inspected what remained of the quill pig after the animal had eaten its fill and vanished as silently as a puff of smoke into the woods. He had eaten only from the stomach, taking most of the body meat, leaving the skin intact; as far as I could determine, not one of the quills was dislodged. An unbelievable conquest.

But the fisher thrives on the unbelievable. (I had learned his name after describing the scene to a game warden the next morning. "You're born lucky," he said. "Not many see a sight in nature like a fisher taking a porky. I never did and I been in these parts thirty years.")

Another fisher conquest was the taking of a gray squirrel —in the treetops! I didn't see this one, but a friend of mine did. A wildlife photographer of talent and patience, he had trailed a fisher for hours hoping to photograph it. He told it this way.

"I had been able to follow the fisher because there was light snow on the ground," he said. "But it was at a distance that did me little good for camera work. After about four hours of this sneaking through the woods, I saw the fisher stop suddenly and stand like a black stone, his head in the air. Then I saw the movement too. It was an old buck gray squirrel moseying along in his treetop domain, leaping gracefully from tree to tree."

The photographer stopped, dramatizing his story. "What I saw next no one will believe! That fisher went up the tree, getting to it in 16-foot leaps, then moving through the trees as gracefully as the squirrel itself. Its tree-to-tree movements were sure-footed; its speed fantastic.

"I think the squirrel knew doom was approaching. It chittered and panicked. The fisher closed in, breaking the squirrel's neck with one bite, getting the little gray animal in a leap of perhaps 20 feet. At least it seemed that far to me. And remember, this was a 10-pound animal pursuing the light and agile gray squirrel in its own territory. I don't expect you to believe me. Of course, I didn't use my camera. I was too fascinated. Anyway, the entire action was one big blur of motion."

Perhaps he was right; perhaps I didn't believe him. But the National Geographic Society does (and I do now, after seeing my own in action on the porcupine): "The fleet marten," observes the society, "can overtake a red squirrel in his leafy backyard, but it takes a fisher to catch a marten.

Faster in the treetops than any other North American mammal, the fisher sometimes dines on his close relative. He is fast on the ground, too, and can outrun a hare. His legs are short, but he can cover 16 feet or more at one bound."

Naturalist Victor H. Cahalane is even more enthusiastic: "Bounding along the ground like the big weasel that he is," he says, "the fisher covers four feet at a jump. It hunts by night, or if hungry, in the daylight. No meat in any form is overlooked. Mice, squirrels, rabbits, woodrats, mountain beavers, dead fish. Even foxes, raccoons, and lynx may be run down, for the fisher has all the persistent endurance of the weasel tribe and is swifter and more powerful than the others.

"Ordinarily, the fisher will not stand and pick a fight with too-formidable opponents. If cornered, however, it can whip any dog, even an experienced bear dog, and make an escape. In the ordinary run of events, it has little to fear from any of the native neighbors. Such a swift climber could escape from an enemy of superior strength such as a cougar, a wolverine, or a wolf pack. A grizzly or black bear is probably too slow or clumsy. A coyote would be too wise."

But like most wild animals, the fisher has one deadly and implacable enemy: man. In our greed, we nearly wiped the fisher out along with the passenger pigeon, the heath hen, the giant mink, the almost extinct sea otter, and the buffalo.

The one weakness of the fisher proved to be his fine, lustrous coat—his greatest enemy being the American woman who liked to feel the silky fur about her throat. The female fisher proved to be the most valuable, a single prime skin commonly brought $125, some as much as $300. Even the male's brought $10 to $50, making the fisher one of the most sought after fur bearers in the country.

Trappers did most of the damage in thinning out the fishers, but every deer hunter who knew the name of the animal also took a fisher with his rifle when he could. This wasn't often, though, for in addition to his other natural talents, the fisher is a master at concealment. But his voracious appetite for the trap baits (even though he often cleverly sprung them) helped lead to his downfall in the thirties and forties.

Forestry officials and lumber companies may be the friend the fisher needs to save him from complete extinction. They led the fight in placing legal restrictions on trapping and hunting the valuable animal, proving with graphs and charts and hard facts that what the trappers were gaining in dollars from fisher furs was heavily offset economically by the damage to our forests by the porcupine, the fisher's normal food supply.

Not really populous anywhere in his natural range (in the deep forests of Canada, the mountains of the United States as far south as the Carolinas, and extending into northwestern Wyoming and central California), it wasn't long until the fisher was a rarity under the heavy trapping and hunting that continued despite repeated pleas from those interested in our forests. The states were slow to act (anything involving people who can sign their names at voting time moves state and local government into ponderous ponderings and massive vacillation) until within the last few years.

Lumbering itself was also partially responsible for the fisher's fate—and forest fires. (The carelessness of campers and forest recreationists has never been clearly pointed to as one of the major contributing causes of wildlife depletion. But fire by the forgetful and the careless continues to be a potent destroying factor.) The deep woods habitat of the fisher vanished or was reduced in some states, thus contributing to his downfall. His slow reproductive processes also hampered the fisher comeback.

A member of the weasel family (mink, otter, skunk, badger, and marten), the fisher breeds once a year, having spring litters of one to five, with three being the norm. In a strange gestation period of "discontinuous development," where the embryo growth is held stationary in the early stage and not continued for months, the fisher usually gives birth to the kits 350 days after the time of mating. Ten days after this whelping, the female (the aggressor) seeks another mating, then returns to her present blind and hairless brood.

The birth place is a hollow tree lined with leaves, grass, and some of that fine fur. At two months the young fishers' eyes open; at three months they climb down the tree and follow their mother. The fisher is such a secretive, non-gregarious animal that little is known about the process that follows, but his hunting skill is so superb that it is the assumption of most naturalists that the mother, like most of the higher carnivores, patiently uses this period to teach her off-spring the facts of life. By fall, they are ready to be on their own, mating at about a year.

The largest fisher on record (in Maine where it is most populous) was a 14½-pound male; the largest female, 6½ pounds.

I have been more fortunate than most in seeing fishers, probably because I make it a habit when in the woods to move quietly and often sit motionless for long periods. The last time I was in the Adirondack Mountains I saw a big male fisher swimming across a lake in the Paul Smith's area. I was sitting silently in a rowboat, waiting for inspiration to strike. He was brownish black, swam well, and hissed at me as I tried to overtake him. I also saw another. It was nearing dusk, and I unleaned myself from a tree and started back along the path to meet a small female fisher coming my way, using the path as if it belonged to her. She stiffened, did a comic double take, wheeled, and fled.

They are supposed to be creatures of the night, nocturnal hunters, but I saw fishers in the daylight, or near daylight, so I assume that they move abroad from their tree-trunk nests whenever hunger urges. They do not hibernate, but like the gray squirrel play it cozy in a warm cavity in a tree when the days are bitter cold, venturing out when the weather is milder.

Also like the squirrel, they are cachers, hiding surplus food in trees and ground holes. They seem to like swampy areas and are reputed to be the best mousers in existence— thus giving man a double bonus.

Master though he is at killing porcupines, the fisher sometimes makes a mistake and gets barbed. But here again, unless he has been directly quilled in the face, eyes, or mouth, the fisher maintains his air of mystery.

Professor Malcolm Coulter, assistant leader of the Cooperative Wildlife Research Unit of Maine, who has made an involved study of the fisher, claims that the dangerous quills, so harmful to all other mammals, have little or no effect on the fisher. He has seen fishers with a hundred quills between the skin and the flesh, in the muscles, even against bones. Yet there was no sign of infection, inflammation, or bodily harm.

This has been projected into a biological mystery. But perhaps nature, which evidently placed the fisher here to balance matters with the porcupine population (it exploded harmfully when the fisher was trapped almost to extinction), has given the fisher a combination body chemistry and skinfold protection.

The good news regarding the fisher today is that he is making a remarkable come back in his old haunts. Maine's Earle Doucette wrote in a news release:

As we have mentioned previously, the fisher is making an astonishing come back in Maine, and nobody knows just why. This, as you may know, is a wonderful furbearing animal. [Author's note: Doucette was unwise to comment on this asset of the fisher in a public release. Drum beating of this sort is what got the fisher in trouble in the first place.] Someone said the other day that there are now almost as many fishers as there are 'coons in Maine, and that is saying quite a lot, because in some of our outlying sections the 'coons outnumber the people.

This has the familiar brass blare of most publicity releases, where facts are habitually fattened. Fishers will never become as numerous as people, they are too smart to breed the way we do.

A zoology professor in New York State's Cornell University, studying the return of the fisher, claims that the animal, said to be strictly a deep forest dweller, has extended its range from mountainous areas to other regions. He also states that the Adirondack Mountains now have a fisher population of more than four thousand, four times what it was twenty years ago.

Canada also reports the comeback. Western states like Oregon are bringing fishers in and releasing them, attempting to protect them with conspicuous signs posted in the wildlife areas, admonishing hunters not to shoot the fisher as he is a valuable ally in porcupine control.

But the biologists are puzzled again: how can the fisher be making such an unpredictable come back: state protection, change of habitat, learning to roll with the punches of civilization, a cycle change?

Maine, who used to have the heaviest population, and now seems to be getting it back again, may have part of the answer—for a while. It closed the trapping season in 1937. By 1960, the fisher had increased his range by 100 percent. So what did Maine do? Naturally, it let the fisher have it again. The trapping season has been reopened.

The New York Conservation Department got even more enthusiastic. In 1949, it opened the trapping season for a month, with each trapper permitted to take three fishers. People took over one hundred that year; the next year the season was lengthened. Each year, apparently upon the demand of the trappers (voters), they lengthen the season with a correspondingly greater take of fishers.

It seems obvious to most students of this extraordinary and helpful animal that abolishing trapping is the only way to keep the fisher in our forests. He never was abundant in any of his range. Each fisher has his own hunting ground, a large area which other fishers respect. It is determined by food supply, but biologists who have studied the problem claim that a single healthy fisher's domain is usually 10 square miles. Their considered opinion: Since the fisher can't stand massing, their numbers even on so-called optimum ranges remains low. Even in his heyday, he wasn't populous.

Another factor in the fisher's survival (in my opinion) is his nondiscriminating appetite (the same asset that has kept the opossum going). If he can't get his preference of fresh meat, he will eat carrion. If he can't find even that, he will eat nuts, berries, and other wild vegetation.

The fisher's hunting skill, courage, ingenuity, and ability to adapt both to terrain and food may save him yet—despite the trappers and the politicians.

17

REMARKABLE RED

The Red Fox

The ancient and respectable sport of fox hunting had a serious setback in England three years ago. So disturbing was the situation that country squires, masters of the hounds, and keepers of the packs called upon zoologists, naturalists, and other experts in animal psychology who might be able to explain what had suddenly happened to a sport that had been baying merrily along for centuries.

Actually, it was a simple matter: The foxes themselves

decided to do something about it. On one chase a red fox approached a railroad track and sat and waited until he heard the express train's whistle. When the hounds caught up with him, he led them across the track in front of the train. Several dogs were killed, the rest fled, howling in terror.

This dastardly deed made the front pages of the English newspapers, arousing comment from readers. Many favored the fox: "What a terrible thing for that fox to do to those hounds that were chasing him trying to tear off his hide! He shouldn't have used a train. He should have turned and fought his battle. After all, Lord luv us, the odds were only twenty-five to one!"

Things got worse. Twice more foxes led dogs in front of speeding trains, killing some of the best foxhounds in England.

Opinion was divided. One group thought that the same fox, having mastered the devilish trick, was responsible; another thought that a single fox was passing on his deadly knowledge, and that if measures weren't taken two things might happen: (1) fox hunting would disappear or (2) soon there would be no foxhounds.

It was a confusing situation—but normal. The remarkable red fox has been confusing man and leading him and his dogs on a merry chase for centuries. The railroad crossing trick was not a new one. In 1910, the American naturalist Ernest Thompson Seton reported a fox leading hounds up a track before an oncoming train in Canaan, Connecticut, then leaping from the tracks and leaving the slower hounds to their fate.

That technique is but one out of the versatile bag of tricks belonging to what many naturalists consider the cleverest animal in the wild. One sportsman reported the following humbling experience. When he was a boy he spent Sunday afternoons running his father's pack of hounds on fox trails. One day the pack picked up a hot scent. He went to a hill and watched the drama unfold beneath him.

The fox headed for a large, hollow log, went into it, then emerged, running, from the other end. The hounds spent a little time sniffing the log, then picked up the trail at the other end and bayed on. Running in a great circle, the fox came back to the log, went in, and came out the other end as before. He kept repeating this until the hounds were, as they say, dog tired, tongues out, their run a shamble. They were exhausted, but the fox was fresher and had more zip than ever. Finally, it dawned on the hunter that something foxy was going on. He went down to the hollow log and poked in a stick—out popped a fox. They were playing relay runner. There were two foxes. When one got tired he came back to the log, and the other rested fox dashed out.

We have done everything in our power to wipe the fox from the face of the earth. We have poisoned and trapped him; we have shot him; hunted him with packs of dogs; blasted at him from airplanes; invented ingenious snares, traps, and deadfalls; and used smoke, fire, and flame. But he still survives. He is even surviving the newer, deadlier mechanical calls that accurately imitate everything from the death scream of a cottontail to the tempting squeak of a meadow mouse.

I am not berating the fox hunters who play the game fairly, running Red through the woods with their hounds, trying him on for size wherever and whenever they can. They usually find that he is too large mentally for them and is smarter and faster than their dogs. In my own bouts with him, I have discovered that the fox just puts up with all of this juvenile hunting nonsense of ours because he really likes to run. He enjoys the chase, one that he usually wins.

But he is hated by man—or by most men—especially by those who haven't chased him fairly or played the game. Why is he hated? In addition to the trapper wanting his hide (which is greed, not hate), we seek to destroy the fox because of his appetite.

Scientists studying that appetite have made several discoveries. First, that it is the fox's catholicity of taste that is responsible for his surprising survival. If he has to, the fox will eat almost anything. An analysis of foxes' stomachs showed that they ate small mammals, mice, shrews, voles, birds, reptiles, fish, turtles, crabs, insects, carrion, strawberries and other fruits, corn, and seeds. He takes what is easiest to find, whatever is offered. Thus, unlike some other wild creatures who are selective eaters, the fox can get along under nearly any circumstance.

Dr. John Wood of Jacksonville University found that contrary to popular belief the fox was not a persistent killer of poultry, that rabbits, rodents, and small birds were about one half of the fox's diet. The balance consisted of insects, mostly grasshoppers, peanuts, persimmons, plums, and other wild foods. He found that foxes will invade the chicken yard only when the farmer is a careless operator, allowing his fowl unlimited freedom, actually tempting wild creatures to come and carry off his poultry.

Southerners, those lovers of hound music who are among the sportiest and fairest of our fox hunters, believing that the seeking is more rewarding than the finding, are aware of the fact that without the fox our southeastern states would be overrun with cotton rats—noisome creatures that not only destroy crops but concentrate on the eggs of birds and poultry.

In 1947, the hunters of New York State, looking for something tangible to blame the pheasant decline on, pointed to the fox as the culprit and demanded that something be done. As they could vote and the foxes could not, the authorities decided to look into the matter—scientifically. They made an in-depth study of two areas. In one, they had an all-out assault mounted on the fox, wiping him out. In the second place, foxes were left alone, actually protected and pampered with no hunting, no trespassing signs, and patrolling guards. Result: Comparison studies proved that the pheasants did not benefit in either area. Fox control did not improve the pheasant population. The reasonable conclusion was that foxes had little to do with the life and death of this game bird.

One scientist who studied foxes for thirty-five years found through examination of dens and droppings that their main food was mice, meadow, white-footed, and harvest.

With 1,300 types of rodents destroying almost everything that isn't metallic in the United States, killing wild and domestic birds, causing more than $700 million in damage to crops, grains, and supplies every year, it shouldn't take much urging to prove what a friend to man is the mouse-and-rat killing fox. Yet, in complete and blithe ignorance of the value of the fox in the overall wildlife picture, some states still offer bounties on this valuable animal, and the race to exterminate him continues.

There have been indictments of the fox as a killer of game birds, quail, grouse, and ducks. Scientists who have studied the problem say that the physical evidence points the other way: the fox actually helps game-bird population. Master hunter though he is, his method is to take what comes easiest, catching what vulnerable birds or animals he happens across. This means that he picks up the handicapped, weak, and sick, the birds and animals wounded by hunters' gunshot. What he actually does is weed or harvest out the inferior stock, leaving the finer strains to survive, giving them more natural food by taking away those that eat and do not contribute to the species.

It is difficult for many of us who hunt to understand the natural situation when we see grouse feathers and blood and fox tracks in the snow—an all too-clear picture of what happened. Yet it is a simple fact that without nature's levelers like the fox, one pair of grouse would pour into our cover 33,000 offspring in less than six years—descendants that would glut the area, stripping the natural food and, in their unnatural numerical strength, bring epidemic and disease. These are facts, not fancies.

Another fact is that the fox is one of wildlife's most interesting characters. As such, he should be considered an object of study and enjoyment, not a creature created to be slain.

I am fortunate in these crowded times to be able to live in the midst of two hundred acres of New England woods. My study is built right in these woods, with the section fronting the wildest area of glass. Several years ago, catching a flash of red from my window, I discovered that a fox had used an old woodchuck den 300 yards from my studio as a place to raise her young. It was well-screened by trees, but by using field glasses and sitting motionless I could watch some of the activity. Unfortunately, I had to go abroad several times during the period when that first litter was born and missed some of the most interesting goings on, but I was able to record a few things.

I learned that after hunting all night, the foxes returned at dawn to sleep near the den, and that, even after the family disbanded, one or more of the fox litter came back to rest near the den that had been home. They would probably have done this all their lives, but a farmer across the road had suddenly acquired a dozen dogs that he seldom kenneled. Despite my protests, his free-roving dogs pushed through the countryside like a plague, and my fox family moved on.

But before the dogs, in the early summer, the foxes left the den and followed their mother afield. I don't think that from that time on they ever reentered the den. But I often saw them bed down in leaves near it. Once while I was watching, the three kits sat looking up at my window. I don't know if the sun threw a reflection from my glasses or what caused it, but they certainly knew that something was up.

One afternoon I saw the mother return with a rabbit, her youngsters following her like she was the Good Humor Man. She waited until they were in a circle, then, like a teacher with blackboard and chalk, she showed them how to skin it. It was then parceled out.

There wasn't much more before the neighbor's dogs and my trips away spoiled the picture of happiness: the kits playing tag with each other; the departure to hunt, all in a single file line; the quiet return; the rest in the morning sun; and the cache. I didn't know before this that red foxes buried and stored food for lean days.

It happened as winter approached. One day, when the foxes weren't around, I went out and looked at the den, hard-packed now, with debris all around. About 25 yards away I saw a place where they had been digging a hole. It had been dug, then recovered. Curious, I pushed aside the dirt and found their winter refrigerator: half a cottontail rabbit, twelve white-footed mice, a large vole, and three short-tailed shrews.

Because of the cache, I made two more discoveries. About a quarter of a mile from the old den, I found another woodchuck hole. Its entrance had been enlarged; it was in use, and it was clean. The fox family had abandoned the soiled old den.

I watched for them at dawn when they returned. The old den was the meeting place, then the two dog foxes in the litter trotted over to the food cache, lifted their legs, and left their family signature so no other fox would mistake it as abandoned food. The vixen sat watching in approval.

Do many of you who read this have favored words, words with a sound that sends a vision before your mind's eye, that immediately flash a meaning, arouse a scent, evoke an emotion? Consider for a moment one of the most beautiful and explicit words in the English language: *vixen*. The female fox. Do you see her dainty in her red coat, with the black stockings and velvety nose and an immaculate white tip on her brush, perhaps sitting in her elegance watching her kits romp? There is something feminine in the word *vixen*, something impish, a coy shrewdness that has an appeal.

There is much more, too, for the vixen is a teacher, a scolder, a stern taskmaster, an adept hunter, a courageous fighter—she is among the best mothers in the wild.

I have seen a vixen, trying to lead dogs away from her den area and her kits, get to a tight place, and turn and fight off two hounds—a 10-pound fox facing two 70-pound hounds!

Dr. David E. Davis of Johns Hopkins University, in a detailed study of foxes, found that they are possibly the only wild species with what he called "a really cohesive family life." He was of the opinion that they mated until death parted them. Other naturalists also claim that the fox is monogamous, basing their belief upon the fact that the male fox takes an active interest in his young and that it seems to be law among the wild that no polygamous male ever cares about his offspring.

According to Dr. Davis (and others), after the fifty-one-day gestation period, when the fox litter is born in the spring (usually four to nine in a litter), from the time they open their eyes at nine days and appear from the den as fluffy balls of red and white in five weeks, the family is joined.

The male stays with the female from mating time through this spring birth, until the young can take care of themselves at the beginning of the next winter. He is not allowed in the den after the first few days of the kits' birth, but he stays in the vicinity, guarding the den and delivering food. (In the family I watched before my studio, I only saw the male fox three times. Presumably, he was near if danger threatened, but he kept himself well hidden.)

It is the vixen that teaches them how to hunt, from the moment they leave the den, starting them on grasshoppers, then, when they are agile and quick enough students, graduating them to mice. She also teaches them the dangers of man and the woods, how to use their scent, sight, and hearing, which is their keenest and the one they depend upon most.

The family stays together for the entire summer. They are living as a unit, the young still learning, long after most wildlife young are on their own. Staying with their mother this long (with an occasional assist from papa), the young foxes receive one of the most extensive trainings of any animal in the wild.

Although there are other species (the kit, gray, and arctic), when most of us think of the fox, in fable or folklore, or in the wild, we think of the red fox, *vulpes fulva*. Actually, the red fox is not always red. He has four color phases: in the normal red also is the "silver," black with a coating of white guard hairs; the "melanistic," black, except for his white-tipped tail; the "cross" is brownish-yellow with black underfur and a black stripe running along his back and crossing his shoulders. A red vixen has been known to have all color phases in one litter.

The eastern United States has mostly all normal red foxes; in the west, cross varieties are not uncommon; and in Alaska, half the foxes are cross, silver, or black.

But it is the flashy, golden-red with the white-tipped brush, moving through the woods like a little Renaissance prince surveying his titled domain, that I admire and respect. He is a fascinating animal, one that I hope will be around for a long time in the wild. One of the saddest of sights is a fox in a cage, pacing, running back and forth, nervous, trying to get out, frightened, tense. Lions, tigers,

polar bears, even wolves and coyotes, seem to take to captivity with more aplomb than the fox—at least the foxes I
have seen. Their attitude in a cage has almost become a
cliché—"as nervous as a fox in a cage." I am told that I am
only partially right in this, that many a fox has been tamed,
some even joining households and living lives like happy
dogs.

Although I am against this trying to tame or make pets
of wild animals, knowing that it always ends in tragedy (as
proved by the glut of recent books on everything from
otters that became man-biting savages to poor lions that had
to be taught to hunt so they could survive), an item I
read in Winchester's *Nilo Newsletter* regarding the hunting
ability of a tame fox is worth reporting:

Whenever you become too prideful of your gun dogs and brag
overmuch, consider the fox. Your trained hunting dog is a marvel. But a hunting fox, just doing what comes naturally, can
make a field trial champ look like a hamster.

Charles Schwartz, artist-biologist-moviemaker of the Missouri
Conservation Commission, once owned a fox that he had raised
from puppyhood. The fox shared the Schwartz' home with Charley's family and hunting dog for two uproarious years.

Although Charley never actually shot over his fox, he frequently took the animal afield with his retrievers and bird dogs,
and had the rare chance of watching them range and hunt together. Dogs and fox got along well; there was no love lost, but
they seemed to tolerate and respect each other as fellow hunters.

The fox was constantly doing things that Schwartz found unusual—probably because Charley has been so well-trained by his
dogs. But although the fox often did things that Charley could
not account for, these things were parts of a thorough hunting
pattern that always produced food. The fox did about everything
afield that a good gun dog would do, but did it far faster and
more efficiently. It would comb a weedpatch or meadow with
infinite thoroughness. It would jump on the tops of brush piles
to flush hiding rabbits, and seemed to know exactly where rab-

bits would flush. It caught these rabbits easily, and the doomed cottontails rarely struggled.

At an interesting tree, the fox (gray) would not simply sniff the trunk—it would climb the tree and investigate each major limb. In the field it would cast and range with great speed and agility. Or, it might just poke along. Either way, with almost electronic precision, the fox would catalog every grasshopper, log, burrow, rabbit, frog and mouse along its route. This was done while the dogs were slogging along at a third the pace.

That fox had not been trained by a wild mother. Its field experience was quite limited. By fox standards it was probably ignorant, but as a hunter it easily outclassed some fine gun dogs and an expert hunter. In Charley's words, it was "tremendously efficient."

What does all this prove?

Simply that we humans and our registered dogs may not be the red-hot hunters we think we are. An unschooled fox may still wipe our eye with instinct alone.

The red fox's sagacity, as many a fable and folktale has illustrated, does not lie just in hunting prowess or ability to out-maneuver man. He uses his head for his own comfort too.

As reported by a respected naturalist, two observers, one of them Peter Kachline from Stockertown, Pennsylvania, saw a red fox come to the water below a sawmill dam, carrying a piece of pine bark in his mouth. He waded into the water until Kachline could only see his nose and the pine bark. He remained immersed for five minutes, then dropped the bark and dashed out of the water. When the pine bark was examined, it was alive with fleas.

W. C. Vogt, also of Pennsylvania, saw a fox take corn-silk from a shock of corn and repeat the flea performance in the pool of a creek. The cornsilk was also flea-covered.

This is the animal we have been trying to outwit for centuries. Gentlemen, it is a losing game.

18

THE STRIPED ENIGMA

The Skunk

Enigma is one of those elastic words used to stretch across the empty spaces in our knowledge. Webster defines it as "anything inexplicable; also, an inscrutable person. . . ."

I met an enigma, or rather several of them, one night while 'coon hunting. It was an early fall night with a September moon round as a coin floating, and it was clear and silent, the kind of night I like for 'coon hunting, for I don't go to kill the 'coon but to listen to the dogs. And this was a listening night. Two black-and-tans and a blue-tick were out there in the woods, getting ready to whoop it up. My partner was with them, or trying to get with them, as the blue-tick was a young dog and he wanted to see how the animal was progressing.

Now the sound of the dogs came as they picked up a trail, starting with a low bay, then rising into a concerted bugling as the three hounds came together and the trail got hotter. I was leaning against an oak tree; before me was a small meadow that ran from the edge of the woods where I was standing. As I listened to the wild music, out into the moon-lit meadow came the enigmas, eight skunks, probably a family. With the dogs providing background music they formed a circle, noses toward its center. Tails flying like fan-dancers' plumes, they hopped forward, legs stiff, until their noses touched; then in rhythm they hopped back, forming the outer circle again. As I watched, the skunks enjoyed their *discothèque,* the 'coon-chasing hounds beating the drums, sounding the saxophone and tooting the trumpet, while they danced. Eight times they performed, much more grace-fully than humans doing the frug, Watusi, and the rest of the sick shambling that passes for dancing in this disturbed age.

Suddenly, as if by silent signal, all tails came down and off they waddled single file, on their way to get a bite to eat before dawn.

"Inexplicable," say the scientists. "We can find no reason for this action other than good nature and social friendli-ness."

That may be the best description of one of our most inter-esting animals. For the skunk is nothing if not good natured and friendly. He can afford to be. Nature has endowed him with one of the best defensive systems in the animal kingdom, one that successfully protects him from just about everything except man, his traps, and his automobile, and the great horned owl, who apparently has no olfactory sense and couldn't care less if his dinner has the worst smell on earth. As a consequence, the skunk seems fearless, knowing that he possesses that built-in armament that can send even the bravest fleeing before its jet stream. Even so, he is amiable about it all.

I doubt if there are many among us who haven't encountered a skunk. And some of us have come away with a lasting impression of this enigmatic creature, perhaps the most famous of our North American animals—or infamous, depending upon the way you look at it. Of course, there are idiot dogs and men who won't leave well enough alone, and they get blasted. Some dogs, however, seem to be born with good sense where the skunk is concerned. I had a Weimaraner named Mark who met many a skunk when we were hunting grouse and walking back to the car along about dusk. He would point and stand motionless; so would the skunk. (Needless to say, at these times I held a classic point myself.) The skunks were never outraged or even curious. Once they saw that we were going to outwait them and offer no resistance to their progress they ambled on, leaving shaken spectators behind.

It would be superfluous to describe a skunk. They are so well known that even the city slicker who walks the woods twice in a lifetime can do a pretty fair job of describing one. But there may be a few facts that many of us don't know. For example, what about that weapon, that devastating spray? That overpowering fume thrower is actually two, for the skunk is a two-gun animal. Located in two anal glands on either side of the rectum in beds of muscle which can compress so strongly that the twin sprays can reach over 16 feet, each scent sac has a duct leading to a nipple-papilla that can be protruded at will from the anus, and this is the aiming device. That evil yellow liquid, fired by muscular contraction, is deadly at 10 feet and dangerous at perhaps twice that distance. The glands can throw two burning bursts of stench simultaneously or singly, depending upon how precarious the situation. And the skunk can shoot six times without reloading. Although the initial shot from the skunk may be just three drops, it comes out in a fine shotgun spray that can be smelled for half a mile, and in damp weather can linger for over a week. It is so strong that it can temporarily blind and cause severe irritation of the skin.

But the striped skunk, as in everything, is fair about this blasting business. Before he decides to go into action he violently stamps his front feet and even tosses his head from side to side and hisses. The little spotted skunk goes even further to warn that if he isn't left alone he means business. He actually whips up, balancing himself in the air on his forefeet, his hind feet sticking straight up and his weapons ready for instant action. A spotted skunk has been known to bluff even a bobcat into retreat with this impressive acrobatic technique. Sometimes, however, spotted skunks will cavort with their fellows, using that position. Naturalists have seen several up-ending like a troupe of circus performers. Only skunks (and hidden naturalists) were present, so it had to be play, not a warning of the spray to come.

That spray, or its contents, known chemically as *nbutyl mercaptan,* contains sulphur, which is the ingredient responsible for the horrible odor, so strong that it can cause even a fox to retch. And apparently this fearsome armament is with skunks almost from the day of birth. There is the case of one fearless photographer being kept at a distance by a blind, two-week-old skunk, whose spray apparatus was in conspicuously good working order. I have approached a nest of skunks at an hour when the mother was out hustling food and the combined defensive odor emitted by six tiny creatures was enough to send me hastening for a region of untainted oxygen. Paradoxically, although skunk scent is an acknowledged leader in the bad odor department, it has often been worn by our fastidious ladies. Science has developed a refining process that converts that malodorous liquid into one used as a fixative in the preparation of perfumes.

Although I haven't been shot by a skunk, and have never had a dog sprayed, friends who have tell me that they have found something that helps. Of course, clothing is burned or buried, but to rid your skin or your dog's coat of the stench a good wash in liberal amounts of tomato juice is said to destroy much of the odor. I have never used tomato juice for anything except mixing with vodka, but it might work. A set-to with a skunk calls for desperate measures. As I write this, skunks and I are still friends, and I have found much enjoyment watching them in the wild. They don't seem to mind and are among the most fascinating of creatures.

Last summer at Lake Keuka, one of New York's Finger Lakes, we discovered that a family of skunks had taken up residence beneath our cottage. Typically, they didn't seem to mind that we moved in over them. There were five, the mother and four half-grown young, a well-bred family if ever I saw one. They were quiet at night, mainly because they weren't there. At dusk, they would come parading out and take off for the woods in a single file. Often they would turn their heads politely as we stood on the porch watching them heading off for dinner. They were always back before dawn and slept under us quietly during the day. They never made a sound or a smell. As a matter of fact, I preferred them to the family that had the cottage next to us.

And like Thoreau, the skunks I have known were aware of the fact that a pond was the place to go and watch for wildlife. We had a pond on our place in Connecticut, deep in the woods where I also used to go and sit quietly. So did a family of skunks. This time there were seven at that age when they were learning the facts of life from their mother.

She would sit patiently at the water's edge, the youngsters

behind her, watching. Skillfully as a tennis player at a net, she would scoop in her clawed paw and flip back a tadpole to the students. She did this four times, then reversed positions and went back and watched them. They knew what was expected, and within minutes they were tadpoling—not so skillfully as their teacher, but they did all right. One day they saw her take a frog, scarcely getting her feet wet; again patience and skill were her weapons. That time the brood didn't do so well. One missed a nimble frog and tumbled into the pond, got out clumsily, and sat sheepishly while the mother sat as if she hadn't noticed a thing. They learned to catch many things there while I watched in silence; beetles under rocks, grasshoppers, careless white-footed mice. I learned from those days of observation that skunks have one of the best of wildlife's parents. And after I had watched what they ate over a period of time, I am of the opinion that this relative of the weasel tribe may be among the most beneficial of our animals.

Although there are a confusing number of species and subspecies, varying in size, markings, lengths of tail, among them the striped, spotted, hog-nosed and hooded, the subject we are concerned with is the one seen by us most often, the common or striped skunk, *Mephitis mephitis,* also classified as *Chincha.* Ranging over the greater part of North America, from the Hudson Bay region in Canada to Guatemala (with other species in most parts of the world), the skunk has appeared in our literature since the early part of the seventeenth century. Gabriel Sagard-Theodat, compiling a history of Canada in 1636, first wrote of them as *enfants du diable,* "children of the devil."

The Algonquins, the most imaginative linguists among our Indian tribes, called the skunk, *se-kaw-kwan,* "from the place where the skunk cabbage grows," and, incidentally, is also what they called Chicago. (Read your own inferences into that.) They believed that the striped animals favored that evil smelling plant. But this wasn't true. There is evidence that skunks don't like the way skunk cabbages smell, which is irony brought to its highest degree.

Scientists perhaps came closer with an accurate name for our striped friend. Their Latin word *mephitis* means an evil exhalation from the ground. But no matter how he came to have his name the animal has given our language a versatile word meaning anything from a villain to defeat. "He's been skunked," may be regarded as a cliché, but it remains a colorful and exact way to say that a man has met defeat—something that rarely happens to the skunk.

Born in late April or early May into a litter of from four to ten, blind, toothless, hairless, 3-inches long, nine weeks after their mother had her fling with father in late February or early March, the young skunks start life off in, for this breed, an unusually helpless condition. But they grow out of that state rather fast, although not so quickly as some, such as birds and mice who are ready to take mates and breed before skunks have even learned what sunshine is. The tiny skunks move restlessly about the den at three weeks; at a month they seek the warmth of sun at the burrow's mouth. In another week they are eating solids, their appetite forcing the mother to hunt even during the daylight hours. In another week they follow their parent outside, and the lessons begin. By fall they are professionals and on their own. The family often remains together until their parent decides to mate again, even though the young have grown from 10 ounces at a month into 8-pound, white-backed beauties, 28 inches long from nose to end of 10-inch, white-tipped tail.

Mating can be quite an active and smelly business, for some skunks play dirty when arguing over a comely female. Two males will hiss, grunt, and groan, and sometimes roll in a wrestling match, until one backs away and decides that if he is to win he had better pull a knife—loose a spray.

This sends everyone out of the territory, including the bad actor who can't stand his own odor.

Male and female usually get together after their partial hibernation in February, when both go topside, pulled by an urge stronger than the dislike of cold. Youngsters, up until their second year, may hibernate most of the winter, but beyond that age they are seldom in burrows after February.

After mating and courtship comes the business of house hunting or building. There is a misconception that although skunks are terrestrial, they are lazy and only have their young in ready-made caves or in the deserted burrows of other animals. Being intelligent, they sometimes do use abandoned woodchuck and rabbit warrens, even crawling spaces under summer cottages and vacant houses. But often they dig their own burrows. And they are well equipped to do so, having long, strong, nonretractable claws that can scoop dirt out nearly as well as that master excavator, the woodchuck. Usually, they dig 12-foot tunnels that slope to the den area 3 feet beneath the surface. The entrance is cleverly camouflaged with twigs or leaves, or the den is dug where there is natural camouflage, such as a rock or stump overhang.

The female begins her responsible parenthood immediately, giving the den a house cleaning shortly after the young are up and about. One week after they are born she gets rid of the old leaves and grass and brings in fresh ones. She also carefully scouts the area for danger, being careful not to come directly back to her den. For this purpose she has already located an emergency lodging. I have seen such a transfer being made, the skunk transporting her kits by the nape of their necks. Of course, few animals, unless starving, would dare attack the litter when the mother was there. But the helpless young, even though they can emit some odor at a tender age, have been known to make a meal for predators.

Their Number 1 enemy is man, the scourge of all wildlife. If man cannot enslave or capture for his amusement or profit, then he destroys. A federal law unknown to most of us, and actually not designed to protect the skunk, or any animal, probably saved the skunk. At the turn of the century, black skunk skins were bringing $6 apiece and more; heavily striped, half that price and sometimes more, depending upon demand. The skins were treated and dyed and sold as Alaskan sable or black marten, and the trappers went all out after the skunk. And they weren't difficult to trap for they are unsuspicious live-and-let-live animals. During the years 1850 to 1890, the Hudson Bay Company alone shipped 250,000 skunk skins to England, and the Astor fortune was on its way. This decimation came to a stop in the United States when the government passed a law demanding an honest labeling of any fur garment selling for over $5. It is an understatement to say that American women did not rush out to buy fur coats labeled skunk, so the market hit a low, and it has more or less stayed there.

But man, the terrible tinkerer, has come up with a new gimmick—pet, deodorized skunks. Being animals with a pleasant personality, skunks do make excellent pets. Selling for $20 and more, baby skunks find a ready market with pet stores that hard-sell them to those who want something "different" around the house.

Here the tragedy again is people. When the children, or misguided adults, become tired of the responsibility of feeding and caring for their deodorized skunk, back he goes to the wilderness. They drive to the nearest woods and dump him. This is somewhat like turning loose before fast young hopefuls, eager to notch their guns and build a reputation, a once-top Western gunman grown old and slow. Reputation can save the now helpless skunk for a while, but the clever and hungry predators soon learn that he is unarmed, and his fate is sealed.

All of us should know that the skunk is much more than

an amiable animal who seems to live to get along with his neighbors. It is well known by naturalists that skunks will often pop into an occupied woodchuck or rabbit warren, or even a raccoon's lair, to pass the time of day and take a nap with the residents. And I have often seen them calmly walking beside opossums. But there is more than friendliness going for the skunk.

Many naturalists claim that he is the most valuable of all animals as a destroyer of the pests that plague mankind. He is without peer as a mouser and ratter, and he seems to especially like those insects that do us the most harm, eating his weight several times a week in tobacco and tomato worms, potato bugs, cutworms, white grubs (our leading lawn and meadow destroyers), army worms, and even the larvae of gypsy moths. I have seen a pair of skunks polishing off dozens of the harmful moth clusters at the base of trees. They'll eat just about anything: frogs, fish, crabs, snakes, wild roots, and berries. Last year, while wandering through the woods, I saw a young skunk on his hind legs throwing his paws around like a boxer. I was puzzled until I heard the droning and saw the beehive broken on the ground. How he knocked it out of its tree is a mystery, but there it was, and he was skillfully swatting the attacking bees to the ground and calmly eating them, even though he was being buzzed and stung repeatedly. (Apparently, he is immune to bee venom.) When he had his fill, he waddled off in his rolling bearlike gait, ignoring the winged warriors that still harassed him.

19

TROUPER OF THE TREETOPS

The Gray Squirrel

Several winters ago, from my home in the Connecticut woods, I watched a gray squirrel gyrate atop a wind-shaken oak. Sleet had glazed the tree, sheathing it in slippery silver, and I wondered how the little animal, even with his amazing agility, had managed to get that high. As I sat fascinated, he suddenly slipped and fell, tail unfurling like a parachute as he plummeted 80 feet. Although it seemed that he hit the frozen ground with quite a thump, he flicked his tail and scampered off, apparently unharmed.

Days later, when I told a field naturalist friend of the incident, he laughed. "Welcome to the squirrel watching society," he said. "But you've got a long way to go. That fall was nothing." He went on to tell me that he had read a report of a gray squirrel jumping off a 600-foot cliff, probably unaware that it was such a drop. "It fluttered rather than fell, legs working like a swimming dog, but quicker, while its tail, slightly elevated, spread like a feathered fan. Another animal that size would have taken 12 seconds to reach the ground; the squirrel took nearly 40. It appeared to hover in space, its tail letting it land as easily as a bird."

That magnificent 8½-inch tail seems to be the gray squirrel's most valuable asset. The ancient Greeks, who seemed to have a word for everything, named the squirrel "Shadow Tail." American Indians called him "He who sits in the shadow of his own tail." Squirrels sit by the hour grooming that bushy appendage; not only does it protect them from falls, but they use it as foil and a shield when fighting, as a sunshade, and to wrap about themselves like a blanket when it is cold. On rainy days, I have even seen them sitting with tails arced over their heads as perfect umbrellas. That tail is also a balance factor, enabling them to make amazing jumps from tree to tree and aiding them when they move gracefully across slender branches much as an umbrella helps a tightrope walker.

This 26-ounce acrobat is America's best-known wild mammal, one of a family of 1,300 varieties. Squirrels are found everywhere in the world, except Australia and Antarctica. The five species of grays have been fascinating and puzzling Americans ever since the pilgrims landed.

I have been a fan since 1935, when I watched an historic mass movement of gray squirrels in western New York. It was an astounding sight: thousands moved down highways, across fields, through towns and villages, crossing lakes and rivers, many of them drowning or being killed on the busy roads. But they kept up their determined, lemminglike trek no matter what the terrain. People gathered by the hundreds to stare at the mass exodus.

Similar mysterious migrations have occurred all over the United States. Robert Kennicott read into the *Congressional Record* his observations in Wisconsin of a half-billion squirrels making a trek that lasted over a month and was repeated at five-year intervals. Naturalist W. J. Hamilton, Jr., saw thousands of squirrels swimming the Connecticut River and moving in formation across Hudson River bridges.

Authorities believe that these mass movements are actually emigration, the desertion by a species of a home territory to which it shows no disposition to return. Mr. Hamilton concluded that it is caused by any one of three factors: lack of food, to find a more congenial climatic environment, or overpopulation occasioned by the extremely prolific nature of the species.

Whatever the motive, gray squirrels always do what is best for them. With perhaps the widest range and highest degree of adaptability of any animal, they are able to survive and increase on mountain or plain, in forest or park. They adjust their diet to the season, eating larch and pine seeds, the scales of pine cones, fungi of all kinds, tree buds and bark, apples, corn, tomatoes, pears, all wild fruits and berries, and even wild honey. I have seen them feasting on the larvae of gypsy moths and Japanese beetles. On rare occasions, when food is scarce, they will invade bird's nests, eating the eggs or even the young.

They'll try anything. I once surprised a gray squirrel rolling goose eggs almost as big as himself away from an unguarded nest. A squirrel in Bournemouth, England, persistently ate the fish placed outside the kitchen door for the cat. One in Cheshire remained healthy eating the remains of a strychnine-poisoned hen carcass, while three rats that had eaten from it lay dead at the squirrel's side.

This sometimes peculiar appetite has caused no end of troubles for Bell Telephone engineers in Wisconsin, where the gray squirrel gnaws through some half-million dollars worth of telephone cable every year. The Bell Laboratories' war dates back to the turn of the century, when they first discovered that squirrels liked the lead sheath in which telephone wires are encased. After the squirrel opens the sheath, moisture gets in the paper insulation and causes a short circuit, disrupting communications. Believing that the animals had a nutritional disorder caused by a lack of calcium and phosphorus, engineers put salt discs on telephone poles. Squirrels tried the salt for a while, then went back to the cable diet. In this battle of wits and tastes, Bell engineers have tried more than one hundred deterrents, including weasel scent, rabbit repellent, tree paint, steel-tape armor, electric shock, and 24-inch barriers of galvanized iron. But at last report the squirrels were still gnawing.

In Washington, D.C., squirrel activity once caused a "national incident" at the White House. The gray squirrels were digging up the grass on then President Eisenhower's putting green without replacing their divots. The President sent out a call for help. An electronics expert came and made high-pitched noises that aggravated everyone but the squirrels. Then the United States Army Signal Corps arrived with even more complicated electronic sound; but the squirrels continued to cavort. Finally, the President sent for a trapper who was successful. But the squirrels had friends in high places: a Senator from the West aroused his public with the cry, "Save our squirrels!" A fund was started to save them from banishment. Result: squirrels are still digging up the White House lawn.

Putting greens and lead cables are not, however, the gray squirrels' normal food preference. They favor nuts of every kind—acorns, hickory, beech, walnuts, hazelnuts, and butternuts. Contrary to general belief, they don't store them for the long winter in a central spot, but bury them haphazardly a few inches under the ground. I watched one gray squirrel bury eight acorns in eight different holes. Naturalist Ernest Thompson Seton estimated that a hard-working gray squirrel will bury five nuts every $3\frac{1}{2}$ minutes and will keep on doing this every morning during the three-month season, probably burying some ten thousand.

Walter L. Hahn of University Farm, Mitchell, Indiana, observed that the white oaks on the farm's 180 acres had been stripped of acorns so efficiently that not a nut was seen. A mathematical analysis put the number of acorns per acre at one hundred thousand. This would mean that from 180 acres the industrious gray squirrels, in two months, had picked up nearly twenty million nuts, burying them in as many holes. Mr. Hahn thought less than one hundred squirrels did the job.

These buried nuts are the result of autumn food abundance and do not, as legend has it, represent premonitions of a hard winter, although the squirrel undoubtedly stores them for future use. How he relocates them during the winter has always been an intriguing question. Most naturalists agree that the squirrels find the nuts by a combination of excellent memory and superior scent, with scent being the main factor. In an experiment, Dr. Robert T. Morris discovered that when acorns were buried one inch the gray squirrels went to them unerringly; those buried $2\frac{1}{2}$ inches were found, but not with the same certainty. Yet, one squirrel went directly to three acorns accidentally buried under 6 inches of wet sand.

Another biologist has observed gray squirrels galloping over two feet of snow, then without error or a trial shaft, dig straight down to the buried nut. Another saw a squirrel eat a hole in a leather attaché case, strapped on the back of a bicycle to get at the food in it.

Yet, they are selective. I watched most of one morning

while a gray squirrel sat under a big oak eating acorns. He grasped each nut with his forepaws, put it to his nose, often discarding it. Examining the pile of discards later, I found every one wormy.

Those nuts which the squirrels do not relocate often grow into trees. Hickories, butternuts, and walnuts will not sprout unless planted underground. Hence, many naturalists claim that most of our wild nut groves have been planted by nature's own gardener, the gray squirrel.

All of the gray squirrel's senses are superb. He is one of the few animals that enjoy uninterrupted vision when looking directly upward; the retina of his eye is composed of cones only, which sharpens perception of movement to an amazing degree. As a result of this vision, skillful squirrel hunters are scarce. Few have the patience to sit immobile for the long periods necessary to deceive these sharp-eyed masters of motion.

Their hearing is also exceptional, enabling them to pick up the snapping of a twig at long distances. If you've walked through woods where there are gray squirrels you know that they are adept at camouflage, freezing to a tree trunk or lying along a branch, almost becoming a part of it, until you have passed. One of their cleverest tricks is "sidling"— being where you aren't, rotating to the opposite side of a tree. I once walked slowly around an oak, 50 yards from it, pacing that nimble maneuver. Moving as if on a greased pole, the squirrel twirled to the opposite side twenty times before he tired of the game and scampered to the treetop. Their agility in trees is astounding, permitting them to leap 50 feet and, surprisingly, they are also fast on the ground. A British biologist clocked one running beside his automobile at 18 miles per hour.

Speed, agility, and woods cunning, however, aren't their only assets. They have two pairs of long, curving incisors which grow continuously and must be honed by daily use

to keep at a normal length. These bladelike teeth that shell
a nut in an instant have other uses. J. F. Bogan of Centralia,
Illinois, tells of suddenly coming upon a tree in which two
gray squirrels were engaged in a fight with a 5-foot black
snake. "Coiled about a limb, the snake was sparring fiercely
with the game little squirrels," he said. "They snapped at
it, then scurried away. With great speed, the snake finally got
a strangle hold on one. Death seemed certain, when its mate
dashed in, biting the snake on the head until it released its
hold and fell limply to the ground."

Squirrels are also protective parents. I saw one, disturbed
by telephone linemen trimming a nearby tree, come tearing
out of her tree nest, three tiny youngsters clinging to her
back, tails and arms wrapped around her neck in the normal infant-carry position. Babies riding easily, she stopped,
glaring and chattering at the intruders, and finally, after
much scolding, holed up in a nest a quarter mile away.
Another time, I saw a gray squirrel beside her nest hiss,
quack, chatter, rise up on her hind legs, and actually box at
a red-tailed hawk who thought he might take a meal. Apparently discouraged by this unexpected aggression, the hawk
sailed off for easier prey. Seconds later, three curious, half-
grown young popped their heads out of the nest.

These young are the result (in a fall or spring litter of
three or four offspring) of probably the most active of animal matings, with several males chasing a female up trees,
across branches, and through underbrush with chattering,
barking, and quacking musical effects. When the fastest suitor
overtakes the object of his acrobatic affection, he turns and
savagely fights off competing males before departing with
the willing female.

The half-ounce young appear blind and naked six weeks
later and are suckled in the nest for seven weeks before
they leave—timidly at first, testing their footing in the treetops, sampling buds and shoots, but still feeding from the

mother. At ten weeks they are on their own for their decade of playful life, the considerate mother making them a gift of the nest home and building another for herself.

Sometimes rebuilt from the shell of an abandoned hawk's nest, these little spherical treetop homes of interwoven leaf and twig are marvels of construction, capped with cleverly thatched rainproof roofs, front and back twig-camouflaged entrances, insulated with leaves and grass, and chinked with moss and shredded bark. Although the grays don't hibernate, if the weather goes far below zero they will often move into the warmer area of a hollow tree, already thoughtfully lined with grass and leaves, where they often sleep out abnormally cold weather for days.

Some class this alert little creature among the most intelligent of animals. Frank E. Fite of Harmon, New York, tells of feeding gray squirrels until they became quite tame. The tamest would sometimes stop feeding and bounce up a tree, meowing like a cat. In each instance, Mr. Fite said, a cat soon appeared. It was obvious to him, happening so often, that the squirrel imitated the cat to warn the others.

At an estate in Yorkshire, England, several gray squirrels quickly discovered how to extract corn from mechanical pheasant feeders by depressing a small wooden platform with their forepaws. In addition, every time the gamekeeper whistled, his signal for pheasants to gather and feed, the smart squirrels came running.

Whenever snow falls, a gray squirrel appears at our kitchen door for a handout. He has been coming for two years now. A friend has three gray squirrels that come out of the woods to his call of "Chow!" Everyone with a bird feeder knows that when natural food is scarce the gray squirrel will help himself to sunflower and other choice seeds. There is every indication that he has a good brain and uses it.

This remarkable little animal has been a familiar part of the American scene since the earliest colonial days. The

Revolutionary War was won against superior forces largely because of the deadly accuracy of our riflemen—and they were hunters who had become skilled by shooting alert squirrels for supper. There was even a regiment of sharp-shooters called the "squirrel shooters," men who could nick a gray squirrel in the head at 50 yards with the "sighted" frontier rifle. Our pioneer forebears, who had no refriger-ators, freezers, or supermarkets, utilized the gray squirrel as a constant source of nutritious food.

Today, the gray squirrel is still a permanent part of the United States scene. There is scarcely a public park in the country that doesn't have its resident treetop troupers whose agile performance delights everyone. Cheered by their bounce, fascinated by their acrobatics, susceptible to their saucy begging, people sit by the hour watching the squirrel show, feeding them nuts, snapping their pictures, and tempting them to climb on their arms and perch on shoulders. I saw an elderly gentleman in elegant attire spend the best part of an hour in New York City's Central Park, convinc-ing a haughty old gray squirrel to come sit on his arm. In his fascination with the game he dropped all dignity, crouch-ing and kneeling, making silly soft purring noises until the squirrel finally seemed to take pity on him and scampered up. The smile on the old man's face was beatific.

From playing with gray squirrels in parks, people have progressed into making them pets—and they make amusing ones. Conservationist Arthur H. Carhart successfully house-broke one, "Dinky," that even ate dinner at the table beside master and wife. Carhart had evening wrestling matches with Dinky, in which the squirrel played like a kitten and would show off before guests with somersaults and spec-tacular leaps. Dinky would take correction from Carhart but not from his wife; if she attempted discipline, he would bark angrily and run up the wall.

Squirrels have even been taught to perform before a paying audience. Opera singer Florence Hinton, presented with two tiny gray squirrels (by a boy who wanted to hear her sing but had no cash), became so fond of them that she finally acquired six. Against the advice of experts who said it couldn't be done, she began trying to train them to perform. It took three years to teach them to play dead, turn somersaults on command, swing on trapezes, take baths in tiny tubs, and walk tightropes. The only act of its kind, it became so popular that Mrs. Hinton gave up singing and toured with her squirrels.

"They were terrific troupers," she says. "Each performance improved, and you could tell that they really appreciated audiences and played up to them."

That appreciation is mutual.

20

HIS MAGNIFICENCE, THE MOOSE

Sun fell upon the water, illuminating the incredible scene
the way sleep does a nightmare. I was in a canoe, crossing a
wilderness lake in northern British Columbia. Beneath me,
on the *bottom* of that clear lake, was an enormous animal.

Completely submerged, he looked like a sea monster
from some ancient myth as he searched for aquatic growth
with his big horse's nose, five-foot spread of shovel-flat antlers bristling with points, and brown-black hide slick as a

seal's. Suddenly, he popped to the surface 30 feet from me, water boiling around him, half-chewed pondweed hanging from his mouth. Glaring and grunting, he tossed a great ax-blade head. Then he came toward me. Easily as an otter, he circled the canoe where I sat, my paddle frozen. In a quick surprise maneuver, an Olympic 180-degree turn, he swam for shore, towing a substantial amount of my fear with him. Water burst from him in a shatter of crystal as he shook, then he took off for the woods on tall legs in a big, hump-backed lope.

That was my first meeting with the moose, the largest and most fascinating member of the deer family, a remarkable wild animal that feeds on the bottom of lakes, walks along city streets, challenges trains, and jousts with jets. A dangerous giant that can weigh almost a ton yet move as gracefully as a cat across swamps, snow, and tree-cluttered terrain, this mysterious dweller of the forests has been considered everything from a killer to an omen for good and a savior of the sick.

The moose looks like a huge, slightly sway-backed mule that has grown strange horns and developed an outsize droopy muzzle. He has a 3-inch tail, humped shoulders, a mane, and a goatee (a pendant, useless hairy strip called a "bell," carried by both sexes, running from a freak 38 inches to a normal 8 to 10 inches). The bull can weigh as much as 1,800 pounds. Often standing 7 feet at the shoulder, his 4-foot, stiltlike legs hike him higher than a horse. During the fall he carries 85-pound palmated antlers, sometimes with a 6-foot spread (record 77⅝ inches), as easily as a man wears a straw hat.

The true elk, this magnificent mammal was misnamed in America by English colonists who called him by the Algonquin Indian "moose," a name that described the sound of his method of feeding on leaves, twigs, and bark. A single species (also in Europe and Asia), there are three sub-

species in North America, differing only in size and named
for locale. The largest is found in Alaska, especially in the
Kenai Peninsula.

It is believed that the moose came here from Asia during
the Pleistocene period, crossing a continent-linking arm of
land at the Bering Strait. Naturalist Ernest Thompson Seton
recorded that the early territory of our moose totaled
over three million square miles. Civilization has shrunk this.
Today, the moose is found in much of wilderness Canada
and is resident in Maine, and there are a few in New
Hampshire and Vermont; he ranges in Wyoming, Idaho,
Montana, and Minnesota and thrives on the Isle Royale
preserve in Michigan. But Alaska holds the largest population (believed to be thirty thousand), and from there come
most reports of the moose's startling behavior.

In 1962, the Associated Press reported that at Anchor-
age International Airport a bull moose became annoyed at
the noise of a Boeing 720 jet. Suddenly, he rushed it, smacking it between its number 1 and 2 engines. Apparently
satisfied that he had proved his superiority, he stepped
back, shook his head, and strolled off into the woods. The
jet was delayed a half-hour while mechanics checked for
damage.

Moose seem completely unafraid of man's mechanical
might. They'll tackle planes, cars, or trains, and seldom even
step aside on the highway for an approaching automobile.
Game Biologist Arthur E. Bratlie, in charge of moose studies for the Alaska Department of Fish and Game, informs
me that there were fifty-four collisions between moose and
automobiles during the winter of 1964. Roads are cleared of
snow, and it is easier for the moose to walk along the highways. As these great animals consider anything theirs by
right of possession, they seldom give traffic the right of way.
Sometimes they are bested by the machines, but they are
so tall and heavy that they often wreck the cars simply by

rolling over on the hood, shattering the windshield and smashing the roof.

Bratlie tells me that the United States Army and the Department of Fish and Game, combining resources to control the problem, have come up with "Operation Moose Mirror." Mirrors are placed on the roadside and angled at 45 degrees to pick up and reflect the highlights of approaching cars into the eyes of the moose, holding him motionless where he stands by the side of the road. Several states have tried the idea successfully on deer. With moose, its success remains to be proved.

The Alaskan Railroad has yet to devise a method to keep them off the tracks. It isn't as bad as it used to be when they were forced to add to the timetable, "Not responsible for train delays because of moose." But in the winter it is a common thing for a train to slow to ten miles an hour to stay behind a moose trotting along the snow-cleared railroad track. Impatience with moose on the rails can cause serious difficulty. In March of 1960 a train hit a moose, hurling it into a switch. Reports Mr. Bratlie, "Two engines, two baggage cars, and a coach were derailed with the resulting damage of $200,000."

Bratlie remembers another old bull, annoyed at the engineer who was trying to get him off the tracks by pelting him with snowballs, wheeling around and charging the engine. The moose hit it with such tremendous power that he broke his neck. There are many cases of moose attacking diesel engines. Some naturalists claim the action is caused by the train whistle that sounds somewhat like the bellow of an aggressive, mating bull.

This could be true, for bull moose take sex very seriously, eating little during the September 15 to October 15 rut, traveling widely to search for willing females, fighting, and often killing lesser bulls that get in the way. Witnesses of the fight between bulls call it one of the most awesome combats in nature. The giants with their sharp-bladed antlers and great strength move in deceptively swift feintings, touching antlers like fencers. Then they back off and rush at one another, meeting in an earth-shaking crash.

An official of Quebec's Department of Fish and Game described for me a fight he had seen: "I watched them for twenty minutes," he said, "and in that time they were pulling over trees three and four inches in diameter. When they had finished, the smaller bull took to his heels. It looked as if a bulldozer had worked over about an acre of ground."

Studying Alaskan moose, biologist Frank Dufresne, in traveling less than 500 miles, found 14 bulls killed in battle, six with antlers locked in death.

Those antlers also are the key to moose survival, the broad-bladed bone structure triggering the reproductive urge. Beginning as small buttons on the bull calf, they grow into six-inch spikes on the yearling; the next year they are crotched and at three years become three-pointed palms— with this set the young bull begins to get ideas. But it is another year before there is significant antler growth; not until he is six will he have the remarkable rack that marks the bull in his prime.

Antler growth begins in April, reaching its amazing size in only three months. During this period, the spongy antlers are covered in "velvet," a fleshy tissue containing blood vessels that nourish the developing bone. In July, the antlers begin to harden, and by August the blood vessels have dried up and the bone is firm. The velvet remains, hanging in tatters as it is rubbed off against trees. By September, the antlers are as smooth and shiny as dueling sabers, which they become.

Now the four-week rut begins and the bull, neck swollen to almost twice its normal size, eyes bloodshot, temper short, becomes a fearsome, belligerent beast with a one-track mind. He bellows, grunts, and moos his desires that rise and end in a sirenlike sound. An interested cow responds in shrill moos and bawlings.

It is during this period that hunters take advantage of the moose by imitating the call of the cow or that of a bull lusting for a fight. But even if the bull will respond to almost any reasonable sound, it is a tricky business. In his anxiety, the love-sick animal may come loping through the woods, breaking branches, sounding like twenty lumberjacks at work with their axes, or he may come sneaking as silently as a leopard.

A friend of mine, hunting in British Columbia, described his first experience at calling up a bull. His guide used birchbark fashioned into a megaphone. They crouched in the brush, waiting for a response as the guide sent a low cow moo every fifteen minutes.

"It sounded much like a domestic cow," my friend said, "and I felt silly hunched down in that thicket for three hours. It was dusk before we got an answer. It wasn't what I was told to expect. The bull didn't bellow his joy at hearing our call. Suddenly, we heard a slashing of brush. Branches flew as if cut with a hatchet. Then there was a godawful bellow fifty feet from us.

"We hadn't heard a sound until then. A monster stood there, ten feet tall, the dying sun coloring him red. He was so close I could see his beard and his angry red eyes. Every second he bellowed. Scared stiff, I couldn't attempt to use my rifle, even though the guide kept motioning for me to shoot. I've been on a tiger beat without batting an eye. But then I was high in a tree. Here I was on the ground with an angry giant screaming and slashing with antlers that took off small limbs like they were thread. Neither my guide nor I made a move, and he finally trotted off grunting."

It has been debated often whether the bull moose in rut is a dangerous animal that will attack man, or just a love-smitten boob who doesn't know what he is doing. The facts are almost as confusing as the moose's character. When I was in Stockholm four years ago, a sportsman told me they called up moose there too—with music. Often, he told me, hunters will hire violinists to lure the moose (called by its true name of elk there) within firing range. Sometimes it does bring the curious creature close enough to shoot; sometimes he becomes dangerous. One moose feeding in willows became so angry at being disturbed by violin music that he rushed out and killed the hunter and the musician.

Two hunters in Maine, canoeing along a river at night, suddenly came upon a bull moose standing in water up to his chest. They managed to get out of the canoe just before the moose jumped in and sank it. Incidents of bull moose in rut charging and chasing men up trees are numerous. In *Nature* magazine, Bill Geagan told of a hunter being attacked and treed by a moose. Later, the same man frightened another bull off his path by hurling a biscuit tin at the animal. A friend of mine came out of his cabin in Maine one night to find a bull moose standing staring at him. The big beast didn't move for ten minutes, then only when my friend's dog began barking.

George Davis, famous New Brunswick guide who has seen more than ten thousand moose, told me he didn't think they were dangerous—at least intentionally. "I have never seen a moose charge a human," he said. "In fact, I don't believe that they will. They'll charge in the direction of a call all right, but that's in the belief that it's another moose—either another bull to be fought or a cow to be courted." He cited the incident of a friend and himself on snowshoes, walking abreast of a bull moose until it finally became frightened and fled.

A long-time student of moose, biologist Adolph Murie, commented in the *Moose of Isle Royale:* "So varied is their behavior that it is difficult to predict what any individual will do when influenced by any of his senses."

These senses or lack of them have put a bull moose in a meadow with a herd of Holsteins only yards from a farmhouse, sent another trotting through the business district of Augusta, and floated one down the Androscoggin River to the town of Auburn, Maine. The latter got out there, sauntered about, then swam to Lewiston, where he got stuck in a canal and was helped out by two policemen. Another got down on his knees on a busy Canadian highway to calmly drink collected rainwater while traffic backed up for miles.

Normally, however, this is a wary, wild animal that only loses his equilibrium for a short time during mating season. The result of that noisy session is a ten-day courtship; then the fickle bull goes looking for another cow. Four usually is his limit before his fire is gone at the end of October. Gaunt then from lack of food and his strenuous schedule, the moose docilely joins a small group of bulls and cows and behaves himself. (The antlers now become a useless weight discarded in late December.)

About eight months after the fall fling of bull and cow, the helpless 25-pound moose calf is born, usually early in June. Sometimes there are twins, rarely triplets. The cow has found an isolated place on an island, deep in a swamp or heavy thicket, where she carefully conceals her offspring for three days until he is able to follow her about. Seven days later the calf can run faster than a man. Mute at birth, he now can utter a shrill bleat and is able to swim. The moose calf might be the fastest growing of wild animals, gaining two pounds every day for the first month, and four pounds daily after that time. The calves stay with their parent until she drives them away or eludes them (outrunning or hiding) the following spring, when she is ready to mate again. It is not unusual, however, for her offspring to stay near her even while she is being romanced by the bull of her choice and then to rejoin her when the bull has moved on. The cow moose has a strong maternal instinct and does much for her offspring. She schools them in the art of back tracking, of standing motionless in thickets, taking advantage of the natural camouflage, and of moving silently and swiftly away when they scent danger from afar. Shortly after they learn to walk she teaches them to swim: instinct instructs them to lay a chin on her back when they tire or to grab her tail and be towed when the going gets too rough.

Moose are powerful swimmers. Andrew J. Stone, author of *The Deer Family*, saw an Alaskan bull swim eight miles without showing signs of tiring. Some observers say that moose are almost as aquatic as beavers, diving, back rolling, and spending much of their time in rivers and lakes during the hot summer. One hunter saw a half dozen in a lake, diving to a depth of 18 feet to feed. Adolph Murie, in his prolonged study of moose on Michigan's Isle Royale, several times saw a bull dive to the bottom of a lake and remain submerged for one minute and a half. Determined swimmers, once they start across a lake, little can deter them. In their search for food, Indians take advantage of this, sometimes jumping from their canoes onto the big beasts' backs and cutting their throats before they reach the shallows. Riding mooseback has even become a sport, with spirited sportsmen seeing how far they can ride before they are dumped. Dr. Thomas Travis from Montclair, New Jersey, rode a big bull across a New Brunswick lake while friends captured the action with motion picture cameras.

That adeptness in water, just like much of the moose's skill, comes from training passed on by one of wildlife's best and bravest parents. The mother will fight anything to protect her calf. Frank Manuel, Newfoundland wildlife biologist, saw a cow moose charge an S-55 helicopter while her calf was being placed aboard. Another drove off two fierce, husky dogs bent on molesting her youngster. In *Hab-*

its, Haunts, and Anecdotes of the Moose, Burt Jones wrote of a mother with her calf in a lake being stalked by a black bear. The bear swam quietly toward the calf and was almost upon him before the cow became aware, whirled, advanced, and struck out as skillfully as a boxer with her forefeet. She batted the bear several times. Then, leaving the bear helpless with a broken back, she made her way to shore, her calf following.

Although the pampered moose calf will grow into the largest antlered animal on earth, his coloring can protectively dwarf him—in the right background, almost painting him out of the sight picture. In spruce, hemlock, or any evergreen, the brownish-black back and sides and yellowish-whitelegs erase telltale outlines and blend him into foliage—and he knows it. Even aerial census has become difficult: when moose hear airplane motors, they vanish into evergreen.

In Canada, I tried to pick out a great bull standing in shadow in a copse of pines less than 100 yards away. Even with the experienced guide trying to help, it took ten minutes to detect that patient and crafty animal—and then I was successful only because he twitched an ear.

This camouflage may be effective against weak-eyed man, the moose's Number 1 enemy, but something special is needed for protection against other keen predators, for example, the wolf and the bear. The moose has this in his superb senses. His only poor sense is sight; his smell and hearing are excellent. One biologist who tested the moose's hearing claimed it is unequaled. In an experiment, he found that moose were aware of the footfalls of a man three minutes before the scientist detected the approaching sound.

They use these acute senses to full advantage, often lying down, tail to the wind, nose guarding them from that direction, hearing and sight from the other. Moose also turn around to hide and rest behind the wind of their own tracks, locating the enemy before he is close enough to cause trouble.

The moose's speed and stamina are impressive. There is the record of a moose broken to harness drawing a sleigh 160 miles on frozen Saint John's River in New Brunswick, on a round trip from Fredericton to Saint John's. It was reported that the moose was slightly steamed up at the end of the trip, but showed no signs of being tired.

For a quarter mile, in continual bursts of speed, a moose can run 35 miles per hour. Naturalists agree that moose can outrun a horse, especially on home terrain. And in a race, the wolf doesn't stand a chance. Considered by many to be the moose's major enemy next to man, the wolf cannot travel more than 25 miles an hour, and then only for short distances.

Durward L. Allen, Professor of Wildlife Management at Purdue University, who is making a ten-year study of moose-wolf relationships at Isle Royale National Park, Michigan, tells me that healthy moose are not worried by wolves. "The wolves quickly sense this," he said. "They may approach a moose, which gives every evidence of being ready for a fight, and quickly give up and go on. Wolves simply do not get into a knock-down-and-drag-out fight just for a meal. They wouldn't last long if they did."

Dr. Allen has found that wolves "test" at least a dozen moose before they make a kill, then usually it is the sick, aged, or unfit that are taken, thereby benefiting the moose population. A photograph by David Mech, Dr. Allen's associate in the Isle Royale study (published in the *National Geographic* magazine) dramatically destroyed the long-held belief that wolf packs pull down any moose they choose. It shows a moose in light snow encircled by fourteen wolves, the big bull bravely standing his ground. After five minutes of jousting with that alert bull and his dangerous hoofs, the wolves gave up.

Those hoofs, with tremendous muscle behind them, can break the back or crush the skull of almost any adversary. E. B. Bailey of the Game Branch of Quebec's Department of Fish and Game, tells me he saw a moose kill a large black bear, actually pounding its head and back with the front hoofs until practically every bone in the bear's body was broken.

Often seven inches long, the hoofs, aided by the additional purchase power of large dewclaws, provide more than defense. More flexible, with a greater division than those of most hoofed animals, they enable the moose to spread his toes, increase his footing, and walk areas that other large creatures (including man) would find impassable. Arthur Graef, a friend, has seen a bull moose weighing 1,000 pounds traverse a swamp where a hunter would have difficulty walking. The speed and grace with which a moose negotiates mossy, slippery rocky terrain and hurdles the tangled hazard of felled trees is almost unbelievable. In one such area that the moose traveled swiftly and easily, I was slowed to less than two miles an hour.

Naturalist Adolph Murie says that moose try any bog or mud flat without fear. He watched a young bull mush through marsh, sunk up to his backline. Slowly and nonchalantly, pausing occasionally to rest, he mastered mud that would baffle a bulldozer.

Those marvelous hoofs and stilted legs permit the moose to move freely in uncrusted snow. (In crusted snow, he has trouble, and the lighter predators can get at him.) Even 30 inches can't stop a moose. It has been reported that these animals in British Columbia sometimes use their forelegs like snowshoes to move across deep snow, kneeling and packing it down before them.

Normally, however, the nonmigratory moose isn't much

of a mover. In winter, in the company of a few of his fellows, he lives in a "yard," tramping down the snow, often staying on less than fifty acres. He is a browser, feeding on leaves, twigs, plants, grass, marine growth, lily pads, and bark. Although he has no teeth in his upper jaw, his eight incisors in the lower jaw and huge molars enable him to handle thumb-thick twigs easily. He doesn't need much space to forage for his 35 pounds of daily food. Many naturalists believe that a moose spends most of his time in a range of no more than ten miles. His summer domain of woodland and brush, near lake, river or swamp, may encompass only a mile or less.

This restricted activity almost brought about his downfall. Sportsmen, Indians, and market hunters killed moose of any age or sex during any season, until in Maine, parts of Canada, and the West, this great mammal almost became extinct. Indians believed the moose to be an omen of good, and also thought that by eating his meat they would gain the animal's strength. In the early days, in Europe, and even in America, it was thought that the left hind foot of the moose was a certain cure for epilepsy. It was worn on the body of the afflicted, burned as an incense, and even ground and drunk in wine. Bone rings from the antlers banished headache and dizziness; mixed with various herbs, ground antler was an antidote for snakebite. Various parts of the moose were believed to cure over six hundred diseases or afflictions. Even his hide was thought to be weapon-proof and was often worn by soldiers.

But as Europe and America came of age and science superceded superstition, the moose finally began to prosper. Most states abolished hunting, even Canada had short and stringent seasons, and in many places the moose was completely protected. Today, the moose population in North America is just under two hundred thousand and is on the rise. This time we awoke to an animal's value soon enough.

Fortunately, unlike the plains buffalo and other animals pushed to the edge of extinction, the moose now seems to be here to stay. Lord of everything he surveys, be it jet plane, diesel engine, or wolf pack, this hump-backed, bearded monarch of the forest promises to continue to bring majesty and mystery to our wilderness.

21

SALT WATER DAFFY

The Porpoise

Several years ago, entering one of the numerous inlets that slash the Florida coast, I saw a sinister fin break the surface. I had unintentionally trapped something big in the shallows. Cutting water fast, the fin started for the little boat. Then, suddenly, a glistening blue-black fish almost as large as the boat was over my head. Jumping 15 feet, he halted for a millisecond in midair, then fell into the water and escaped to the sea. That was my introduction to the bottlenosed dolphin or porpoise, not a fish at all but our most fascinating animal.

My second meeting came as I walked a beach gazing seaward. Suddenly, strange swimmers appeared in the froth of the evening surf: three porpoises riding the incoming tide of breakers, enjoying themselves like surfboarding vacationers.

The third meeting involved a life-and-death drama. I was in a motorboat escaping the shore and its complications, drifting quietly, staring at the still, clear water. Suddenly, 50 feet from me, a big mako shark hurled from the water, then plopped back. Drifting closer, I saw that six porpoises had him surrounded. One darted forward striking with such force that it sent the mako out of water again. Now the porpoises circled like a raiding Apache gang. One by one they went in for attack, punching just behind the gills and in the stomach. The mako finally collapsed, sinking in the clear water. Following him to the bottom, they nudged his white belly several times and then swam off to sea.

Last summer I sat in a charter boat near Stuart, Florida, talking with a professional fisherman who had been afloat for forty years, when suddenly something appeared on the surface—as if walking on water: a big porpoise. Balancing on his tail, he delivered an audacious Bronx cheer and vanished, his mouth spread in a huge grin.

The old fellow laughed and shook his head. "No respect for man *or* shark, *those* characters! They're either daffy or the smartest things in the sea!"

Recent involved scientific experiments have proved that *Tursiops truncatus,* the bottlenosed dolphin, or shallow-water porpoise, is indeed not daffy and may be one of the smartest creations on land or sea.

A member of the warm-blooded clan of mammals, *cetacea,* and the subspecies *odontoceti,* or prehistoric toothed-whale family, the bottlenosed dolphin (so-called because his nose is shaped like an old salt's grog bottle) is not a porpoise. And he is not to be confused with the true fish, *coryphaena hippurus,* also called a dolphin. The word "porpoise" (sea hog) comes from the French *porc-poisson,* a name given to the bottlenosed dolphin by immigrant fishermen who, sighting it in our bays and inlets, mistook it for their common harbor porpoise.

Of the more than twenty-three species of dolphins and small whales along the Atlantic and Pacific coasts, the one continually clowning for the public is the bottlenosed. This 300-pound pelagic playboy is quickly identified by his gunmetal hide, eight- to twelve-foot length, gin-bottle beak, laughing face—the smile frozen by the curvature of the mouth, somewhat like the one painted on a circus clown.

Biologically closer to man than any of the fishes, the bottlenosed dolphin possesses rudimentary hind legs buried within the musculature of the body, the framework of its flipper contains five jointed fingers; he has no gills, must breathe air into his lungs to live, gives milk to the young, and at an early stage has hair on his head.

The mouth is simply a fish-catching mechanism with forty teeth in each jaw. Breathing is done through a peculiar single nostril, a crescent-shaped blowhole atop his head, an ingenious organ which closes upon contact with water. It is also his "voice" which he vibrates like a human lip.

Eyes, set just back from the mouth, contain a greasy substance that prevents water irritation and, like a human's, are "ranging." I saw one photographed out of water carefully watching the photographer, then me. His ears, tiny holes behind the eyes, are the keenest of any animal.

He has a single dorsal fin with horizontal tail flukes—a true fish's fin is vertical. In motion most of his thirty-year life span, he catnaps only when necessary, partially submerged, eyes usually closed for 30 seconds, but sometimes as long as 5 minutes.

There is controversy about his speed. At the Scripps Institution of Oceanography, Dr. Sholander worked on a theory that the porpoise is expending much more energy than he possesses. I clocked one at seventeen miles an hour; some marine scientists claim they've seen porpoises doing thirty. Our Navy has logged them at forty knots, overtaking and even keeping ahead of some of our fastest ships.

Scientists believe this speed and agility is partially due to skin containing tiny ducts filled with a spongy material permitting the entire surface to undulate according to water turbulence.

The animal's shape assumes the contour of the flow rushing past—configuration of skin-matching wave form. The result, "laminar flow," reduces friction drag by as much as 90 percent. Unlike a ship's hull, a porpoise's body adjusts in accordance to pressure variations of fluid around it.

Dr. Max O. Kramer, one of many working on this theory, has perfected a rubber skin that fits sea craft, reducing water drag by 50 percent.

A skillful marine hitchhiker, the porpoise seems to possess an uncanny knowledge of hydrodynamics. Setting his tail fluke at a precise 28-degree angle to get the full forward thrust of a boat's bow wave, he is scientifically shoved great distances without expending energy.

Living on live fish—mullet, squid, cod, and herring—the bottlenosed porpoise hunts by cruising until he sees the meal he wants and then putting on his spectacular burst of speed. Often porpoises hunt in pairs or groups, rounding up fish much as a cowboy herds his cattle. For their size, they are moderate eaters, taking only 18 pounds of fish a day. Averting an all-out war in 1947, biologists at Marineland, Florida, proved, with illustrated "balance of life" charts to a politically vocal group of disgruntled commercial fishermen, that porpoise were not stealing quantities of their food fish.

Porpoises can even exist out of water, but their skins burn

fatally if not kept wet. One pair, wetted down and transported on hospital stretchers, were out of water for twelve hours without ill effect. Another pair were flown to Silver Springs, Florida; wetted, and fitted with oxygen masks over blowholes, they arrived in good shape.

They have elaborate and often complicated sex play. Although these sexual activities continue throughout the year, they mate in the spring at the age of four years, becoming restless and noisy, the male sidling up, whistling a courtship tune, or yelping like an excited puppy. Males compete for attention with masterful jumps and intricate underwater maneuvers.

The result of the noisy session is one 3-foot calf, weighing 25 pounds. At birth, the youngster is almost fully prepared to face life, showing little of the helplessness of other newborn mammals. He swims to the surface, immediately gulping life-giving air; he can see, hear, talk (whistle and grunt) and recognize his mother's call. The long 12-month gestation period is believed responsible for this independence.

Unlike other mammals, the porpoise is born tail first, a necessary position because the baby would otherwise drown during delivery, which takes twenty-one minutes to two hours. At the moment of birth, the mother twists, breaking the umbilical cord and releasing the young one who immediately surfaces. In two hours the baby begins nursing from two nipples set in grooves near the mother's tail.

Long nursing underwater being impossible, the parent contracts abdominal muscles squirting milk into her offspring's mouth every twenty minutes. The tested milk is six times as rich in protein as a human's, increasing the youngster's weight eight times in six months.

An adult female porpoise always joins the new mother, keeping her company, staying with her and her offspring until both seem able to ward off danger.

But even with the help of the "assistant" parent, the

young porpoise couldn't survive if it couldn't keep up with its mother who shields it, interposing her body between curious porpoises, sharks, strange fish. When she swims from danger the baby follows, sometimes at 15 miles per hour.

So complete in every other respect, the young porpoise has no teeth at birth but manages to get along after weaning by munching small squid until teeth appear in six months. The transition from milk and squid to whole fish isn't easy. When the mother brings the young porpoise the first mullet he plays with it for a while, often losing it to another porpoise, but finally working up enough nerve to swallow it. The first fish gives him indigestion; he vomits. The mother rubs his stomach. This goes on until he can keep the mullet down. If frightened, the young swim in fast, tight circles, whistling shrilly for their mothers.

There are few other animals with so strong a maternal instinct. One night a young porpoise died at Marine Studios. The next morning the mother was found supporting it on the surface. One carried a dead baby on her back for three days. Another raised one stillborn infant to the surface, grasping its fin with her jaws; when a six-month old calf died, its parent tried to lift it from the bottom by grasping it with her pectoral fins.

They live a community life, helping one another when a shark or a barracuda swoops in after a newborn baby. Whistling, they form a circle around mother and offspring, then polish off the shark, pulverizing his liver and rupturing his internal organs with powerful thrusts. Yet several porpoises have lived amicably in a tank with a shark for several years. In one aquarium, just after the curator had told guests how well his shark and porpoises got along, he was surprised to see three attacking the big tiger shark. It was impossible to stop the fierce, ramming battle. The shark was dead in an hour. In his stomach they found a young female porpoise.

A marine biologist told of placing two injured porpoises in a pool with two that were normal. One couldn't move its fins; the other had a brain injury which made it veer to the right. Immediately, the two healthy animals hoisted the sick ones to the surface. Then, satisfied that they had enough air, they submerged, one swimming against the right side of the one with brain damage, setting it on a straight course. The other went beneath the paralyzed porpoise, scraping its fins to produce a reflex action that brought it to the surface. They continued to help for hours until one died, the other recovered.

The porpoise's serious enemy is the grampus or killer whale, actually a cousin. Zane Grey reported seeing a pack wipe out a herd of fifty porpoises. But, fortunately, the killer whale is a rare creature, and the carefree porpoise spends most of his life free from danger, eating well and playing.

Wild ones will make up a game with a floating pelican feather, one balancing it on his nose, another coming in and catching it before it falls, another scooting in to keep the feather in the air—the game often lasts over an hour.

Observers claim porpoises are spontaneous frolickers, that they don't play for any expectation of reward. I saw a captured porpoise create a game by picking up a stick, tossing it several feet forward, swimming to it, and then throwing it again. This went on for several minutes. Dr. F. C. W. Olson watched a porpoise in a mischievous mood grab a red snapper by its tail, swim backward with it several feet, then release it unharmed. I've watched a young female place a turtle on her nose and give it a ride around the pool. She did this at the same hour for three days.

They play catch, going a dog one better by actually throwing the object back, then awaiting its return. Stale fish are flung back in the attendant's face. Porpoises love having their backs rubbed. One at Marineland surfaced to have his

back scratched and I stood there like a fool scratching until
we both got tired. I've watched them playing basketball,
tossing the ball to one another, making baskets; one even
took a handkerchief from my pocket, then "laughed" as I
reached for it.

"Flippy" in Marineland, trained by Adolf Frohn, blows
a rubber horn so gently that his sharp teeth don't leave a
mark. He also gets into a harness, pulling a dog or a man on
a surfboard. The dog and Flippy got so friendly that the porpoise would surface to have his head licked. Flippy also
jumps through a paper target on command, hurtles any
object, and twirls in a fast barrel roll until ordered to stop.
Another porpoise, Cha Cha, does a hula atop the water;
Corky catches, passes a football, sings a tune, raises the
American flag, and rings a bell when it is time for dinner.

Calling them "man oriented," one scientist says that unlike most other wild creatures who flee at the sight of humans,
the porpoise wants to be near us—actually seeks our company.

Plutarch wrote more than 2,500 years ago: "The dolphin
is the only creature who loves man for his own sake. Some
land animals avoid man altogether, and the tame ones such
as dogs, horses, and elephants, are tame because he feeds
them. To the dolphin alone beyond all others, nature has
given what the best philosophers seek: friendship for no
advantage. Though it has no need at all of any man, yet it
is a genial friend to all and has helped man."

Four centuries before Christ, philosophers Pliny and
Aristotle wrote of the animals saving lives. Pliny wrote in
detail of a wild dolphin taking a boy for a ride at Hippo, a
Roman settlement in Africa. Roman coins of 74 B.C. show
small boys riding dolphins. But modern historians and
scientists doubt the old stories.

Mrs. Yvonne M. Bliss of Stuart, Florida, doesn't. She
fell overboard near Grand Bahama Island in the West In-

dies and was most explicit in her description of a porpoise guiding her out of shark-infested waters to safety.

Another case, documented and reported in *Nature* magazine, told of a woman wading waist deep off the Florida coast when an undertow pulled her down. Floundering, she swallowed water and was unable to regain her footing. "As I gradually began to regain consciousness," she said, "I felt someone give me a terrific shove. I landed on the beach, face down, too exhausted to turn over. It was several minutes before I could do so, and when I did, no one was near, but in the water about 18 feet out a porpoise was leaping about. When I got enough energy to get back up the steps, a man who had been standing on the other side of the fence on the public beach came running over. He said that when he arrived I looked like a dead body and that the porpoise shoved me ashore."

Marine scientists point out that the porpoise's spirit of play is responsible, that he doesn't really save lives, he just likes to push things. Among other proof, they offer photos taken in 1928 of four porpoises working desperately to push a waterlogged mattress ashore.

But Dr. George Llano in *Airmen Against the Sea* tells of a porpoise pushing four airmen in a rubber raft. He pointed out that there was wreckage floating and the porpoise had a selection of things to push. Also, the animal didn't push the raft seaward, but toward the nearest island. The irony was that the island was Japanese held, and the airmen had to drive the helpful porpoise off with paddles.

From 1888 to 1912, a porpoise dubbed Pelorus Jack appeared in Pelorus Sound, New Zealand, guiding ships through the treacherous waters of Cook Straits and French Pass. He met incoming and departing ships, wouldn't take reward food and, finally, through grateful seamen's efforts and his diligence as a harbor pilot, was responsible for having a bill passed protecting porpoises.

In 1955, a wild porpoise appeared in Hokianga Harbor, near Opononi on the northern coast of New Zealand, and started swimming with the bathers. Called Opo, she finally became so tame that she would play games with the swimmers, going between their legs, upsetting them, rolling in to have her back rubbed, even permitting herself to be lifted out of the water and photographed. Opo preferred children and would immediately leave an adult when a child entered the water. Her special friend was thirteen-year-old Jill Baker. She took the child for short rides, even letting Jill place a couple of toddlers on her back for a sprint in the surf. Untrained, Opo played with a beach ball, tossing it to Jill and catching it on return. For the scoffers, New Zealand reporter Antony Alpers recorded and photographed Opo's activities, one day counting two thousand people at the beach watching the famed dolphin play with the children.

Opo was found dead at Koutu Point, March 8, 1956, jammed in a rocky crevice. Theory had it that she was feeding and became trapped when the tide went out. All New Zealand mourned; a sculptor was commissioned to create a monument to her memory.

Now, we have discovered that a porpoise can talk and may even have a brain that is potentially better than ours. A dozen top scientists, foremost among them being Dr. Winthrop N. Kellogg and Dr. John C. Lilly, have been conducting sound-and-intelligence experiments for several years.

After nine years of study, Dr. Kellogg, professor of experimental psychology, Florida State University (supported by the Civil Aeronautics Authority, the Office of Naval Research, and the National Science Foundation), discovered that porpoises have had a sonar system for 500 million years that makes man's recent invention obsolete.

In man-made sonar, our fundamental method of submarine navigation (sound, navigation, and ranging) a train of repeated sound signals is emitted by an underwater trans-

ducer. Echoes are reflected to the source from targets on submerged objects, then electronically translated to give distance and shape. The problem, one reason for Dr. Kellogg's
studies, is that man's mechanical sonar confuses steel ships
with wooden ones and submarines with whales—sensitivity
and selectivity are limited.

Hydrophones, special tape recorders, and a pair of dolphins named Albert and Betty, donated by the Marine Laboratories of Marineland, Florida, were Dr. Kellogg's scientific tools. In a 55-by-70-foot test pool at Alligator Harbor
on the Gulf Coast, he found that his porpoise subjects, using
strange clickings, took less than 20 seconds to zero in on a
B-B shot $1\frac{1}{64}$ of an inch in diameter dropped at the far end.

Taking months to define sounds, Dr. Kellogg described
them as birdlike whistles, Bronx cheers, rapid clicking pulses,
and a noise like a door on a rusty hinge. He found the porpoise cerebrum has a supercoustic development with a capacity for sound perception that exceeds all animals.

Discovering that Albert and Betty were getting tired of
their ration of mullet, Dr. Kellogg originated a selective
test. "They were fond of 'spot,' a fish the same size as mullet," he says, "so I had two assistants hold a mullet and
a spot in the water. It took ten seconds, in turgid water,
where sight was impossible beyond 20 inches, for the porpoise to locate the spot." From a distance Albert could immediately tell the difference between a hand and a fish of
the same size.

Trying to prove that porpoises "see with their ears," that
sight and scent are not important, Kellogg lowered half-
inch plate glass into the test pool. Two fish, one a food
fish, were held in the muddied water, one behind the invisible screen. Without a mistake in two hundred tries, Albert,
oscillating his head from left to right, "auditorily scanning,"
took only the "preferred" fish outside the barrier.

"Then came a really complicated one," Dr. Kellogg says,

"a tough, diploma test." In the pool he arranged a maze of forty steel poles which would give bell-like sound if touched. This obstacle course was set up on a day when the test-pool was muddied by incoming tides and vision was impossible. To further complicate matters, Dr. Kellogg tried to "jam" their impulses by flooding the pool with the taped sound of porpoise sonar. Ignoring the "false" impulses, Albert and Betty touched the musical poles four times in 24 hours, then just lightly with their flukes after their bodies had passed the obstructions. In minutes they were almost perfect.

A light splash, or even sudden rain upon the surface of the water, triggered a series of porpoise sound pulses—the sounds stopping if nothing entered the water, continuing if the object remained, until size and distance had been computed. Targets silently placed in the pool were discovered by short 20-second bursts.

"Porpoise echo location is not merely sensing an echo," says Dr. Kellogg. "This animal has the ability to interpret, evaluate, and identify that echo—something man cannot do."

Dr. Kellogg and the Navy are hoping that maybe someday man will have this ability. During World War II, porpoises annoyed and confused our submarine operations with sonar mimicry—imitating the sound of motors, clanging of bells, and other underwater sounds we couldn't identify as porpoises until recently.

If probing the porpoise's brain will unlock secrets of that strange area under the sea, occupying almost four fifths of the earth's surface, then perhaps psychophysiologist John C. Lilly will one day have some answers. At his own Communications Research Institute in Saint Thomas in the Virgin Islands, he tried to understand the animal's language, teach him ours, and discover if he has a better brain than we have.

To accomplish this, he hammered a small length of hypodermic-needle tubing (using his own head to discover if the pain was severe; it wasn't) into the porpoise's skull, so that the brain cavity was penetrated, but not the brain itself. Then he inserted an insulated, shielded electrode with bared tip into the brain, probing pleasure and pain centers and studying reaction under various conditions.

Rigging a switch that the porpoise could push to get a pleasure-reward stimulus, or to turn off an unpleasant one, Dr. Lilly was startled in early tests. He noticed the porpoise closely watching his procedure. Before he could finish assembling the rods necessary to push the switch (which was out of water), the porpoise started pushing on the rod. By the time he hooked up the switch, the animal had already learned the right way to push it to start stimulation. It had taken weeks in a similar test for monkeys and chimpanzees, considered among the most intelligent animals, to learn what the porpoise learned in minutes.

Dr. Lilly once had a porpoise experiment on him. "I was attempting to make him whistle a burst of a given pitch, duration, and intensity, in order to obtain brain-stimulus reward," he says. "When he cooperated, I immediately rewarded him; at which point he would whistle again and get another reward. Then he began to raise the whistle pitch so high that I couldn't hear it, but I could see the blowhole twitching as it gave voice. I stopped rewarding him and he rapidly gave up the supersonic experiment and came back into my range. From that time on he didn't go out of it. He discovered what my hearing range was and stayed within it for the remainder of the tests."

Working on the theory that nerve centers control both sensitivity and behavior, and that a large and complex brain indicates advanced capacities and potentialities, Dr. Lilly found that the average porpoise's brain weighed 1,600 grams or 3.5 pounds against a 150-pound man's 3.1-pound or 1,400-gram brain. Findings resulting from the study of five brains sent to Johns Hopkins University bore him out. The cell count is the same as ours per cubic centimeter, the brain being so highly developed that it is uncertain if man is still at the top so far as cerebral structure is concerned.

By wiring porpoises' tanks and taping their sounds, Dr. Lilly eavesdropped scientifically. Two porpoises in a tank made continual whistling and buzzing talk; conversation between male and female was in barks, yelps, and squawks. If separated and placed in nearby tanks, one would whistle until the other answered.

Porpoises talk fast and in high frequencies, so Dr. Lilly slowed his tape recording to one fourth of normal speed with amazing results: off the tape came high-pitched Donald Duck laughter, the words "one, two, three" and "323," "yes, it's a trick," or "yes, it's six o'clock," the letters "T, R, P," the sound of a banjo, a baby crying, two cars passing, the buzz of a transformer, and the whir of a movie camera. The doctor believes the animals associated these sounds with the pleasure-giving stimulation of the electrode and were trying for food reward. Most of the words were falsetto imitations of his own voice.

Dr. Lilly once snapped back at a porpoise who was making irritated noises at him. "He mimicked my voice so well," he said, "that my wife began to laugh. Then he gave a fine imitation of *her* laugh."

As this is being written, there have been developments that would seem to bear out the scientists' thinking. One is a report that a porpoise has been trained to perform on command simple tasks in the open sea. According to a report by Kenneth S. Norris of the Los Angeles campus of the University of California and the Oceanic Institute in Oahu, Hawaii, this achievement opened "a new way to a variety of experimental possibilities."

He wrote, "It may prove possible to insinuate a trained animal into schools of wild animals and to observe and record various kinds of behavior." Mr. Norris did not say so, but this ability might also prove useful in doing exactly what the scientists foresaw, herding seafood and doing a variety of other human-directed chores in the sea.

Keiki (Hawaiian for "child") was the porpoise Mr. Norris and his colleagues trained. It was taught first to stop in front of an experimenter in a Hawaiian lagoon at the sound of a police whistle—and the presentation of food. Later, Keiki learned to swim away and return to a clicking noise in the open sea.

In the Navy's 1965 aquanaut experiments they took porpoise training several steps farther. One was taught (by buzzer command from the aquanauts on the bottom of the sea) to swim down and deliver equipment and its own food, performing the task a dozen times. He was also taught (and executed several times) a life-saving action, carrying a life-line from one diver to another who feigned distress. The Navy isn't divulging all that its porpoises can do. But the future looks bright for porpoises—and for men. We finally may have established communication with another species. The potential of this staggers the imagination.

22

THE SAVAGE IN THE SEA

The Shark

Perhaps the most frightening word in the English language "Shark!" came snapping at me as I was fishing for sailfish off Pompano Beach, Florida, not long ago. We had come through the early morning mists after sails every day for a week without hanging up a big fish. The fish were there, and I was with a couple of professionals in a beautiful boat complete with flying bridge, fighting chairs, big equipment, and even a tuna tower. But the luck wasn't there until I got this spine-shaking strike and counted three in accepted sail-fishing technique, giving the sail time to "kill" the baitfish with his bill, make his gobble, and set the hook. I started to reel in when the captain in the tower shouted, "Shark!"

I'm not much of a man with sharks, having caught only a few of the small, so-called sand sharks in Long Island Sound, but I had seen them in tropical waters, the big tigers and the whites, and they are not exactly my favorite creatures, but this one didn't let me do any choosing about whether or not to fight. Trying to keep my rod up, I managed to get to a fighting seat, anchor the rod butt in the metal socket on the swivel chair, and the battle began. There weren't any aerial acrobatics, and there wasn't anything dramatic about the fight, except I knew the fish was enormous and strong, many times stronger than I, even with my barbed steel in his mouth—despite the fact that I was belted to a solid steel reinforced chair bolted by heavy metal to the deck.

The contest went on for nearly three hours in the fierce sun until the captain said, "If he's that tough maybe we better just cut him loose. He's takin' up the whole afternoon!"

But there is that cruel stubbornness in man that makes him want to win, especially if he feels he is losing, forcing him to face an antagonist as strong and determined as this one was. So, muscles sore and back aching, with a red haze in my brain and black spots before my eyes, I kept at it until the fish, resting for the moment, was reeled close enough for identification. I was too weak to rise out of the chair to look at it.

"Mother! Mother!" said the mate. "It's the biggest hammerhead I ever did see!"

He swirled to the surface, a nightmare from the bottom of the sea, a gruesome throwback on evolution, his head five

times as wide as it was long, obscenely flat, his eyes and nostrils located on the outer ends of a weirdly misshapen head.
He was at least ten feet long, and as he lay there near the
surface, the captain said, "That monster will hack up our
new teak deck and the owner will throw a fit. I'll have to
shoot him."

He fired four .22 hollow point long rifle bullets through
the head, the blood came like underwater roses suddenly
blooming on the surface. The giant fish thrashed for five
minutes and then went limp.

Using block and tackle, we hoisted him aboard. He hung
there dripping blood on the deck like some impossible monster dreamed up by the property men in Hollywood. Ten
minutes later, excitement subsided and we headed shoreward,
cold cans of beer in our left hands, our right hands waving
to accentuate adjectives describing the might of the hammerhead. I was standing less than three feet from the "dead"
shark on the hoist. Suddenly, he came to life. He lifted his
head quick as a dog and grabbed my right hand. Instinctively
I jerked back, leaving quite a bit of the flesh from my index
finger on two of the creature's teeth that looked as long as
a lead pencil. Although the finger became infected three
times and I was unable to tie a necktie or punch a typewriter for many weeks, I was one of the lucky ones. Most
people who have been bitten by a shark lose much more
than time or an ounce of flesh.

One of the unlucky was William J. Dandridge who was
scuba diving in 20 feet of water off Fowey Rock Lighthouse
near Miami with Mr. and Mrs. James Quillian. They had
been swimming about a half hour and Dandridge, who had
gone below to explore, had been submerged for ten minutes. Suddenly, he rose to the surface, his face mask gone,
shouted "Shark!" yelled for help, and disappeared. After
much courageous searching by Quillian, his body, the right

arm missing and the left side mutilated, was found in a split of coral.

Wading in shallow water off Pawley's Island, South Carolina, William Lee Bailey was attacked by a shark without warning, bitten so badly on the left leg that amputation was necessary and 163 stitches were required to close the wounds in his right arm.

Albert Kogler, swimming with a friend, Shirley O'Neil, off Baker's Beach, San Francisco, was treading water only fifty yards from shore when he shouted "Shark! Go away!" to Shirley O'Neil, then began crying for help as the underwater attack continued. Risking her life, Shirley swam to him and saw a huge shark tearing at Kogler. In his pain and desperation, the attacked boy fought his girl friend off, but she finally managed to get one arm around him and tow him to shore. Help arrived as she was giving him oral respiration. But his entire left shoulder had been ripped, and his back, shoulders, and arms were deeply lacerated. He died two hours later in the hospital.

Gerald Lehrer lived through the horror of watching his friend, Robert Pamperin, being swallowed alive by a twenty-foot tiger shark. They had been looking for abalones in La Jolla Cove, not far from San Diego, when Lehrer saw a fin cutting through the water toward his friend who was 50 yards away. He shouted a warning, but it was too late. He saw his friend rise out of the water as if he was being pushed. Pamperin was waving his arms and seemed to be fighting to stay afloat, but he was pulled under and quickly disappeared. Swimming to the scene as fast as he could, Lehrer put his head under the water and looked for his friend. What he saw will haunt him as long as he lives. Just a few feet beneath him was an enormous tiger shark with the torso of Pamperin protruding from its mouth. Lehrer swam toward them, flailing the water, but the shark ignored him. Horrified, Lehrer made for the surface, alerted the other swimmers, and went for help. But the shark had vanished with Pamperin by the time Lehrer returned with expert scuba divers.

It is believed that a single man-eating shark attacked five people off the New Jersey coast. The attacks started with Charles Vansart at Beach Haven, a few miles from Atlantic City as he was swimming with several friends close to shore in five feet of water. One of the swimmers, Sheridan Taylor, heard Vansart scream and saw him violently thrashing the water. There was blood in the water and Taylor saw the fin of a shark as he got closer. Grabbing Vansart by the arm, he tried to drag him to shore, but the shark, a big one of ten feet, hung on, and Taylor was having trouble. Seeing the commotion, other swimmers came, and they dragged Vansart to shore, with the shark still hanging on until they got in two feet of water. The shark had stripped all the flesh from Vansart's left leg, and he died shortly after he was admitted to a hospital.

The second attack came at the seaside resort of Spring Lake, when Charles Bruder was swimming a distance from the other bathers. Two life guards who had been watching Bruder because he was in deep water heard him scream and went to him in a boat. He shouted, "I've been bitten by a shark! Hurry! Hurry!"

They got there as fast as they could, lifted him into the boat, stunned at what they saw: both Bruder's feet were gone; the left leg had been stripped of all flesh; the right side of his abdomen had been ripped away. They got Bruder ashore and sent for a doctor, but he was dead before help arrived.

The next attack was even more frightening because of its location, Matawan Creek, a shallow tidal stream thirty miles from Spring Lake where the shark had butchered Bruder. Ten-year-old Lester Stilwell and a dozen others were in the stream swimming when Stilwell suddenly started screaming.

Stanley Fisher, who had just entered the water, heard Stilwell, saw him flailing the water, and dove in to try to help him. When he reached the area Stilwell had disappeared, and Fisher made a half-dozen dives trying to locate the boy. Finally finding him, he rose to the surface with him in his arms and swam toward shore. As he got to shallow water he started wading. Suddenly the shark darted in, viciously attacking him until he was forced to drop Stilwell so he could fight back. Dozens of people watched from the beach, but apparently no one had enough courage to go to his aid. Stilwell was now lost, sunk in the deep water again, apparently pulled below by the shark. Dragging himself ashore, Fisher fainted from shock, his right leg was fleshless from the hip to below the knee.

As he regained consciousness he told how the shark kept trying to drag him back into deep water. Fisher died before he reached the hospital.

By now the Matawan area was aroused, and police were racing around warning everyone to get out of the water. Less than a mile down the river from where Fisher and Stilwell were attacked, several boys were still swimming. When they heard of the shark attack they rushed out of the water, with 12-year-old John Dunn the last, trying to climb on a dock near a brickyard at Cliffwood. He wasn't fast enough. On the way out, the shark ripped away most of the flesh in the knee region of his left leg. Rushed to a hospital, the leg was amputated and John Dunn's life was saved. He was the only one of the five to live after the shark attack. Two days later Lester Stilwell's mutilated body was found in the creek.

The tales of horror continue. Men who have survived shipwrecks tell of shark attacks that lasted for days. Children have been attacked while wading in shallow water off busy beaches. Yet the menace is still ignored and scoffed at by many.

There are several schools of thought on shark danger, some experts claiming that sharks won't attack unless there is blood in the water; others say that they attack only rarely, then only when molested; others point out that the shark danger is greatly overstressed, that the creature only goes for people in muddy, murky water thinking they are fish. The American Institute of Biological Sciences thinks otherwise and is so certain that the shark is an unpredictable menace that it has organized a Shark Research Panel that not only is constantly studying the creature and its attacks, but is conducting tests to develop an effective shark repellent. The panel also summarizes and analyzes research reports from scientists in all parts of the world who are investigating shark migration, the anatomy and physiology of shark sensory organs, and the shark's methods of attack.

Some statistics of the Research Panel follow. Sharks made thirty unprovoked attacks on humans during 1961, injuring thirty-one persons, six of them fatally. There were four other attacks, on boats, in which no one was injured. Attacks were made in waters off both coasts of the United States, off Hawaii and other Pacific Islands, off Bermuda, Australia, South and East Africa, the Philippines, in the Mediterranean Sea and the Persian Gulf, and 150 miles upstream in the Limpopo River, East Africa. At least seventeen different species of sharks made the attacks on fishermen, swimmers, or boats. The smallest was a two-foot Banjo shark; the largest was a 2,500-pound White Pointer shark.

African and Australian waters were the scenes of most of the unprovoked attacks. There were three attacks in Florida waters, one off South Carolina, one off California, and one off Oahu, Hawaii. The report includes all attacks reported by world newspapers, and otherwise, which could be authenticated after investigation by scientists or physicians, cooperating with the panel, at the scene of the attack.

Confirmed unprovoked attacks included six in the United

States with one person killed and the others wounded. There were nine attacks in United States waters in 1960 and ten in 1959; United States casualties were one killed and nine injured in 1960 and three killed and seven injured in 1959. There were nine attacks, on ten persons, by sharks which had been provoked by being caught, trapped, speared, injured, or pursued: seven in Australian waters, one off South Africa, and one at Oyster Bay, New York. All ten people were injured, none fatally. There were twelve provoked attacks in 1960 and four in 1959.

Four boats were attacked by sharks during 1961. No injuries resulted, but one 35-foot launch had its rudder damaged by a huge shark, one canoe was torn and turned over, its occupant forced to swim to shore, and a dinghy with two aboard was used as a toy by a school of sharks which swirled it around and around. During the year there were four air and sea disasters in which sharks were reported active among victims. In the sinking of the United States Navy vessel, Pacific Seafarer, off the coast of Colombia on January 6, three persons were recovered, three perished. There were many deaths among the hundreds of hurricane victims who were attacked by sharks northwest of Acapulco, Mexico, November 17.

Are there more sharks in our waters now, or does it just seem that there are more because their attacks are for the first time being scientifically investigated and reported? Some experts explain that there are more shark attacks on humans today simply because there are more sharks. Before the discovery of synthetic vitamins, shark liver was considered one of the best sources of Vitamin A, and a large industry was built around its production. Now, with no commercial reason to hunt sharks, there is a population explosion—at least in United States waters. Orientals still fish for them and convert their fins into a delicacy, shark-fin soup, and many people eat shark. I have had delicious fish and chips in Australia and was later told that the fish was school shark. A large mako that I caught off Miami was quickly claimed by several Negroes who said that it was just as good as swordfish.

But there is little concerted and no commercial fishing for sharks in this country; thus, there are more sharks now than ever. Taking a summer shakedown cruise with Hank and Diane Hunter in their speedy *Huntress* on Long Island Sound, we counted three dozen big mako sharks sunning themselves atop the water in less than four hours of haphazard observation. Trying to get a bluefish or two for supper, we hooked into a mako that took the bait with a mad rush. Hunter, who is six feet five inches and muscular, was quickly whipped, his rod broken, and his reel ruined. We saw the fish at close range; it was at least 12-feet long.

Although it certainly couldn't be proved from Hunter's and my experience, fishermen can help in this battle against one of man's most dangerous enemies. When teenager Billy Weaver was killed by a shark while surfboarding off Oahu, Hawaii in 1958, the community was so outraged that a group of fishermen decided to charter the sampan *Holokahan 1* and scientifically fish for sharks for a full year and determine if, by this method, they could decimate the creatures.

Their weapons were long lines (originated by the Japanese for ocean fishing for tuna, marlin, and swordfish) of a half mile of main line, consisting of ten fathom lengths of nylon rope. Ten to twenty hooks were suspended from the long line by three-fathom branchlines at intervals—a strong and usually effective technique.

Planning carefully, setting up spaced fishing stations, keeping accurate records, fishing in planned periods on the stations, the *Holokahan* caught 684 sharks and destroyed 641 unborn ones. The long line proved terribly effective, taking 33 tiger sharks the first time out; 29 the second; 11 on the third; and 9 tigers on the final trip. Nearly 200 sand sharks were taken on the first trip. This experiment proved that it was reasonable to expect that sharks could be kept under control if programs of this kind were initiated whenever needed.

Unfortunately, experiments like the *Holokahan*'s are rare; fishing for sharks either scientifically or as a hobby seems to be an exercise that doesn't catch on. I am told that the real reason is fear. It has always been a frightful creature, difficult to catch and land, and nearly impossible to handle unless you are a highly skilled fisherman using the proper equipment. I saw a giant tiger shark winched aboard, tear up the deck, splinter the cabin, and ruin a fighting chair. The amount of damage it caused in less than five minutes was unbelievable. The shark has been causing man trouble for a long time.

Actually, the shark is a prehistoric monster. One species, the Cladoselache, has been in the ocean for three hundred million years and is a terrifying creature one hundred feet long with teeth the size of daggers. Scientists call the shark the most perfect living creature, nature having designed it so wonderfully that, unlike other creatures, its evolutionary position has changed only slightly since it was created.

Shark teeth from the Miocene and Eocene ages are almost indistinguishable from modern teeth. Their fossils date back from the Upper Devonian period with little change. By contrast, bony fish, dating back from the same time, have developed many specialized forms, and where there are less than three hundred species of sharks today, there are upwards of thirty thousand species of ray-finned fishes.

No one is certain where the name "shark" came from, but there are some educated guesses. The ancients knew of the shark's existence. Pliny the Elder called it the dogfish; and in 492 B.C. Herodotus recorded that survivors of shipwrecks were killed and torn apart by monsters off the Thessalian coast. The name "shark" began to be used after an English sea captain exhibited a white shark in London, and the guess is that English sailors picked up the word from the German "Schurke," which means villain. They couldn't have selected a more apropos word from any language.

Belonging to a varied family, *Selachians,* which include rays, sharks in some form are found in most waters of the world, ranging in size from a few inches to the sixty-foot whale shark and in form from an eel-like creature to the striped tiger and spotted leopard. Unlike fish, the shark has no bony skeleton, but a cartilaginous frame covered with tougher-than-leather dermal dentricles, a hide so coarse that it can mark a man's skin more effectively than sandpaper. Lacking the air bladder of a fish, the shark's gills take oxygen from sea water. In order to remove this oxygen, they must be continually on the move—from the moment they are born until the day they die sharks must be in constant motion.

All but a few of the three hundred species give birth to living young; the exceptions lay eggs in clusters which cling to underwater objects until hatched. The young born alive have a full set of teeth and are equipped to look after themselves from the moment they enter the sea. They leave their parent immediately and start the eternal foraging for food; they had better, for their hungry mother often eats them soon after they are born. This appetite is remarkable. A full-grown shark tries to eat its own weight at every meal and can digest just about everything, including tin cans and wooden boxes. In one shark, the intact body of a walrus was found. The digestive juices of the tiger shark are so strong that a single drop will blister human flesh.

Although sharks have small brains and are not particularly intelligent or sophisticated creatures, some of their senses are remarkably keen. Smell is probably the leading sense, as a shark has an ability to pick up the scent of blood or fish oil a quarter mile away. Scientists tested lemon sharks that detected the minute fluid from a tuna, estimated at one part in 1.5 million, at seventy-five feet. This sense of smell coupled with the shark's sensitivity to vibrations is what makes him so dangerous to shipwrecked men. Vibrations are picked up on the lateralis system, a network of canals filled with fluid supplied by nerves near the skin on the head and both sides of the body that meet in a certain area in the brain. It is this system that enables sharks to gather from great distances when a ship is sunk by explosion. Actual distances for which the lateralis system is effective haven't been accurately determined, but tests with schools of fish and men splashing in water have indicated that a shark is extremely sensitive and responsive to underwater sounds from remarkable distances.

With all of man's ingenuity, he hasn't yet been able to develop a foolproof shark deterrent, a method which would use the shark's own sensitive sense of smell to keep it away from humans. World War II made the need for such a deterrent imperative because troop ships were being torpedoed or dive-bombed and surviving American servicemen returned with gruesome stories of men torn to pieces by schools of ravening sharks that became so excited in their blood orgy that they often turned on one another. To die on the battlefield was one thing, but to be eaten alive by sharks in the ocean was quite another, and tremendous pressure was brought to bear on the War Department to come up with a shark deterrent that worked. The best the chemists could conceive in the short time they had was a cake of a soaplike substance which dissolves as a black water-soluble dye and which kept a single shark at bay for five hours and has been known to discourage several sharks for a period. But it is the rare case when only one or a few sharks are in on a shipwreck, so this deterrent is not the answer.

A couple of years ago a series of shark scares along the New Jersey coast, with several people being attacked, brought into being a new safeguard for bathers, a bubble curtain that was supposed to offer protection from sharks by blowing a curtain of bubbles around them constantly and thus, in theory, keeping the sharks at bay. This system used a perforated pipe or hose that lay along the ocean bottom with compressed air forcing bubbles to the surface. Several resorts used them and proclaimed them sharkproof; but experiments made by the American Institute of Biological Sciences Shark Panel with bubble curtains at Bimini proved that sharks swam through the curtain as if it never existed.

The panel and its worldwide membership are currently working on a deterrent, but have not yet come up with anything that they want to call effective. At the Lerner Marine Laboratory in the Bahamas, a field station of the American Museum of Natural History, special pens have been constructed that contain sharks constantly under study. They can be anesthetized, brought up with special hoists, and placed on the pier for as long as twenty minutes while eye shields are attached, nostrils plugged, and other scientific tracking and computing devices adjusted. They are also observing and photographing captive sharks from underwater with the use of steel cages and special breathing apparatus.

Investigations of the same sort are underway in South Africa, Florida, and Hawaii; but as yet the most effective measure to ward off sharks is the one invented by Australians, whose shark menace seems to be on the increase. It is a nylon mesh hanging from a buoyed line completely encircling a bathing area. The only failure in this system occurred during heavy storms when great swells actually lifted sharks up and over the nylon mesh into the bathing area.

Out of this involved study of sharks, the Shark Panel has

proved that the attacking shark doesn't roll in to bite its victims as was believed, but comes head on. Six lemon sharks were photographed attacking a freshly caught 400-pound marlin placed in the pens at the Lerner Laboratory. They came in head on, protruding their upper jaws, grasping the marlin fiercely, then violently shaking their heads like dogs, yanking off twenty pounds of meat at one bite. It was also noted that the shark group circled for a while, seeming to study the situation before a single shark darted in; then, one by one, the others followed until the water was bubbling with blood and flesh, and the sharks went into the feeding frenzy so clearly described by servicemen surviving shipwrecks. The sharks were hitting, biting, striking, and eating anything near them; in one case, the scientists saw the sharks swallowing boxes and cans and attacking one another.

Which of these seemingly indestructible monsters of our seas are dangerous? One student of sharks and shark behavior, a qualified professional observer, a former commercial fisherman, and a writer and photographer who has compiled an excellent book on sharks, says, "Any shark with the teeth, jaws, and instincts necessary for a rapacious way of life can be termed a man eater. Among these will be found the white, mako, mackerel, tiger, lemon, blue, bull, white tipped, and all sand sharks, including the common Ganges River and grey nurse and most of the hammerheads."

But Perry W. Gilbert, professor of zoology at Cornell University, a member of the Shark Research Panel, says, "In 1959, the first year for which statistics were prepared, there were just thirty-nine shark attacks in the entire world. In contrast, 183 people were struck by lightning that year in the United States alone." He feels that just 10 percent of the three hundred kinds of sharks around today are dangerous.

Actually, the sharks that are considered dangerous to man

are sometimes grouped under the heading "requiem sharks," taken as far as I can discover from requiem mass or mass for the dead, which makes it quite an accurate grouping. These include twenty-four sharks, all of those mentioned by the first shark expert we quoted who believes that just about any shark with teeth is dangerous. He is of the opinion that the man eaters are a great deal like other man-eating animals, such as the tiger, the lion, and the leopard. They get a taste of man, like it, are attracted by such an easy meal, and concentrate on people from that point on. The experience I mentioned of the white shark killing four and maiming one on the New Jersey coast is an example.

Regardless of Perry Gilbert's calm words regarding the unlikeliness of shark attack, the search for a way to stop sharks goes on, with several scientific groups involved, including the Office of Naval Research. The American Institute of Biological Sciences Shark Panel, realizing that swimming is our most popular sport, with water skiing and scuba and skin diving running a close second, bringing millions of people into the water every year, has prepared a set of rules for those who go down to the sea to swim, boat, water ski, skin dive, or just wade. I offer it as an integral part of any profile of the shark.

Advice to Bathers and Swimmers

1. Always swim with a companion. Do not become a lone target for attack by swimming away from the general area occupied by a group of swimmers and bathers.

2. If dangerous sharks are known to be in the area, stay out of the water.

3. Since blood attracts and excites sharks, do not enter or remain in the water with a bleeding wound.

4. Avoid swimming in extremely turbid or dirty water where underwater visibility is poor.

ADVICE TO SKIN AND SCUBA DIVERS

1. Always dive with a companion.

2. Do not spear, ride, or hang on to the tail of any shark. To provoke a shark, even a small and seemingly harmless one, is to invite possible severe injury.

3. Remove all speared fish from the water immediately; do not tow them in a bag or on a line cinched to the waist.

4. As a rule, a shark will circle its intended victim several times; get into a boat or out of the water as quickly as possible after sighting a circling shark before it has time to make an aggressive "pass." Use a rhythmic beat with the feet and do not make an undue disturbance in the water as you move toward the boat or the shore. If wearing scuba, it is best to remain submerged until you have reached the boat.

5. If a shark moves in and there is no time to exit from the water, try not to panic, and keep the shark in view. A shark can often be discouraged by releasing bubbles or, at close range, by deliberately charging it and hitting it on the snout with a club or "shark billy." Since the hide of a shark is very rough and may cause serious skin abrasions, hit the shark with your bare hands only as a last resort. Shouting underwater may or may not discourage a shark.

ADVICE TO SURVIVORS OF AIR AND SEA DISASTERS

1. Do not abandon your clothing when entering the water. Clothing, especially on the feet and legs, is your only protection against the rough skin of a shark.

2. Place the wounded in a life raft; all should use the raft if there is room.

3. Remain quiet—conserve energy.

4. If you must swim, use regular strokes, either strong or lazy, but keep them rhythmic.

5. Do not trail arms or legs over the side of the raft.

6. Do not jettison blood or garbage, for this attracts sharks.

7. Do not fish from a life raft when sharks are nearby. Abandon hooked fish if a shark approaches.

8. When a shark is at close range, use Shark Chaser (U.S. Navy repellent) if available—the black dye will repel many species of sharks.

9. If your group is threatened by a shark while in the water, form a tight circle and face outward; if approached, hit the shark on the snout with any instrument at hand, preferably a heavy one; hit a shark with your bare hand only as a last resort.

Advice to All

1. Always swim with a companion.

2. Avoid swimming at night, or in extremely turbid or dirty water, where underwater visibility is very poor.

3. Keep your head when a shark is sighted; leave the water as calmly and quickly as possible.

4. If an attack does occur, all possible effort should be made to control hemorrhage as quickly as possible—even before the victim reaches shore. If the wound is serious, the victim should be hospitalized as promptly as possible.

5. Adopt a sensible attitude toward sharks. Attack is almost assured when one deliberately grabs, injures, or in some other way provokes even a small and seemingly harmless shark.

23

LORD OF THE JUNGLE

The Tiger

A big, shaggy, black buffalo came clumping up the jungle road beneath me, his hoofs sending up smoky spirals of dust. The dying Indian sun shined up his horns so that they gleamed like a pair of polished ivory tusks. From the carefree way he ambled, I knew that this was a domestic animal strayed from a herd, probably heading homeward to the village three miles beyond.

As I watched from the *unjun* tree, where I had climbed

to try to photograph peacocks that fan danced in this area, there was a wind-whisper of movement in the pale grass 20 feet from the road. With a motion that came as quickly and startlingly as a bad dream, a tiger thrust his whiskered, orange-white head out of the grass. He was so close that I could see the wet gleam in the amber-hard eyes and count the five stripes that crossed his forehead.

Twisting out of the cover as sinuously as a snake, he stood in the road in breath-taking beauty. His coat was a delicate golden-rust, his stripes so vividly black and well-defined that they looked freshly painted.

Not a muscle quivered in his superb nine-foot body. I could sense his reserve and depth of strength. That marvelous control was a terrifying thing to watch as the cat flowed down the road as gracefully as a run of water.

The only sound I could hear was the plop-plop of the buffalo's feet hitting the dusty road. As the tiger went softly as a shadow after the unsuspecting animal, I thought of a poet's words: "The great cat goes on fog-feet, moving as lightning strikes."

Now I could see the tiger's muscles bunch. He stopped, motionless as marble. The sudden, 30-foot leap, frightening in its fury of motion, catapulted him upon the back of the buffalo. Lurching and staggering, the enormous animal probably never knew what hit him.

The tiger sank his claws into one shoulder, his long canine teeth in the back of the animal's neck, and hooked his other paw in the nose, drawing the head down. With the bull plunging forward in panic, the cat then tripped him with his hind feet. Falling, the buffalo's neck was broken instantly.

I had heard that the clever cat often conserves his own energy, using his victim's strength and speed to make a kill. Less than 100 feet from me was a chilling example. I remembered thinking that if this is the way death in the jungle must come, I was thankful that it was so swift, so surgically skillful.

I was able to witness this death in the afternoon due to the only weakness I have been able to discover in this magnificent murder machine: the tiger's sense of smell is inferior. He didn't know I was there. But this extraordinary cat's hearing, sight, strength, speed, agility, and cunning combine to make him lord of everything he surveys.

Actually, I was fortunate to see this stalking of the buffalo, for the tiger is a master at masking his movements. His handsome golden coat, with its transverse brownish-black stripes, is perfect camouflage in the country he travels. I once sat and stared for fifteen minutes trying to locate a tiger 30 yards away in *cheen,* brown dwarf palms, where an agitated Gond native tried to point him out. It was bright sunlight, but the tiger was in such harmony with his surroundings that I couldn't see him until he came forward. At night, when color does not count, he is almost impossible to see; he becomes part of the shadows themselves.

In order to survive, the tiger needs this camouflage and every physical asset, talent, or trick he can muster. Every hand in the jungle is against him: crows, peacocks, and other birds scream a warning when they see him from their high vantage points; langur monkeys go howling mad; deer and sambur bark. So, in addition to his stealth and strength, which often are not enough, the tiger needs a brain. And he has a good one.

Old jungle hands say that the big cats perfectly imitate the call of the sambur stag, enticing the elklike animal near. They will even splash their paws in a pool to attract the curious creatures. In the book, *In the Grip of the Jungles,* George Hogan Knowles describes a tiger luring a wild bull-buffalo. Crouching in high grass, the tiger imitated the bellow of a bull spoiling for a fight. The clever cat even set the scene by scratching the earth and making the dust rise, much as the hoofs of a mad bull would. When the bull gave a responding bellow, the tiger challenged from his ambush again until the angry animal came thundering up. Then, as quickly as an assassin's knife, the cat killed.

I discovered that the tiger has a variety of abilities that make him lord of the jungle. He never kills unless he is hungry, but when the time comes for the cat to take a meal, he has more than his killing talent and his talons working for him. Tigers can sprint with incredible speed for 40 yards, chasing their quarry that distance but not much farther. I watched a young tiger run down a black buck, one of India's fleetest antelopes, catching it within 35 yards in a flashing spurt that was unbelievable.

Often tigers will work in pairs, the male moving through the jungle with the tigress waiting perhaps a half mile in front of him. Proceeding noisily, stopping from time to time to roar or moan, he drives the prey before him into the jaws of his hidden mate.

The tiger is said to kill every five days, eating up to 200 pounds of meat at a sitting. Dunbar Brander saw one consume three quarters of a buffalo. Several times I have had a cat take a 200-pound bullock bait every other night, almost completely stripping the carcass.

Many training sessions, from the time he is a tiny cub, perfect the tiger's adult skills. After a fifteen-week gestation period, the terror of the jungle is born into a litter of from two to six cubs, in November or April. He enters his domain the size of a small house cat, fuzzy but with a full complement of stripes. His father leaves promptly after the mating and his mother finds an isolated place (often in an old silver mine or an abandoned temple) near water and shade where other tigers can't molest her offspring. Adult males will kill any cub they see.

At the age of two months, the cubs leave the den for brief periods, but they don't follow their mother for another two months, when they are about the size of cocker spaniels. At five months, when her milk no longer satisfies, the tigress brings her litter small game, mouse deer, jungle fowl, peacock, and pieces of pig which they mangle in play and learn to eat.

When the cubs are a year old, their mother cripples game and introduces them to their lifetime of killing—and survival. My friend Rao Naidu, a professional hunter, who spends most of his life in the jungle, once watched a tigress show her three cubs how to stalk and chew up a helpless barking deer that she had evidently disabled for her students.

At eighteen months, young tigers begin making their own kills and are given polish in the arts of hunting silently, utilizing cover, and using their remarkable eyes, ears, and poor noses to test and work against the wind for proper approach. This is important, for tigers have a strong, musky odor that betrays them to horned game having a superior sense of smell. They are also taught to swim—unlike most felines, they are fond of water. Many a tigress has been seen up to her neck in a stream with her cubs splashing nearby.

Ready to mate again, the tigress deserts her offspring when they are two years old (sometimes before), but the cubs may remain together, aiding one another in the hunt, until they get their own reproductive urge. Maturing at five, they become solitary stalkers and killers (except when mating) for the rest of their thirty-year life-span. They grow large quickly—most run from eight to nine feet in length and up to 500 pounds in weight, with the female considerably smaller. But males as large as ten feet, measured from tip of nose to end of 3-foot tail, have been shot. The sexes look alike except for size, although the female is more lithe and elegant, with a narrower head. She is also the fiercer, the one who rarely falters in her charge.

English sportsman F. C. Hicks had a tigress charge out of the grass and leap on his elephant's hindquarters to get at him. He shot her; she circled and again leaped on the elephant, clawing and biting the huge beast until she died. The elephant, ten times the size of the cat, trembled and trumpeted in terror throughout the attack.

It is not only because of courage like this that I consider the tiger the true king of cats. More than three times the size of a leopard, he has the smaller cat's agility and can actually jump 18 feet vertically. I saw a tiger leap a 30-foot gorge without seeming effort. I also think the tiger is fiercer than the lion. The Masai and other African tribes successfully hunt lions with spears. Indian aboriginals have as much courage and more intelligence than the Africans, yet the tiger is never hunted by their tribal groups—with *any* weapon, even guns. The natives respect and fear the giant cat too much to go after him in his own territory, where he usually dictates his own terms.

Often larger and stronger than the lion, the tiger is credited with driving it from India, usurping the maned cat's territory, keeping it from the jungle, and forcing it to live in open areas where game was scarce and humans with weapons abounded. Where the lion with his dun coat and mane has an almost doglike air and is gregarious, often traveling the open plains in packs or prides, the tiger is all cat: stealthy, secretive, solitary, keeping to the shadows and the heavy jungle where his invisibility is his protection. The tiger always appears suddenly, dramatically, then melts away into the forests of the night as mysteriously as he came.

There is this air of mystery about the tiger that the other cats don't seem to have. Perhaps it is this not knowing, this seldom seeing, that inspires fear throughout his vast range: Siberia, the Caucasus, Northern Iran, Central Asia, Manchuria, Mongolia, China, Korea, Burma, the Malay Peninsula and India. Everywhere in these lands the monstrous striped cat is highly respected, greatly feared and, in some places, even worshipped. Other animals may be as danger-

ous and as powerful, but the tiger has always been synonymous with terror.

I admit that one of the varying emotions I have always
felt toward the tiger is fear. That feeling was born one sunlit afternoon when Rao Naidu, India's foremost hunter, my
wife, and I were walking through a *ringal* jungle of young,
gold-stemmed, feathery bamboo toward an enormous fan of
vultures unfurling in a cloudless sky. There we found the
remains of a gaur, India's giant wild ox, saw that a big cat
had been at it, and wondered aloud how even a tiger could
pull down an animal that weighed nearly a ton.

"See," Rao said, "the hind legs are hamstrung. I have
watched tigers team up to take a gaur this way. One engages
its attention from the front while the other creeps in behind
and severs the tendons. The big beast is then at their mercy."

We stood staring in horror at the killers' gristly work, when
Rao nudged me. I looked where he was facing.

The wheat-brown grass rose hip high. Less than 100 yards
away, head above it, was a huge black-and-gold tiger. He
stood sculpturesquely still, glaring at us, fearful symmetry
without motion, just the white tip of his tail twitching like
a hovering bird behind him. Tense, in a block of fear, I
thought suddenly of Kipling, who knew the tiger and the
jungle, and who described fear unforgettably:

Do you know what fear is? No ordinary fear of insult, injury, or
death, but abject quivering dread, a fear that dries the inside of
the mouth and half of the throat, fear that makes you sweat on the
palms of the hands, and gulp in order to keep the uvula at work.
This is fine Fear—a great cowardice, and must be felt to be appreciated.

Although we had rifles, I remembered that one tiger with
its heart shot out had charged 100 yards and taken the top
off a man's head with a sweep of his paw. I was feeling Mr.
Kipling's great cowardice now, gulping and sweating. Then

the tiger moaned, a deep *ahhh-hhh,* turned in a graceful movement and vanished in the golden grass.

We ran for the nearest tree and went up it, fear making us as agile as monkeys. While we sat carefully searching the terrain, I learned from one of the world's cat experts about two more of the tiger's characteristics: the sounds he makes and his incredible strength.

Sher, as the Indian tiger is called, moans when he is disappointed or displeased or to warn animals that he is approaching either to avoid tangling with an irritable old wild boar or to herd animals into a trap. They also bark sharply, "pooking," to call to one another; cough to frighten animals away from their kill; and make a hissing, bellowslike sound when blowing on a carcass to try to dislodge stinging insects. Naidu claimed that he had heard them make a distinct whistle, which he believes is used to call a mate. A tiger roars to show his good feelings or his anger; the two sounds are easy to distinguish: one a bold, buglelike sound, the other is peevish rage. His most frightening sounds are a series of irate roars when he is about to charge, his tail lashing sideways.

The tiger's strength is remarkable. One hunter found the carcass of a 1,200-pound bull that the striped cat had moved a quarter of a mile over rough terrain. Another leaped a 7-foot stockade, killed a man and, with the body in his mouth, sailed easily over the fence again.

Rao Naidu and I have had baits tied to tough hemp ropes that the tiger snapped like thread; once, when a tiger couldn't break the 4-inch ropes that we had doubled, he yanked down the tree, dragging it along with the bait. Another tiger charged back through a line of advancing hunters, killing and wounding eleven men in a matter of seconds.

The great cat's vitality is also astounding. After Clifford Batten shot a tigress through the brain with a .450 high-velocity rifle, she traveled over a mile and was still alive and ready to fight twelve hours later. Both shot through the heart with a .470 elephant rifle, two tigers ran more than 60 yards. Another charged 100 yards to kill the shooter, even though his heart was blown apart. A tigress drilled through the stomach with a .577 lived without food for eleven days to attack again in a fierce charge.

If you could use one word to describe the tiger, it would probably be awesome. Anyone who has sat in a tree in the Indian jungles at night as I have, watching this magnificent animal walking along a cartroad in the white moonlight, knows what I mean. So beautiful and perfectly proportioned that he seems cast in gold-bronze, the tiger is a living sculptural masterpiece that even Rodin would envy. He is so suddenly gigantic there beneath you that he doesn't seem real; so lordly and graceful as he glides in a movement that I liken to moonlight itself.

Picture the most handsome, well-brushed, coat-gleaming, pedigreed house cat you have ever seen. Make it one hundred times larger; place it in a wild place where moonlight and shadow meet dense jungle; then examine your emotional reaction. If it includes admiration, surprise, awe, fear, even frozen wonder, then you have an admixture that describes exactly how I feel every time I see a wild tiger in his own land.

I have gotten used to the sight of a leopard; I have sat blasé in my car several times and watched lions feasting on a zebra or wildebeest. But the tiger is the supreme feline that stirs strong and varying emotion whenever I see him: each time seems like a first meeting. In two months I saw one particularly beautiful, beige-gold tiger nine times. At each view, I had all I could do to keep from falling out of the tree. Three times when I saw him in sunlight (driven out on a beat), I never had the presence of mind to use the camera I had strung around my neck.

In the ancient battle of man against beast, the tiger is

unequaled in his ability to instill this sort of hypnotic fascination in his enemies. In India, three armed hunters in a tree were so petrified with fright that they did nothing while a tiger climbed and carried one man away. Another cat leaped to an 18-foot platform and killed a man before he could fire a single shot.

In *Shikar and Safari*, veteran hunter Edison Marshall observes: "No tiger, not even the staidest old cat, can be trusted after nightfall. He is infinitely bolder then, quicker on the trigger, hungry and savage, and full of adrenalin from his big glands, and is likely to jump on anything that moves. Between five and ten thousand people are killed by them on the jungle fringes of India every year."

Has man ever defeated an attacking tiger in hand-to-hand combat? Five years ago in the central jungles I had tea with three men who had. Aboriginals, Gonds, with loincloths and flashing brass earrings, their shiny sepia chests and arms were welted with white scars and one of them dragged a useless leg. With Rao Naidu translating, I heard their story.

Several years ago when they were on a beat, a huge tigress had broken back through the line of men, swatting as she ran, knocking down one of these three men. Instantly, his two companions rushed in, swinging their crescent-shaped, homemade axes. (Think of the last tiger you saw in a zoo, and you'll realize what they faced!) The three fought the tigress until she was dead and they themselves were bloody messes. Today, these men are revered throughout the jungle villages, songs are sung around campfires telling of their courage, and they have been given the status of headmen.

When a tiger turns man killer, he does it with a vengeance. One tigress in the province of Scinde killed 127 people, stopping all use of the main roads for months. The Indian man eater of Champawat killed 436 people; another brought such terror that thirteen villages were abandoned and 250 square miles of agricultural land were left uncultivated. In the province of Bengal, 4,218 humans were carried off and eaten by tigers in six years.

However, those who know tigers best, *shikaris* like Rao Naidu, Vidya Shukla, and Bobby Kooka, believe that the magnificent cat prefers his own game and wants to ignore man and is in fact afraid of him. India's famed taxidermist, Van Engen of Mysore, has a hobby of collecting the skulls of man eaters. He told me that without exception all of his man eaters had been wounded or were crippled or badly incapacitated by old age. Of the fifty-odd specimens he has collected, forty carried severe bullet wounds. Thus, he believes that all man eaters are man-made.

Another factor that drives tigers toward man and his cattle is that throughout the Far East when natives with traps, poisoned arrows, speared pitfalls, or even nets kill off the game, taking the tiger's food, the cats are often forced into unnatural killing to survive.

Currently, the situation has worsened, especially in India, which remains the stronghold of the tiger. During the rule of the British, all firearms were collected from the villagers after the crops were harvested. Today, many of the jungle people own firearms and poaching has become a problem that is rapidly thinning out wildlife, thus destroying the tiger's normal food supply. In addition, villagers are placing massive doses of fast-acting poisons in the carcasses of slain cattle, killing large numbers of tigers. They claim that they do this as a simple matter of protection and retaliation, but tiger skins are becoming increasingly valuable, and the big cat's whiskers and claws are used for everything from aphrodisiacs to a supposed cure for rheumatism.

If the Indian government doesn't face the problem soon, the tiger may not be able to hold his own much longer. If he goes, one of India's most precious possessions goes with him.

24

IN DEFENSE OF THE WOLF

I am one of the lucky ones. I have seen the vanishing wolf in India, Canada, and Alaska, and I have listened to him at night, sounding one of the wildest, freest, most haunting calls I have ever heard—and I have heard everything from an angry tiger to six hyenas fighting over a carcass.

But the last wolf I saw is the one I remember. It was at an airport in Canada. Two hunters had just returned from the wilderness and were dragging the body of a fine gray wolf off the plane. Even in death he was majestic. Perturbed, I asked the hunter why he killed an animal that was fast disappearing. He grinned. "They kill game animals, don't they? I figure that I did a good turn. Besides, how many people you know got a timber wolf rug?"

Those three sentences summed up what most of us think of the wolf. I have been trying for years to tell his story, attempting to clear up the myths and misunderstandings that surround him. Now, I will try again.

A Canadian biologist also learned the hard way that it is probably a losing battle to work in defense of the wolf. He had spent months studying the animals in Canada's wild barren land. To the annoyance of hunters and trappers, he had uncovered facts proving that the wolf was an asset to the dwindling caribou herds, not the destroyer that many claimed he was.

When he returned to civilization at Brochet (northern Manitoba), the game warden there angrily told the scientist that less than twenty years ago local residents had been able to kill fifty thousand caribou every winter, but that now, because of wolves, they were lucky to kill two thousand.

Antiwolf feeling was high, and the "wolf lover," as the biologist was called, was not received with enthusiasm. A few days after he arrived, a man came to his cabin saying that he had heard that he was looking for evidence that the wolf killed caribou indiscriminately.

He had proof, he said, just discovered by a trapper on a nearby lake. Fifty caribou were dead on the ice, killed by wolves. Moreover, few of the carcasses had been touched— a chilling example of the wolf's savagery and blood lust.

The biologist rushed to the lake to find a sickening scene: twenty-three caribou dead, blood everywhere. And the trapper had been right: It was senseless slaughter, little of the meat had been taken.

But he had been wrong about everything else. There were

no wolf tracks in the snow; no sign of attack; no evidence that wolves had been within fifty miles of the lake when the mass killing occurred.

There were other tracks though: the ski-tracks of a plane. Hunters had shot the herd from the air, firing at the animals as they massed in terror from the swooping roar of the plane. After they killed the caribou, the plane landed and the few prize heads were taken, along with some choice hindquarters for camp meat.

The bloodthirsty wolves turned out to be men, as so often is the case, and the world's most maligned animal had been falsely accused again. Biologist Farley Mowat reported this incident in a revealing book, *Never Cry Wolf*. That cry has sounded so often over the centuries, fiction clouding fact, fable and folklore fogging reality, that the wolf, actually among the most interesting and noblest of animals, has emerged as wildlife's worst villain. Never has a creature been hunted and exterminated more relentlessly and deserved it less.

Instead of concentrating on wiping out the wolf, man could learn social lessons from this animal that would better his own life. Here is an animal that seldom kills its own kind, an animal that mates for life, one that hunts and lives in harmony with its family group. So intelligent that he still survives with all of mankind against him, the normal wolf observes a strict moral code, respects his fellow wolf, educates his young, provides for the old, and never kills needlessly.

Yet no country during recorded time has passed any law to give the wolf protection. Aside from the influence of the character-destroying fairy tales, "Little Red Riding Hood," "The Three Pigs," and many others and the largely unsubstantiated and often ridiculous horror stories that came from abroad (a wolf the size of a pony was reputed to have killed over a hundred people and terrorized Paris for years and Russian serfs were supposed to have flung themselves from

sleighs into packs of wolves to enable their masters to escape),
the wolf's bad name in the United States was actually established through greed—man's.

Our Western pioneers discovered that the grass of the
plains was a perfect livestock food and determined to kill
off the buffalo to obtain this free pasture for their sheep
and cattle, launching the most pitiless slaughter of wild
animals in the history of the world. Buffalo were slain
by the thousands for their tongues and hides. Within a few
years, the main food of the Indian and the wolf was gone.

But the wolf fared better than the redskin. With his natural food gone, the wolf turned to the livestock that began to
graze the plains in huge herds. As the law of nature decreed,
cattle and sheep became his food. The bloody battle to the
end began.

Traps, guns, and poison were used. It became the unwrit-
ten law of the West for the cowboy or stockman to never
pass a carcass without placing strychnine in it. That the
poison also killed harmless animals other than wolves didn't
seem to matter.

But such was the wolf's intelligence that he soon learned
to avoid the poison, spring the traps, and stay out of shooting range. During this period in our Western history the
tales of the renegade wolves began, amazing stories of the
old plains or buffalo wolves who became leaders of family
groups, clever animals that outwitted man at every turn.

Ernest Thompson Seton made one of these outlaws immor-
tal in his story, *Lobo—The King of Currumpaw,* detailing
some of the feats of this remarkable wolf. Once men tried
to kill Lobo by placing poison in small blocks of melted
cheese sunk in the kidney fat of a recently slaughtered heifer.
They dragged the bait of fresh kidneys and liver, placing
poisoned meat every quarter mile for ten miles. In the morning, when they examined the trail, they found three baits
gone and thought Lobo would be dead at the fourth.

"But Lobo had just carried these three baits to the fourth," Seton wrote, "and then he had scattered filth over them to express his utter contempt for the devices."

Lobo carefully dug up buried traps, exposing them so other wolves wouldn't be caught. They laid an H-line of traps along a run that they knew he used—the traps were placed on each side of the trail, with one across it. Lobo apparently saw the trap in the runway, then carefully backing out, placing each foot in its old track behind him, he got to a point of safety. Then he went to the side of the trail and scratched soil and stones on the hidden traps until he sprung every one. They finally got old Lobo when he came looking for his trapped mate Blanca.

Even with man and his ingenuity against him, the wolf probably wouldn't have been defeated except for one thing —money. Spurred by the bounty system (governments or agencies offering payment for dead animals) that the Greeks originated against the wolf before the birth of Christ, wolf hunting became a profession practiced by many. Started seriously by our Western stockmen who offered $5 for an adult wolf and $2.50 for a pup, the system quickly put the wolf in a losing battle. Cattle producer and Wyoming Senator Thomas B. Kendrick spurred his men into trapping and poisoning 150 wolves in three months. Five hundred animals were taken in one year, just on his ranch property.

Then, in 1896, the bounty went up to $9.50, the ranchers paying $5 and the county $3, the hide bringing another $1.50. Wolf hunting became a profitable business. In the early 1900's, Colorado stockmen raised the bounty to $35 for each adult wolf and $10 for the young. Later that year, wolf trappers were paid $200 a month plus board, leaving a new bounty of $50 per wolf pure profit.

The bounty finally spiraled to $150 for each wolf (Colorado trapper William Caywood earned $7,000, delivering 140 wolves in less than a year). By 1914, a million dollars was being paid annually. Alarmed by the cost, that same year ranch interests got a Congressional act passed making appropriations for the Department of Agriculture to expend money ($1 million a year by 1931) "on experiments and demonstrations in destroying wolves, prairie dogs, and other animals injurious to agriculture and animal husbandry."

Forest rangers were instructed to trap and poison wolves in our thirty-nine national forests (where there was no domestic stock), an area of 72,760 square miles, plus the 145,520 square miles that encircled the forests, one tenth of the total region inhabited by wolves.

Spearheaded by experts in the United States Bureau of Biological Survey (who conceived the idea of tracking wolves to their dens and destroying entire families with poison and gas), by 1941, 24,132 wolves had been killed just in the western United States.

Actually, this "monster" that mankind has been trying to exterminate for over three thousand years is a dedicated homebody devoted to mate and family. A naturalist saw this dramatized when five wolves routed from their den area a one thousand-pound grizzly bear, a fearsome animal that can kill a wolf with a glancing blow from one almost wolf-sized paw. They bravely risked death, herding the giant from their home territory by dashing in and snapping at his heels.

Canus lupus, of the wild species of dog family *Canidae,* the wolf, looking startlingly like the German shepherd, is so closely related to the domestic dog that scientists can't find any important structural differences.

Unlike most carnivores, wolves mate for life. Their spring litters of from four to fourteen pups (average seven) is whelped in a den after a sixty-three-day gestation. Born with fuzzy grayish-brown fur and blind, their eyes open in nine days, and they are weaned at three weeks by the mother disgorging partially digested food. At ten weeks they are capable of handling meat and begin working on bones. By fall, when the youngsters' teeth and strength are sufficiently developed, they are taken to the family runway, where they are taught the arts of survival.

They mature rapidly: in five months they stand 24 inches at the shoulder, and at a year are able to sever the spine of a moose calf in a quick snap or cleanly cut a 2-inch juniper limb in a bite. Then they can run in bursts at twenty-five miles per hour or trot all night at half that speed. But now they need parental guidance; and they get it.

The parents bring food to the young wolves at various points along the runway, with the distance points becoming progressively longer until the youngsters actually engage in the taking of a game animal.

A Canadian biologist watched an early stalking lesson—on mice. The young wolves sat and watched, like cocker pups at an obedience training class in a kennel, as their mother and father hunted meadow mice. The skills were speed and coordination: the patient waiting, then the pounce. The Canadian said the adult wolves were graceful and cat-like and never missed a mouse. They worked with the young for two hours until they seemed to be satisfied, then trotted back to their den where the adults regurgitated all of the mice they had caught—the menu for tomorrow's dinner.

This same biologist discovered (and was disbelieved at his headquarters in Ottawa) that the family of wolves he spent many months studying made mice, not caribou, their principle food.

An adult wolf, although always called gray, runs in color phases from white and black to red, the colors changing with the light, humidity, and temperature of his wide range, which once covered the entire North American continent to within a few hundred miles of the North Pole.

Running in weight from 60 to 175 pounds, with the largest found only in Alaska and the Mackenzie River area in Canada, the wolf lives in family groups (not packs as reputed), usually consisting of mother and father and offspring, that stay with the parents until they are three, and perhaps two or three stray adults that attach themselves to the family. Sometimes these family groups will join another for a short period, but they spend most of their fifteen-year lifespan living within their own runway territory that can encompass one hundred miles. This area is respected by other wolves, who recognize the "scent" lines of demarcation.

Wolves have another lesson for man: They practice birth control. A biologist learned that many wolves of breeding age remain bachelors, apparently realizing that there isn't enough hunting territory to take care of too many bitches with litters. Overpopulation of wolves above the capacity of an area would result in a food shortage and subsequent starvation. So some wolves remain mateless for years while waiting for a territory, often attaching themselves (and lending support) to family groups as "aunts" or "uncles."

An older, mateless female often "baby sits," guarding the pups in the den while the mother and her family are off hunting.

They also have regard for the old and the weak. Naturalist Adolph Murie watched a young black wolf kill a caribou calf, then share the meal with an old, crippled wolf.

A touching example of the wolf's regard for his own kind was described by a naturalist who spent many months observing these fascinating animals. He told of a new litter of seven pups whose mother had been killed by a hunter. A local Eskimo boy wanted to see if his Husky dog would adopt them, but was told by his father that the pups would be taken care of—by the wolves themselves.

Hidden, they watched while a strange male and the father came to the den, and in several trips, whelps in their mouths, carried the entire litter to the den of a female with young of about the same age.

This is the animal the poets have plagued and the writers have maligned until much of mankind has come to regard a dead wolf as the only good wolf.

In reality, the wolf is a shy and wary creature that long ago learned to avoid man. The countless stories of his attacking man—at least in this country—are fiction. I have been unable to find any documented account of any wolf in North America attacking a human. This research is strengthened by most biologists (among them, Lorenz, Mowat, Crisler, Murie, and Stanwell-Fletcher), who ridicule the idea of wolves attacking people. In fact, the Crislers lived with wild wolves in their tent in Alaska and later at their Western ranch; Adolph Murie had one as a pet, a companion to his child.

To test the theory that wolf and man in our national parks and forests are compatible, biologist David Mech traveled by snowshoes to a wolf kill of an adult moose. Several times he shooed the feeding wolves off, then stood motionless on the carcass until the wolves returned. When they saw him, they stopped abruptly, raised their heads, sniffed, then vanished. This experience has been repeated by many naturalists and hunters.

Rewards have even been offered if a wolf attack could be proved. James W. Curran, a wildlife expert and editor of the *Sault Daily Star,* Sault Sainte Marie, Ontario, near the huge wilderness area of Algoma (with a wolf population) which fronts on Lakes Huron and Superior, has offered $100 to anyone who can establish that a wolf has attacked a person. The offer ran in all Canadian and many United States newspapers. Ninety claims were made for the reward, but none could offer conclusive proof of the wolf's hostility to man.

According to Curran in *Wolves Don't Bite,* the famous Canadian hunter Sam Martin summed up the feelings of most wildlife experts regarding wolf attacks: "Any man that says he's been et by a wolf is a liar."

The United States Bureau of Biological Survey says that its files contain no record of wolves killing people in North America, adding, "All reports of such killings proved, upon investigation, to be unfounded."

One fact about the wolf that most people get straight is his howl, his call of the wild. The wolf does indeed make music in the night that once heard is never forgotten. In the deep wilderness of British Columbia, I sat by a campfire, enthralled as a wolf sang to the stars.

It was past midnight, the night was chilly, the sky was frosted with white stars, and there was a wind. It began as a humming call; starting howl-low it became a rising sound, actually a sad, wild song. You could sense a plea in it, the call for companionship. It trebled, then sank so low that you could scarcely hear the notes die. I had heard wolves in India, but never anything as stirring as this. Then it began again, low, then rising to that high, wild song that stiffened the hairs on my neck and made my heart hammer. Only one other call approaches it: the cry of migrating Canada geese, but it doesn't compare in its wonderful, wild sound.

According to two naturalists who lived for an extended period near wolves in Ontario, they are the only wild mammals in North America that actually sing, often giving voice for no reason except to produce sound. The singing is done by solitary wolves and by choral groups. Frequently, they gather before and after a hunt and have a social sing, the howl fest begun by one, keying in on a low note until he is joined for a 20-second period.

But wolves also use their voices for communication. They have a mating call (the one I heard), a lonesome, melodic sound; a hunting call with a two-note pitch; the full family cry on a game scent; and the combination of howl and bark, a signal of closing in for the kill. The female has a many-trebled call for summoning her young, and the leader gives a low, penetrating howl interspersed with sharp barks to reassemble the pack for help, new hunting direction, or strategy.

Even the wolf's most vocal detractors admit that he is among the most intelligent of all carnivores and that he works in remarkably close concert with his own kind. Examples of this teamwork and strategy are impressive. One hunter, Enos Mills, describing how wolves use the relay runner system to catch the fleet antelope, tells of a wolf cleverly cutting an antelope out of a herd. After a stiff chase, the wolf dropped behind, but his place was immediately taken by another, fresher animal. The antelope outdistanced this one, but it was a losing game, for a third wolf soon joined the chase and the exhausted antelope was run down.

Another wildlife observer saw two wolves standing quietly, then watched while one went into a ditch and laid down and the other trotted off across the plain toward a herd of antelope. Without any show of speed or fierceness, the wolf went to the opposite side of the herd and then, like a collie herding sheep, guided the antelopes toward the ditch. As they jumped the ditch, the concealed wolf leaped up, easily catching an antelope.

The wolf also makes organized game drives (as men do), several getting behind deer in the woods and driving them into the jaws of waiting hunting companions. But the old buffalo-hunting technique of a wolf team cutting the slow, the old, or the too young out of the herds, then converging for the kill, is the one usually practiced.

Lois Crisler observed in *Arctic Wild* that often wolves would sit and carefully study a herd of caribou before attacking, looking for the weak to cull. In her studies she found that healthy caribou (even two-week-old calves) outran the wolves and that her young pet wolves were frightened by the enormous, antlered caribou.

Adolph Murie, biologist for the United States Fish and Wildlife Service, spent three years observing wolves in Mount McKinley National Park in Alaska. His primary task was to determine the relationship of wolves, Dall sheep, and caribou. Before his involved study, it had been assumed that wolves were taking a large toll of these animals and should be removed.

Murie found that wolves prey on weak classes of sheep, the old, the diseased, and the young in their first year who can't keep up with the flock. He came to the conclusion that wolves actually stabilized and benefited Dall sheep flocks. He discovered that caribou was the main food of the wolf, but that the McKinley herd of thirty thousand maintained its numbers. After the first few days, the caribou calves are strong enough to lead the wolves a chase in which only the weak fall.

Murie's belief is that wolves act as a necessary balancing factor and, by weeding out the weak, the old, and the crippled actually improve the health of the herd, giving them more grazing land and keeping them fit—for only the fit survived.

Two scientists from Purdue University carried on the same sort of studies on Michigan's Isle Royale National Park where wolves and moose were living together. They found that wolves had a prudent fear of an adult, healthy moose, that the group of sixteen wolves tested twelve moose for every one they finally downed. Examining sixty-eight moose kills, the scientists found some kind of physical disability in over 45 percent; the remainder were the easily caught, young or old. Their conclusion was that the wolves practiced a rigid culling of animals that were inferior due to age or infirmities.

In another experiment on the Kaibab Plateau in northwestern Arizona, all wolves were removed to protect the mule deer. Within a few years the deer population had increased to such an extent that the pasture was stripped and even the forests were severely damaged. As a result, thousands of deer starved.

Today, the still misunderstood wolf lives on the borderland of extinction. Authorities claim that there are less than one thousand left (outside of Alaska and Canada) in the northern wilds of Wisconsin, Michigan, and Minnesota. Minnesota has the largest population. According to Milt Stenlund, northeastern Minnesota game manager, that state has about four hundred wolves left.

President Truman inadvertently helped save these few remaining wolves when he signed the Wilderness Air Ban, preventing hunting from aircraft. But most states still have wolf bounties, and wolves are still hunted from planes in Canada.

We must change our thinking about the wolf, a symbol of the beauty and mystery of our shrinking wilderness, of courage, and of proud, wild independence.

Austrian naturalist Konrad Z. Lorenz points out that the much-slandered wolf knows the meaning of the mercy that man should have. He watched wolves engage in fierce battle (recorded in *King Solomon's Ring*), hurling at one another, slashing with those ripping fangs. The defeated wolf finally stretched on the ground, offering, in an attitude of humility, his throat and the jugular vein he had skillfully shielded while the fight was on, knowing that the victor would not make the death bite if he appealed for mercy. (He didn't; the winner snapped within an inch of the exposed throat, then stalked away.)

Lorenz thinks it a magnificent thing that the wolf finds it impossible to bite the unprotected neck of his foe, but still more commendable that the defeated wolf confidently depends upon the winner for this remarkable restraint.

He warns that naturalists must be careful not to insert human moral standards and situations into animal behavior, but makes an exception of the wolf, claiming that mankind can learn a lesson.

"I have a new and deeper understanding of an often misunderstood saying from the Gospel," he says, "which hitherto had only awakened in me feelings of strong opposition: 'And unto him that smiteth thee on one cheek offer also the other.' A wolf has enlightened me: not so your enemy may strike you again do you turn the other cheek toward him, but to make him unable to do it."

25

THE KING'S LAST STAND

The Lion

For over an hour we sat in our car in Kruger National Park watching the scene that seemed to have come alive from a wildlife artist's drawing board. Morning mist was rising from the damp grass in little gunsmoke puffs and a herd of graceful antelopes, impala, foxy-red animals with milk-white bellies and black stripes along their sides, now stopped cropping the grass and kept throwing up their heads in quick, nervous motions, like an advertising agency vice-president looking behind to see who was gaining. The South African sun on the males' sweep of horns made them gleam like pirate cutlasses. Two giraffes, legs propped at an impossible angle, drank from a small pool caught in a dip of earth. Four zebras stood behind them, heads in the air, as still and as perfect as porcelain.

Suddenly my wife gasped and pointed. Coming out of the high grass to the left of the herd was a big male lion wearing his yellow mane like a golden crown, shuffling along head down as if he couldn't care less about the antelopes a few hundred yards from him.

"We're about to see something spectacular," the South African in the rear seat said softly. "There is a lion with a plan!"

The plan seemed to be for him to sit like a big dog and stare. He sat for fifteen minutes, and then on the still morning air came the sound of coughing from beyond the nervous herd. The lion's ears twitched. He got to his feet, and in a quick burst of speed started toward the impala. Panicking, they fled in bouncing leaps directly away from the lion, passing between two grassy rises into a little valley. We drove as close as we could, following the great cat who now had slowed to a walk but was still moving after the vanishing herd. There, in the middle of the valley, lay two dead impalas. Beside them three creamy-tan lionesses awaited the lion before beginning their meal.

Thus does a pride of lions use cooperation and high strategy to outwit the fleet antelope. That lion we watched actually herded the animals into the death trap when the lionesses coughed to signal that they were in position. The planning and execution were perfect.

This was my dramatic introduction to Africa's largest carnivore in action on his home ground. Probably the world's most famous animals, the huge, tawny, amber-eyed cats need little description. Most of us have seen them in zoos and watched them perform in circuses. The lion was the first wild animal exhibited in the United States (September 26, 1720). We have seen the lion in architectural and heraldic designs, in history, religion, and fable. There are more than seven hundred descriptions of him in Arab literature; the lion is mentioned sixty times in Homeric tales; and he appears in every chapter in the Bible, from Genesis to Revelation. Since the beginning of recorded time he has been associated with strength, nobility, and courage.

But there are facts about this popular cat few of us know. Not many realize that right now the lion is fighting for existence in his last stronghold in a portion of Africa, a continent that has had 90 percent of its wild animals destroyed during the past 50 years. Few know that a lion is a sultan with a harem, that he can swim skillfully, carry twice his weight by using his tail as a balance factor, is the most social member of the cat family, and that the female uses baby sitters.

Felis Leo, the largest member of the cat tribe, the most highly developed and specialized of all carnivores (with the tiger), is one species with nine (sometimes questioned) territorial subspecies whose manes, colors, and sizes differ slightly. Among them is the Cape lion (now extinct) with his black mane so full that it skirted his back; the smaller, fiercer Senegal; the light-maned desert dweller, the Kalahari; and the best known, the East African or long-legged Masai with a full, face-framing mane.

The lion's domain was once large: all of Africa, India, Greece, Persia, Syria, Palestine, Armenia, the Balkans, and even the British Isles and Russia. Man has always been his greatest enemy, annexing most of his territory, harassing and driving him out wherever he could. Egyptian, Assyrian, and Persian monarchs considered it their kingly duty to war on lions, usually seeking renown as lion killers under the guise of protecting the peasants.

Assyrian King Tiglath Pileser I personally killed 920 lions; Moghul emperors of seventeenth-century India hunted lions with armies of 200,000 men. Most rulers had the cats netted alive, caged, and then released in palace arenas where they perfected killing techniques with spears and bows and arrows. The Romans used more than 50,000 lions for their Colosseum entertainments. When the French occupied Algeria, they found that the two Arab tribes specializing in lion killing were exempted from taxes by the Turks and had become wealthy from high bounties paid for lion skins.

With this concentrated slaughter, by the end of the last century lions were extinct everywhere except Africa, and even here they were gone from the north and south and the forest tracts of central and tropical West Africa. In South Africa, with the spread of farms and civilization, they were shot, trapped, and poisoned until by 1865 the most handsome of all, the Cape lion, was exterminated. Boer farmers boasted of killing one hundred in a season. In India, where the lion was common, today there are only three hundred, living under protection in the Gir Forest.

After the publication of President Theodore Roosevelt's African safari story in 1910, his hunt organizer booked three hundred parties the following year. Records of lions killed in the next few years were appalling: several white hunters claimed over two hundred; *one* party killed sixty-five lions on the Serengeti Plains; an Indian Maharaja sat up one night over a dragged bait and shot eighteen; Paul Rainey brought his pack of trained cougar dogs from America and quickly bagged one hundred lions. Sportsmen took over one thousand lions in less than twelve years just in Somaliland.

No one is certain what the lion population is today, but currently the king of beasts is making his last stand, momentarily protected in national parks in the Congo, South Africa, Uganda, Kenya, Tanganyika, the Serengeti Plains Park, and the Ngorongoro Crater and in a few game reserves where he can be hunted only with special, expensive licenses. No one can say what will happen when the new governments are in full control, but given a fair chance the lion is a cat that can take care of himself.

Records show that when he was being hotly pursued in Africa, the lion killed more men than any other animal. Sir Alfred Pease, a dedicated lion hunter and author of *The Book of the Lion,* tells of the courage of a lion charging three men with high-powered rifles after the animal had been wounded four times.

That charge is one of nature's most awe-inspiring sights. When the big cat decides to rush, he drops his head, his tail switches, and then he stands stiffly erect; he utters a series of rumbling growls, his yellow eyes flame, and he moves forward at an amazing speed. The impact is shattering. A professional hunter had a lion charge out of the brush at his truck, nearly knocking it over. Englishman George Grey tried to run a lion down while on horseback. The lion doubled, coming back in 20-foot leaps, and although he was hit three times, he easily bowled over Grey's horse and killed the hunter. Gordon Cumming told of a lion he was hunting that entered his camp and carried away his guide; Major B. R. Glossop wrote of a hunted lion in Somaliland that jumped into a 7-foot enclosure, killed one of the hunters, and leaped back out with him. The lion's list of retaliation is long.

Frederick Selous, Africa's most famed hunter, along with Theodore Roosevelt, Sir Alfred Pease, and many others experienced in lion hunting, claimed that when molested the great cat is the most dangerous animal in Africa. They base this on a number of factors: talent at concealment, might, speed, and determination to attack. One hunter searched for an hour for a wounded lioness who virtually wrapped herself around an anthill on the open plain, blending with the background so perfectly that she appeared to have vanished. Black shading on the ears breaks up the lion's head outline, and his coat resembles burned, brown plain's grass. Lions take advantage of the smallest cover and flatten so closely to the earth that they seem to be part of it. But their main weapon is strength—few men have lived after having been rushed by a lion. An animal that can kill an ox three times his size, breaking his neck with a quick combination of fang and claw, has as little trouble with a man as a cat has with a mouse.

C. A. Guggisberg saw a lion drag a full-grown zebra stallion away, with two tugging lions at the other end. Biologist D. R. Gromier watched two lions dragging a horse uphill through grass and heavy brush. "It was a feat of strength," he said, "that would have taken twenty men to duplicate."

One observer, A. E. Brehm, saw a lion jump an 8-foot *zariba* (thorn fence) with a two-year-old cow in its mouth; another noted that a lion leaped a barrier with a 660-pound donkey.

Lions have been seen tackling the hippopotamus, a tank of flesh which few animals have the courage or strength to molest. Two full-grown hippopotami were destroyed by lions at Mzima Springs in Tsavo National Park. In Uganda, lions have even been observed killing the fearsome crocodile, and one lion was seen outmaneuvering and tearing in half a giant python.

A Boer hunter, Michael Engelbrecht, told of a lion attacking a formidable elephant, the fight lasting for hours, with the elephant badly wounded, the cat unhurt. A Swedish naturalist saw three lions attack and kill in a terrible battle the indestructible rhinoceros.

I watched a lion and lioness team try to outsmart a female rhinoceros with young. The lion did his best, faking rushes, growling, dashing in, and flicking his paws to provoke the adult animal into attacking and chasing him so the lioness could take the youngster. They tried for an hour to tempt the rhinoceros to charge the lion and leave her calf, but the technique didn't work. The rhinoceros wouldn't budge from her baby's side.

It is the exceptional lion that weighs 500 pounds, standing more than 3 feet 6 inches at the shoulder. Most go to about 400 and are 9 feet 6 inches or less in length, including the 3-foot tail. The record, listed by Rowland Ward, was a 516-pound, 10-foot 7-inch lion. How can an animal this size accomplish such remarkable acts of strength?

According to J. A. Hunter, dean of African white hunters, the lion's ability to kill animals much larger than himself is due to method. "I know it sounds incredible," he wrote, commenting on a lion jumping a fence with a cow in its mouth, "as the lion weighed no more than 400 pounds, the cow probably twice that. Yet a male lion can perform this exploit with no more trouble than a fox carrying a chicken. A lion shows a special knack in getting partly under the carcass, shifting the weight on his back while holding the cow's throat in his mouth. When jumping the barricade his tail becomes rigid and seems to act as a balance. The Masai have assured me that a lion without a tail could not possibly perform this feat."

Their killing methods are skillful. I saw a lion suddenly appear amid a herd of wildebeest, quickly separate one animal, run easily beside it, then flip a paw and slap its neck. The cat ran a few paces ahead waiting for the wildebeest to fall. It tumbled, neck broken, precisely where the lion waited. The timing was perfect.

This isn't the usual technique. Experienced hunters claim that lions kill horned game as the tiger often does by putting a paw on the nose of the victim to prevent it from using its horns and then pull the head to the chest so that when the animal falls it breaks its neck. Hornless quarry like zebras, donkeys, and horses are downed by a bite close to the ears that breaks the cervical vertebrae.

When the lion changes these tactics he sometimes runs into

trouble. A hunter in northern Rhodesia found the remains of a big male lion and a gemsbok whose stiletto horns had penetrated the lion's ribs.

Lions are not wanton killers. Colonel Stevenson-Hamilton who studied them for many years at Kruger National Park claimed that a pride of six lions kills on the average two big antelopes a week and that a single lion takes only twelve animals a year.

They don't harm domestic animals if wild game is available. Exceptions are the old and incompetent lions. One famous lion specialized in goats. When she was killed, they found a front paw missing; another that killed goats and chickens was very old, without teeth.

There have been man eaters, created through old age or lack of food. The most publicized were two maneless lions at Tsavo who stopped the construction of the Uganda Railroad for weeks, killing 135 Indian coolies and becoming a much-debated subject in London's House of Parliament before they were destroyed by Colonel J. H. Patterson. Another lion in Mikindani, Tanganyika, took three hundred people before he was stopped.

Things become confused when a man eater appears. Even today many Africans believe in the existence of werelions; they say that lions never kill without human motivation and that the man eater kills and then resumes human form. Witch doctors have taken advantage of this superstition, and men draped in lion skins in one instance killed two hundred of a witch doctor's enemies before authorities stepped in. The African's superstitions about lions would fill a book. Some currently believe that if you eat a lion's heart you will defeat your enemies and that wearing a lion's claw makes you bullet- and spearproof. I have seen African porters search the grass after a lion had been shot looking for the ball the cat is supposed to spit out. A piece of this regurgitated lion ball worn on the person is reputed to give protection from all wild animals and to bring health and courage. Most of the lion charms seem to be designed to protect the wearer from the lion itself. The cry "man eater" brings terror to Africans in many ways. In reality, the lion is so skillful at taking wild animals almost at will that it is seldom necessary for the normal cat to become an eater of men.

The lion doesn't acquire his killing skill easily; he spends years learning the art of survival. The day he is born it begins. After a two-week courtship (with a polygamous playboy who usually leaves her after the cubs are born), the lioness brings two to six fluffy-grey, striped and spotted, 12-inch, 1-pound cubs into the world after a 108-day gestation period. She leaves her pride of 6 to 20 lions, seeking a secluded place near water. Normally, unless there is an unusual supply of game, never more than three (more often two) cubs survive—nature's method of selection, perpetuating the lion race from the finest specimens. Their enemies are rickets, hyenas, and the greatest predator of all, man. Leaving the cubs only to seek food (at which time hyenas sneak in and often carry off entire litters), the lioness nurses them for five weeks, then begins bringing pieces of meat, also disgorging her own partially digested meal which is easy for the young to assimilate. When they are three months old she usually rejoins her pride where another female (sometimes two with families join forces) becomes the official baby sitter and guardian. Contrary to general opinion, it is the old-maid baby sitter who is the most fierce.

Lionesses are devoted parents, often making unprovoked, protective attacks when with cubs. But Steward Edward White, who spent much time in Africa, observed wryly that it was usually the cubless female who made the most fuss about protecting the youngsters. He had a baby-sitter lioness charge him repeatedly (while the mother stood in the background with her cubs), so savagely that he had to shoot her, while the other moaned and fled into the brush with her brood.

Lions use a number of sounds for communication: coughs, grunts, roars (although even long-time African residents have seldom heard this), and moans. The female often controls her offspring with this moan that sounds to me as if it were strummed from a bass viol. One early morning my wife and I were sitting in a car watching the animals in Nairobi National Park when we saw two spotted lion cubs looking like they had just stepped out of a toy shop. We drove near them, enticing them to come closer with the soft mewing noises that domestic cats seem to like. Curious, they came within 20 feet, then there was a stirring in the brush by the roadside and their mother poked out her tan, gold-eyed head and moaned. At this sound the cubs fled to her side and the family vanished in the underbrush.

At four months the cubs become her shadows and are taken to a kill where they attempt to imitate her as she eats, but they can't quite manage it and spend most of their time mauling and growling. But even here there are lessons. An English major saw a lioness at an oryx carcass carefully instructing her cubs in using claws to strip the skin off the meat and dewclaws to hold it down when eating. The youngsters sat like schoolchildren watching a teacher's pointer trace cities on a map.

At six months they are weaned, but as their canine teeth don't develop for another six months they remain completely dependent upon their mother. But now serious training begins.

Safari organizer Donald Ker once watched an advanced training lesson illustrating superior skill and practical application. He saw a lioness casually strolling along the windward side of Thomson's gazelles, ignoring the drinking herd until it was between her and a reedy swamp. Then she streaked into the herd, scattering the panic-stricken animals. Twenty gazelles fled into the gum of the swamp, moving in short, ineffectual leaps. At this, lions, lionesses and half-grown cubs (an entire pride) poked their heads above the high grass where they had been hiding and rushed after the trapped animals. Ker saw eight gazelles killed in less than a minute, with the cubs inexpertly assisting. This was an involved lesson, containing several techniques: hunting at the right place (near waterholes), pride cooperation, using the wind properly so cut-off advance can be made, killing method, and, above all, patience. Patience has always been the hunting cat's greatest asset.

The lioness is the better hunter, fiercer than the male and more lithe and active. She usually attacks enemies first and is the scout and executioner of game, with the lordly, maned sultan lending his superior weight and power only if needed. Even when the lioness is hunting to feed herself and her cubs the male takes his share first. I saw a lion gorge, until his belly was so full that it dragged, before he permitted his mate and family of three cubs to eat.

I have watched a lioness teach her cubs the meaning of water, dipping her paw into a pool, then letting the cubs lick it. Lions are unafraid of water and become skillful swimmers. Even in this action they show superior intelligence, avoiding crocodiles by crossing streams only where the water is swift and shallow.

Lions' favored territories are open plains, grassy areas where herds feed, lightly covered savannas, and places where acacia trees and brush border the water. (But lions can never be taken for granted. They have also been seen hunting in the 12,000-foot Aberdare Mountains in Kenya.) Hunting in such terrain means that the cat has to be fast, agile, and crafty.

Most experts agree that the wild lion can run forty miles an hour for at least 100 yards. A couple of years ago I watched a lioness rise out of the yellow grass of an East African savanna and rush after an impala. She lifted her legs like a race horse in a golden blur of motion, moving at terrific speed. The antelope, fast as he was, had a difficult time outdistancing her. It took 150 yards of straight chasing to stop the lioness. She was within 50 feet of the fleet impala before she gave up, panting and spent.

Theodore Roosevelt didn't believe that a lion could move as fast as a forty-mile-per-hour horse. But there are documented cases of lions overtaking men on good horses, and one observer saw a lioness break all rules. She was chasing a herd of gazelles (known to get up to sixty miles per hour), trying to cut off a young male. She raced for 500 yards and caught her quarry.

I lay observing three lionesses stalk a herd of topis and saw them suddenly move into a covey of quail that flushed wildly. In the initial bursting flight, quail are the fastest of game birds, but they weren't fast enough for one lioness. She flicked out a paw and caught and ate a quail while the other cats waited; then they resumed their stalk.

Many people claim that lions, once they have reached maturity, can't climb trees, but I saw a full grown lioness in a tree the first time I went to Africa, and others also question this long accepted "fact" of naturalists. A Tanganyika game warden saw a leopard cache a Thomson's gazelle atop a 30-foot tree, when ten lions moved in, sat around the tree and, growling and leaping, tried to bluff the spotted cat into flight. They succeeded. When the leopard went, a big male climbed the tree and got the gazelle.

Captain C. R. S. Pitman, when a game warden in Uganda, saw a slightly wounded lion climb a tree with 6-foot girth. He said the cat moved quite easily to the higher branches, up at least 30 feet.

For large animals, lions are amazingly agile. One hunter measured a lion's leap at 52 feet; Lieutenant Von Hohnel saw a lion hurdle a gorge 24 yards deep and 12 yards wide. Lion expert Vaughn Kirby watched a lioness jump without effort to the top of a 12-foot embankment. But all of this physical ability comes only with time.

The young stay with the mother (who may mate again meanwhile) until they are two and their canine teeth fully developed, their sheathed claws, five on the forefeet, four on the hind, strong; and their stalking and killing techniques advanced. Two-year-old males often form a bachelor's pride, working together to secure food. (By now a strange, horny spike has developed under the dark tuft on the tail. Natives in Kenya told me that the lions use this tail spike to whip themselves into fury before charging, but biologists have been unable to account for its presence.) Their manes grow at three years and they mature at five years, living in the wild for fifteen years—and often twice that in captivity, where they seem to thrive.

Lion trainers have assured me that they prefer the wild lion to the zoo-bred lion, claiming that tame animals quickly develop a knowledge and often a contempt of man, thus becoming dangerous.

The big cats have always fascinated people, and the list of stories of house pets and self-trained lion tamers is long. George J. Keller, an American college professor with no professional knowledge of training, taught himself how to put together a lion and tiger act. It nearly cost him his life. Part of the act was putting his head in lion Leo's mouth. Once Leo didn't cooperate. He wouldn't let go, and Professor Keller had a bad moment until he kicked Leo in the haunches and was able to withdraw his head. Winston Churchill acquired a lion war mascot, Rota, who gave him "enlivening diversion." Charles Hipp of Graham, Texas, had a 200-pound lioness, Blondie, who ate at the dinner table, took bubble baths, went motorboating and played with the neighbor's children. Currently the most famous lion is Joy Adamson's Elsa. Mrs. Adamson has written several books about her lion, dramatizing how she and her husband, an African game warden, taught the cat to hunt so it "could be free and go back to its wilds." Mrs. Adamson had a point: that's where lions belong.

It will be a sad day when lions are seen only in cages in zoos or as the confused pets of people who don't seem to know any better. As writer Alan Moorehead noted in *No Room in the Ark,* "The hunting lion, the herds of elephants, the migrations of antelopes—these are some of the last great natural spectacles left in the world, and they have a fascination which is beyond value."

Experts like Mervyn Cowie, who was the director of Kenya National Park, don't think we will have this spectacle much longer. The lion can survive only where the wild grazing herds are kept intact. With the new Africa emerging, hungry for meat, land, and the spread of civilization, it appears that the days of the king of beasts are numbered. The national parks remain his last stronghold—how long the lion can last is a question only the African nations can answer.